Hans-Christian Hagman

European Crisis Management and Defence: The Search for Capabilities

Adelphi Paper 353

Oxford University Press, Great Clarendon Street, Oxford OX2 6DP
Oxford   New York
Athens   Auckland   Bangkok   Bombay   Calcutta   Cape Town
Dar es Salaam   Delhi   Florence   Hong Kong   Istanbul   Karachi
Kuala Lumpur   Madras   Madrid   Melbourne   Mexico City
Nairobi   Paris   Taipei   Tokyo   Toronto
and associated companies in
Ibadan

Oxford is a trade mark of Oxford University Press

Published in the United States
by Oxford University Press Inc., New York

© The International Institute for Strategic Studies 2002

First published December 2002 by **Oxford University Press for
The International Institute for Strategic Studies**
Arundel House, 13–15 Arundel Street, Temple Place, London WC2R 3DX
www.iiss.org

Director John Chipman
Editor Mats R. Berdal
Assistant Editor Matthew Foley

British Library Cataloguing in Publication Data
Data available

Library of Congress Cataloguing in Publication Data

ISBN 0-19-852799-3
ISSN 0567-932x

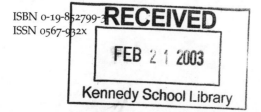

Contents

Glossary

ABCCC	Airborne Battlefield Command and Control Centre
ALSL	Alternative Landing Ship Logistics
ARRC	Allied Command Europe Rapid Reaction Corps (NATO)
AWACS	Airborne Warning and Control System
C³	Command, Control and Communications
CBRNE	Chemical, Biological, Radiological, Nuclear and Enhanced high explosive
CDM	Capabilities Development Mechanism (EU)
CFSP	Common Foreign and Security Policy (EU)
CJTF	Combined Joint Task Force (NATO)
CONOPS	Concepts of Operations
COREPER	Committee of Permanent Representatives (EU)
COP	Contingency Operations Plans
DoD	Department of Defense (US)
DCI	Defence Capabilities Initiative (NATO)
DSACEUR	Deputy Supreme Allied Commander Europe (NATO)
EC	European Community
ECAP	European Capabilities Action Plan (EU)
ESDI	European Security and Defence Identity
ESDP	European Security and Defence Policy (EU)
EMU	European Monetary Union
EU	European Union
EUROCORPS	European Corps

EUROMARFOR	European Maritime Force
FAWEU	Forces Answerable to Western European Union
GDP	Gross Domestic Product
GPS	Global Positioning System
HFC	Helsinki Force Catalogue (EU)
HHC	Helsinki Headline Catalogue (EU)
HPC	Helsinki Progress Catalogue (EU)
HTF	Helsinki Headline Goal Task Force (EU)
HQ	Headquarters
ICC	International Criminal Court
ICRC	International Committee of the Red Cross
IFOR	Implementation Force (NATO)
IMF	International Monetary Fund
J-STARS	Joint-Surveillance Target Attack Radar System
JV	Joint Vision (US)
KFOR	Kosovo Force (NATO)
LPD	Landing Platform Dock
NAC	North Atlantic Council (NATO)
NATO	North Atlantic Treaty Organisation
NBC	Nuclear Biological and Chemical
NGO	Non-Government Organisation
NRF	NATO Response Force
OCCAR	Organisation Conjointe de Coopération en matière d'Armement
OPLAN	Operations Plan
OSCE	Organisation of Security and Cooperation in Europe
PfP	Partnership for Peace (NATO)
RMA	Revolution in Military Affairs
SACEUR	Supreme Allied Commander Europe (NATO)
SACLANT	Supreme Allied Commander Atlantic (NATO)
SAS	Special Air Service (UK)
SEAD	Suppression of Enemy Air Defence
SFOR	Stabilisation Force (NATO)
SG/HR	Secretary-General of the Council of the EU/High Representative for the CFSP
SHAPE	Supreme Headquarters Allied Powers Europe (NATO)

SITCEN	Joint Situation Centre (EU)
UAV	Unmanned Aerial Vehicle
UN	United Nations
UNPROFOR	UN Protection Force
WEAG	Western European Armaments Group
WEU	Western European Union

Introduction

For decades, the countries of Western Europe depended on US protection for their security. Today, the European Union (EU) has become a net exporter of security. The question that now confronts European governments and institutions is how much *more* security they should be producing and projecting, and with what means. Much of the debate over European and transatlantic capabilities has focused on institutional labels, defence expenditures, costly procurement projects and comparisons between European military potential and US military power. However, the real question is how much more individual European governments can and wish to do in the security field, and which new formulas can produce greater output. The debate about capabilities is really a debate about the extent of Europe's ambition for an active, responsible role in international security, and whether Europe's societies deem acceptable the risks and sacrifices that this would entail.

The outcome of this debate will be shaped by wider changes in the old paradigms of security. The boundaries between military and civilian security and between external and internal security have become more fluid, and economic and social inter-dependence, both within Europe and between Europe and the rest of the world, has increased. As the US focuses increasingly on homeland defence, counter-terrorism and crisis regions beyond Europe, Europe itself must be prepared to take more responsibility for its own security. That governments and publics on both sides of the Atlantic have different perceptions of the shape of the threat and the meaning of multinational cooperation only adds to this complexity.

The EU's approach to security has been based on the conviction that military means are just one element of an effective, sustainable security policy, and usually not the most important one. While this may in part reflect perceptions distorted by the specific experience of the East–West confrontation in Europe, it also corresponds with the belief that not every problem has a military solution. This leads to a broader understanding of capabilities: the ability to 'manage' crises, or better still prevent them. Europe's advantage is seen as lying in precisely this cocktail of security-related measures and activities.

The EU's priorities and modes of operation will never be the same as those in the US, in NATO or in US-dominated war-fighting coalitions. It is not sufficient to compare European and US defence spending or military assets. European capabilities must be judged over the whole spectrum of security-projection measures, and in relation to accepted political goals. Hoping for significantly increased defence budgets would be unrealistic in the current political climate in most European countries. The corset of macro-economic performance imposed by European Monetary Union (EMU), together with high unemployment, ageing populations and growing healthcare costs, leaves little room for defence-related growth. Besides, structural changes are often slow and politically painful, and rarely produce rapid savings. For added capabilities, coordination and cooperation need to increase in all areas relevant to security, including diplomacy, the military, the police, civil emergency protection, post-conflict reconstruction, international trade and economic measures. The issue is how to get more out, with limited resources.

This paper answers this question by looking at both the military and the civilian components of conflict prevention and crisis management. It argues that the main opportunities for increasing European capabilities lie in expanding national and functional coordination within Europe; enhancing the EU's strategic decision-making; developing the spectrum of European non-military and military capabilities; and establishing rational and pragmatic cooperation mechanisms between the EU and

NATO, and between the EU and the US. The paper has four objectives:

- to assess the substance of military and civilian capability initiatives by both NATO and the EU;
- to analyse the development of EU instruments and capabilities, and their operational consequences;
- to assess the prospects for strategic partnership between the EU and the US, and the role of European capabilities therein; and
- to identify the major challenges and opportunities in increasing European capabilities for conflict prevention and the management of international crises.

The first chapter describes and assesses initiatives to strengthen European capabilities up to and including NATO's Prague Summit in November 2002.[1] The second chapter discusses likely short-term developments, including a detailed scrutiny of the EU's crisis-management tools. The next chapter analyses US reactions to the European Security and Defence Policy (ESDP) and transatlantic burden-sharing after 11 September, and looks at options for a new strategic partnership between the EU and the US. Chapter four deals with the long-term operational and strategic limitations that Europe faces, and the final chapter enumerates five areas where European capabilities could be significantly increased.

In its use of key terms, this paper assumes that crisis-management *capabilities* are more than just an assembly or catalogue of *assets*, be they mechanised infantry battalions, mine-sweepers, strike aircraft, civilian rescue helicopters or police officers. First, there are both military and civilian crisis-management capabilities. Second, in addition to field capabilities, national and institutional planning and politico-military coordination and decision-making capabilities must be taken into account. Third, just because a state or organisation has an asset, this does not mean that it has a capability: a capability exists only when the asset is relevant to the task at hand.[2] An asset must have the relevant level of training, equipment, deployability, sustainability and effectiveness for it to be a capability in a particular operation or function. This also means that the term 'capability' is relative; there is no exact or comparative qualitative dimension.

Defining *crisis management* and *conflict prevention* – and thus the ESDP's sphere of application – is particularly difficult since individual EU member states have their own definitions and ambitions. Indeed, even within national governments different ministries have different agendas and definitions. The pragmatic solution, adopted in this paper, has been to not define these terms at all, thus granting a degree of constructive ambiguity. Instead, this paper distinguishes between three broad categories: 'military crisis management', 'civilian crisis management' and 'conflict prevention'.[3]

Of course, all of these categories are of secondary importance next to vital interests, including collective and common security commitments and the territorial defence.[4] However, even within the EU and NATO, one member state's crisis management can easily be another's safeguarding of vital interests. Consequently, commitments to crisis management and conflict prevention, and the underlying perceptions of risk, morale, values and acceptable costs, have considerable implications for core aspects of defence and alliance strength in the pursuit of international peace and security.

Chapter 1

Capability Initiatives

NATO's Defence Capabilities Initiative

NATO's Defence Capabilities Initiative (DCI) is often perceived as a reaction to the European deficiencies highlighted by *Operation Allied Force* in Kosovo in 1999.[1] According to the US Department of Defense (DoD), the European allies were particularly weak in precision strike, mobility and command and control and communications (C^3), and lacked sufficient strategic lift and aircraft for intelligence, surveillance and reconnaissance (European nations did, however, have sufficient tactical and operational airlift).[2] Poor doctrinal and technical interoperability among the allies were seen as further challenges.[3]

In fact, the DCI began as a US initiative in June 1998, designed to address the growing technological gap between the US and its NATO allies, the strategic de-coupling of Europe and the US and declining European defence budgets and procurement. Increased European defence spending and off-the-shelf procurement of capabilities were seen as the solution. By late 2002 and the NATO Summit in Prague, however, little had changed in US and European perceptions of capabilities.

The DCI was seen in the US as a blueprint for NATO's response to the US-led Revolution in Military Affairs (RMA) and Joint Vision (JV) doctrines.[4] However, faced with obvious European weaknesses during the Kosovo campaign, the DCI was transformed into NATO policy just ahead of the Washington Summit, and was adopted with little debate.[5] Significantly, the goals were not the result of a comprehensive NATO assessment, nor were they linked to any specific scenarios.[6] With hindsight, the DCI was narrowly focused on military capabilities and towards conventional military crisis management. Nevertheless, the DCI did add momentum to European defence restructuring, and its effects will be felt throughout the decade.

The DCI identified 58 vital upgrade goals in deployability and mobility, sustainability and logistics, effective engagement, the survivability of forces and infrastructure and command-and-control and information systems.[7] Several involved the military use of commercial sea and airlift, the sharing or pooling of transport assets, establishing multinational logistic units and expanding logistics and support forces. Other goals included acquiring precision-guided munitions, all-weather weapon systems, unmanned aerial vehicles (UAVs), stealth aircraft, cruise missiles and non-lethal weapons. Nuclear, biological and chemical (NBC) protection and C^3 were also covered, as were 'softer' areas to do with concepts, policies and doctrines. Several goals related to battle-field ground surveillance (such as Joint-STARS) and theatre- and ballistic-missile defence.[8] The DCI was noticeably similar to the 'wish-lists' of the US and the Western European Union (WEU), and the French and British after-action reports on Kosovo.

Of the 58 goals, a number were seen as 'low-hanging fruits' – delivering additional capabilities reasonably quickly, and without great cost. Most coordination, cooperation and training objectives fell into this category. The DCI was also seen as a mechanism for increasing interoperability in peace-support operations. A majority of the goals were applicable to NATO partners, and were channelled to the Partnership for Peace (PfP) planning and review process.[9]

Different perceptions of the DCI

Within the alliance, national interpretations of the DCI varied widely. In general, most Eastern European NATO members saw it as a long-term project to be dealt with after they had adapted their own armed forces, a process expected to take ten years or more. Thus, the DCI was seen as geared mostly towards the UK, France and Germany, because most of its elements are expensive, involve advanced technology or take for granted a certain degree of interoperability. Smaller NATO countries welcomed the DCI, but claimed that there was little prospect of them contributing to its large, high-tech projects. France and the UK seemed to interpret the DCI as a confirmation of their own defence-restructuring efforts and as support for some of their pet national projects; the big gain for Europe, they argued, would be if Germany transformed its armed forces in line with DCI goals. Germany took a selective approach to the DCI, stating that only three elements were of interest: strategic lift, command and control and intelligence. Much could be done through increased interoperability, joint doctrines and multinational exercises, and not everything had to be high-tech. In both France and Germany, there was a widespread perception that the DCI was a US shopping list, not least since the only way to quickly acquire new and advanced combat systems was to buy them off the shelf, and that essentially meant buying American.

The US has seen the DCI as a way of getting its allies to 'field a 21st century force'.[10] The problem is that the US and Europe have different perceptions of what such a force should be. For the US, there is a direct parallel between the DCI and its transformational JV 2010 and 2020 ('net-centric warfare') doctrine. The two are part of a common US understanding of the kind of capabilities 'required to address the future security environment as seen by the US and NATO'.[11] Although many of the buzzwords from JV 2010 have found their way into the UK's Strategic Defence Review, NATO's Strategic Concept, allied communiqués and the DCI, European willingness to sign up should not be taken for granted.[12]

It would be wishful thinking to believe that all NATO allies agree with the interpretations of the RMA prevalent in the US debate, and much less with a US-led RMA for the alliance. While there is recognition of the need for interoperability with US forces and a growing realisation that technological advances ought to be better exploited for European defence and security, few if any European states have indicated that their own acquisition priorities match those of the US.[13] Furthermore, not all Europeans are yet prepared to accept US-designed concepts for future joint warfare or the US military transformation model.[14] Although these transformation concepts contain valuable components and guiding ideas, for the majority of European defence forces, with a different baseline, different missions and different priorities, the US vision in its entirety lies far over the horizon.

Regardless of the vocal US agenda and the DCI's preoccupation with high technology, its emphasis on interoperable, mobile and effective military capabilities is relevant in most types of international coalition warfare, whatever its nature. Several of the DCI goals – strategic airlift, for example – have less to do with NATO missions in the Euro-Atlantic area or with net-centric warfare visions than with land-based coalition warfare of the kind seen in Iraq in 1991 and in Afghanistan in 2001, and the kind which will characterise future large-scale US-led war-fighting coalitions. Where such DCI goals match EU scenarios and ambitions, the prospects for implementation are probably the best. However, the DCI has enjoyed only limited progress, at least in relation to US objectives. From its launch in 1999, few in NATO's International Staff in Brussels or at the Supreme Headquarters Allied Powers Europe (SHAPE) have been optimistic about the process. The DCI has made little if any difference to the development of European military capabilities.

The WEU audit of assets

In late 1999, European states finalised an audit of the assets and capabilities available for Petersberg tasks.[15] The audit was based on the Forces Answerable to WEU (FAWEU – a catalogue of national forces potentially available for WEU operations), and those committed to the NATO/PfP planning and review process. Although much of the terminology was the same, the audit differed from the DCI in that it focused more on what Europe would need for autonomous operations.

Although the WEU had the necessary forces in terms of numbers to conduct military operations across the Petersberg spectrum, the audit identified a number of capability gaps and weaknesses.[16] 'Severe gaps' were found in airborne C^3, suppressive electronic warfare, combat search and rescue, stealth technology and precision-strike capabilities. The audit concluded that European forces were 'very weak' in military strategic heavy lift, and relied on civilian assets in this area. Capabilities were 'very limited' in intelligence provision at strategic political and military levels, and in deployable secure tactical communications in theatre, air mobility, psychological warfare, deployable combined joint head-quarters, deployable combined air operations centres and elec-tronic/signals intelligence. There was also a serious shortfall in the capabilities required for evacuation operations. The audit pointed out that European forces depended on roads for their ground mobility, and that air mobility (helicopters and tactical air lift) was lacking. Although few states reported on civilian assets, the audit concluded that civil–military coordination was also unsatisfactory. Reconstruction and administrative capabilities were weak, and only one country claimed to be able to provide full assistance to a population affected by an NBC attack. Surprisingly, the audit concluded that interoperability, readiness and sustainability were acceptable – a point which questions its credibility given that these remain huge challenges.

In 'realistic' quantitative terms, the audit counted 66 infantry battalions, 18 armoured regiments, two special-forces battalions and four field hospitals.[17] Maritime forces included three aircraft carriers, ten amphibious ships, 75 destroyers and frigates, 59 mine-countermeasures craft, 34 submarines and 62 sealift and support ships. Ship-based air power was deemed sufficient for self-defence, but extremely limited in any strike or area air-defence capacity. In the air, European forces could muster some 152 air-defence fighters, 137 attack aircraft, 144 light-to-medium trans-port aircraft (C-130s and smaller), 126 small-to-medium lift helicopters, 24 reconnaissance aircraft, 26 air-to-air refuelling aircraft and seven airborne early-warning (AWACS) aircraft. Only one mobile combined air operations centre was committed. While the capability of this asset would initially be limited, it would increase to a level of 600 sorties a day after three months in theatre.

These assets were compared with the 1996–97 WEU Illus-trative Profiles/scenarios, drawn up by the WEU and elaborated and developed by the NATO Combined Joint Planning Staff. For the high-end Separation of Parties scenario, involving two divisions (with equivalent air and maritime forces) in a 12-month operation 6,000 km from Brussels, it was concluded that Europe had sufficient land forces, but lacked air assets for strategic lift, suppression of enemy air defence (SEAD) and electronic warfare. For the conflict-prevention scenario (involving a brigade and equivalent air and maritime components, for less than a year, up to 3,500 km away) Europe had all the assets and capabilities required. In the lower-end scenarios, including humanitarian aid and assistance and evacuation operations, European forces could meet almost all of the requirements. In short, in 1999 Europe had the capabilities to manage a small, high-intensity operation, and any lower-intensity conventional military operations. European forces were not capable of larger, complex and/or distant land operations like KFOR, or major air operations like *Allied Force*.

The audit was solely a quantitative exercise based on conventional military forces earmarked for the FAWEU, or identified in NATO's planning processes. Qualitative issues – whether forces were available, deployable, sustainable and interoperable – were not assessed. A majority of declared forces were already double- or triple-hatted or more, and a significant proportion were deployed in peace-support operations. For WEU operations, many assets would have had to be taken out of NATO reaction forces. WEU military staff complained that much of the national data were superficial, and information provided by some states was clearly unrealistic. Unconventional capabilities beyond the traditional Petersberg spectrum (for example defence against chemical, biological, radiological, nuclear and enhanced high explosive (CBRNE) weapons or counter-terrorism) were generally not included in the audit.

The audit was generally critical and realistic in its assessments of Europe's conventional military capabilities. Both WEU military staff and the nations reporting their assets knew that the findings would not be binding, nor would they form the basis for any operational planning within the WEU. The audit also appeared to have been less influenced by national defence-industrial politics than the DCI. By applying the WEU label, which was seen by NATO and the US as relatively harmless, the EU could also use the audit as a springboard towards the Headline Goal, which was agreed at Helsinki in December 1999.

The Headline Goal and the Helsinki Catalogues

The Headline Goal added the first real substance to the European Security and Defence Policy (ESDP).[18] Under the Goal, by 2003 EU member states committed themselves to being able to deploy and sustain forces capable of the full range of Petersberg tasks as set out in the Amsterdam Treaty, including the most demanding, in operations up to corps level (up to 15 brigades or 50,000–60,000 personnel). These forces should be militarily self-sustaining, with the necessary command, control and intelligence capabilities, logistics, other combat-support services and air and naval elements. Member states should be able to deploy in full at this level within 60 days, and to provide smaller rapid-response elements more quickly than this. They must be able to sustain such a deployment for at least one year.[19] The following year, in November 2000, the EU Capabilities Commitment Conference resulted in the Helsinki Force Catalogue (HFC), which constituted the current sum of national commitments. In addition, the Helsinki Headline Catalogue (HHC) represented an assessment of what the EU would need to fulfil the scenarios developed from the Headline Goal. In effect, the HFC and the HHC reflected what EU member states wished to commit to the Headline Goal in 2003, and what capabilities they wanted to create.

At the Cologne Summit in June 1999, EU members agreed that action would be taken 'without prejudice to actions by NATO'.[20] At Helsinki, the phrase 'where NATO as a whole is not engaged' replaced this formula.[21] This wording guarantees the EU full freedom to act autonomously. In EU operations that can be conducted without recourse to NATO assets, the EU is not dependent on NATO consensus, although US and NATO support would be a bonus. The single institutional framework and decision-making autonomy of the EU in EU-only operations is considered non-negotiable. As in any other organisation, the members are sovereign in deciding if, when and with whom they are prepared to cooperate. This includes inviting non-members to participate in EU operations.[22]

The HFC included only a fraction of the EU's 1.8 million soldiers, 160 destroyers and frigates, 75 tactical submarines and 3,300-plus combat aircraft in 2000.[23] The majority of EU member states committed just about all the interoperable capabilities they had, and these states would be hard-pressed to fulfil their commitments. Nevertheless, what has been committed to the Headline Goal represents the elements of a major fighting force, albeit a rather traditional one. The EU Military Staff initially concluded that member states had committed more than enough HQs, combat brigades, combat aircraft and manpower, but not always the right kind of units. The flaws lay in in-theatre transport, AWACS, air-to-air refuelling, SEAD and electronic warfare, plus strategic airlift and sealift. Psychological-operations battalions, cruise missiles, airborne battlefield command and control, UAVs, airborne signals and electronic intelligence and satellite intelligence elements were also lacking.[24] In 2002, Europe did not own a single military wide-body or long-range strategic transport capable of lifting a main battle tank or transporting the bulky *Patriot* missile system. In addition, the quality and/or availability of some of the committed HQs (five operational HQs and four Force HQs) are questionable.

Most force contributions were double-hatted, and had already been offered to UN standby forces, FAWEU, NATO rapid-reaction forces and multinational constellations such as EUROFOR and EUROCORPS. Only a handful of countries committed new or more capable forces to the EU. Almost all countries put severe restrictions on their forces; the majority of supporting units were limited to supporting national contributions, and would only be used to support European allies if paid for their services. As for commitments by non-EU allied and EU candidates, Turkey limited itself to what had previously been listed in the FAWEU, while Norway offered a new contribution to non-NATO European operations of 3,500 soldiers – a significant number, given the country's size and its location in relation to most areas of European crisis management.

Although essentially symbolic, the Europeans offered more forces to the HFC at the Capabilities Commitment Conference than they had assigned to NATO. Greece and Belgium offered a whole brigade to the HFC and only one battalion to NATO-sustained operations. The Netherlands provided one brigade to the EU and two battalions for NATO, and both the Netherlands and Belgium offered considerably more ships to the Headline Goal. The UK, Germany and Turkey provided more than twice as many combat aircraft to the EU as they did to NATO. Although there is a difference between NATO forces allocated to non-Article 5 missions (which in part correlate with NATO rapid-reaction forces) and the Headline Goal, the US took this as a further warning that the EU may increasingly be taken more seriously than NATO. As was the case for assets announced to the WEU Audit, many Headline Goal commitments would have to be taken out of NATO reaction forces for EU use – which would challenge NATO's traditional 'right' to a 'first pick'.

In June 2001, the gap between the HHC – the capabilities deemed necessary – and the HFC – the forces actually committed – was assessed in the first version of the Helsinki Progress Catalogue (HPC). In greater detail than even the WEU Audit, the HPC identified what further capabilities were needed from EU member states, and added some 'new' capability gaps, such as theatre-missile defence, which cannot easily be categorised as part of the traditional Petersberg spectrum.

The higher-profile shortfalls listed in the HPC included carrier-based air power, sea-based theatre-missile defence, SEAD aircraft, cruise missiles, precision-guided munitions, air surveillance, attack and reconnaissance helicopters, medium and heavy support helicopters, light infantry and multiple-launch rocket systems. Early-warning and distant-detection requirements (UAVs, AWACS and airborne early warning, airborne ground surveillance and intelligence satellites), sealift, airlift and amphibious shipping were also highlighted as acute gaps. Other shortfalls included special-operations forces, NBC battalions, psychological operations and electronic warfare. There were also gaps in less spectacular areas, such as transport, general support logistics, medical units, recovery and maintenance, engineering, signals and surveillance and target-acquisition units, and a shortage of military observers and military police.

The Capability Improvement Conference

The HPC paved the way for the November 2001 EU Capability Improvement Conference, which pledged to address the flaws it identified. Although the Western European states made additional contributions, there was essentially no progress in the areas demanding major procurements.

Significant acquisitions and procurements cannot be changed overnight – most acquisitions take several years to plan and finance and major projects can take a decade or more to develop and produce. No matter what the political process or Headline Goal may demand, assets such as strategic airlift, satellites or communications equipment will not be developed or financed in the space of a few years. Besides, as long as most European states feel secure and crisis management is not seen as a matter of defending vital interests, developing capability for distant autonomous high-tech enforcement operations will not be given priority (unless of course it is a question of national prestige, industries or jobs).

At the 2001 conference, member states committed more than 100,000 soldiers, some 400 aircraft and 100 ships. In quantitative terms, levels increased from those reached at the 2000 commitment conference, and gaps relating to bridging-engineer units, electronic warfare and multiple rocket launchers were addressed. Gaps not addressed included logistics, force protection, operational and strategic mobility (air and sea), combat search and rescue and precision-guided munitions. Command, control, communications and intelligence capabilities remained of questionable quality, and shortfalls persisted in surveillance and reconnaissance.

The European Capability Action Plan

Further steps were taken in February 2002, when EU member states agreed on a voluntary European Capability Action Plan (ECAP). The ECAP aimed to incorporate all the investment, development and coordination measures executed or planned, both nationally and multinationally, with a view to improving existing resources and gradually developing the capabilities deemed necessary for the EU's activities. It offers a forum for identifying requirements, enhancing multilateral coordination and encouraging national initiatives on capabilities. It specifically states that multinational solutions might include the co-production, financing and acquisition of capabilities, particularly for large-scale projects.

The ECAP establishes a number of panels, each focusing on a specific capability such as strategic airlift, UAVs, air-to-ground missiles or communications. Each panel is chaired by a member state (a 'pilot country') or two, responsible for leading, coordinating and summarising the panel's work. This adds impetus to the whole process since national prestige is at stake. Unfortunately, there is a tendency for member states to focus on projects that they have a direct interest in developing, or to participate in order to minimise the potential damage to other national pet projects. On the other hand, the prospects for coordination are greater than would have been the case without the ECAP.

EU non-military/civilian crisis-management goals

Non-military or civilian instruments of crisis management and conflict prevention were also highlighted at Helsinki, though they were not directly linked to the Headline Goal. In recognition of the EU's comparative advantage in this area, member states agreed that: 'A non-military crisis management mechanism will be established to coordinate and make more effective the various civilian means and resources, in parallel with the military ones, at the disposal of the Union and the Member States.'[25] At the EU summit at Feira in June 2000, the EU decided to focus on four aspects of civilian crisis management: police, the rule of law, civil administration and civil protection.

EU members made it their goal to provide up to 5,000 police officers for international missions by 2003, with 1,000 available at 30 days' notice.[26] The Police Action Plan agreed at the Gothenburg summit in June 2001 called for the establishment of operational headquarters, interoperability criteria, training programmes, the development of interfaces with military and other civilian components of crisis management and the development of a legal framework for police operations (including Status of Forces Agreements). Since then, the development of common concepts, command-and-control arrangements, selection and training criteria and compatible equipment lists and guidelines, for instance for criminal procedure and civilian administration in crisis-management operations, has made significant progress. The EU has even been able to offer the UN help in improving its guidelines, for example in the rule-of-law field. This development of common European standards and training will eventually enhance internal police and civil-emergency cooperation within the EU.

The Ministerial Police Capabilities Commitment Conference in November 2001 received commitments for 5,000 police officers for crisis-management operations by 2003 – though remarkably without any explicit reference to the changed international environment after 11 September. Of these, 1,400 will be deployable within 30 days. By any measure, this is a major undertaking. The EU police capability is meant to cover the full range of missions, from training, advice and monitoring to executive tasks. In 2003, the EU is to take over the UN police mission in Bosnia, with almost 500 officers. Even if the pledged numbers are available as promised – which is not yet fully the case – it is not certain whether the available assets will be adequate to the task at hand, and whether their deployment will be given sufficient political and financial importance by the states sending them. Language requirements as well as the reluctance of national police forces to make their core personnel available for international missions are further complicating factors.

The development of *gendarmerie*-type heavy police has made little progress on the European level, but further headway is likely as more European states acknowledge the value of such capabilities for counter-terrorist operations and engagements where traditional police forces are too weak and military combat forces too provocative or expensive. It is likely that the impact of 11 September will in the long run lead to a number of new forms of European internal-security and police cooperation, perhaps including integrated border controls and coast-guard forces.[27]

During the first half of 2001, civilian crisis management overshadowed the military elements of the ESDP, and the scope of EU crisis management and conflict prevention was significantly broadened, in some eyes beyond the traditional Petersberg range. Members committed themselves to an additional pool of 200 officials for crisis-management operations (judges, prosecutors and correction/penitentiary officers) to supplement the police. The pledging conference in May 2002 actually exceeded this target, with a total pledge of 282 officials. Lead elements are to be deployable within 30 days. The basic idea behind such rule-of-law missions is to ensure that the area of operations has a complete and functioning criminal-justice process. Although these missions will most likely complement police operations, the capability could in theory be deployed on its own, or with other EU capabilities.

EU members also agreed to create a pool of experts in civil administration, ranging from elections and taxation to health services and waste management, and to establish a 2,000-strong civil-protection capability for major natural, technological and environmental emergencies. Key functions would include search and rescue, the construction of refugee camps, logistical support and communications. Although not envisaged at the time, EU states' civil-protection capabilities will also be relevant in the wake of large-scale terrorist attacks. EU member states had already decided at Gothenburg to develop common standards and modules for training, and common exercises.

By the EU Summit in Seville in June 2002, further progress had been made in implementing the Police Action Plan and in civil protection/emergency relief. The non-military aspects of ESDP became more prominent, and the link between civilian and military crisis-management capabilities was reinforced. The EU also reaffirmed that it was prepared to take over the UN police mission in Bosnia from January 2003. Member states agreed that the development of the ESDP and Headline Goal must take fuller account of the capabilities that may be required to combat terrorism. These include enhancing EU instruments for long-term conflict prevention, political dialogue with third countries, non-proliferation and arms control, and providing assistance to third countries so that they can increase their capacity to respond to terrorism. The EU also plans to include anti-terrorism clauses in EU agreements with third countries and to re-evaluate relations in the light of these countries' attitudes towards terrorism. However, although counter-terrorism falls within the realm of the Common Foreign and Security Policy (CFSP), it is questionable whether it can be regarded as part of the ESDP under the 1992 definition of the Petersberg spectrum of tasks. Arguably, counter-terrorism may affect territorial issues and states' self-defence, which do not come under the ESDP – at least for now.

Interim modalities for financing EU crisis-management operations have also been agreed. In principle, the EC budget will pay for institutional administrative costs, while operational expenditures for national military forces engaged in the operation are paid for by the troop-contributing nation. This is the same principle that NATO has used for years. The Council will decide on a case-by-case basis whether deployment and lodging expenses should be regarded as a common or a national cost. Individual states are responsible for deploying and sustaining forces in crisis-management operations. There has been debate over whether the EU should have a separate budget for common costs relating to crisis-management operations, and whether a start-up fund for operations should be established.

EU structures for security and defence cooperation

In parallel with these capability initiatives, developing security and defence cooperation within the EU has also required structural change. In 1999, EU member states agreed to establish new working bodies. These were set up in March 2000, and made permanent in January 2001. They included:

- the post of Secretary-General of the Council of the European Union/High Representative (SG/HR) for the Common Foreign and Security Policy (CFSP) – filled by Javier Solana – and the associated SG/HR Policy Unit;
- the Political and Security Committee (comparable to NATO's North Atlantic Council (NAC));
- the Committee for Civilian Aspects of Crisis Management;
- the Military Committee;
- the Military Staff; and
- a Police Unit in the Council Secretariat as part of the Police Action Plan.

A Joint Situation Centre (SITCEN) was also established, with an embryonic intelligence and assessment cell. This has since developed and grown, with an increased capability to manage intelligence from member states. It has even started to assign tasks to national intelligence services, either informally or, on a voluntary basis, formally. To an extent, the SITCEN can produce its own assessments and analyses in support of the Council and the Council Secretariat. Input from the EU Military Committee, and above all the 120-strong Military Staff, has meant that the quality of concepts, procedures and structures for coordinating crisis management within the EU has vastly improved. The formal mission of the Military Staff is to perform 'early warning, situation assessment and strategic planning for Petersberg tasks',[28] to provide military expertise and to conduct EU-led military crisis-management operations.[29]

The Political and Security Committee, which is subordinate to the EU Council, deals with all aspects of the EU's foreign and security policy, including the ESDP. It is the focal point for crisis management. During EU operations, it will exercise political control and provide strategic direction. With the exception of EU operations, the Political and Security Committee is not a decision-making body, though it is the prime decision-*shaping* organ in the CFSP/ESDP realm.

Additional forums have also been established, such as the EU Headline Goal Task Force, a Working Group on Capabilities and the Politico-Military Working Group.[30] Since the attacks in the US in September 2001, ESDP institutions have also fed into assessments of the terrorist threat, and have contributed to the Political and Security Committee's position. ESDP processes, procedures and structures were tested in early 2002 in a crisis-management exercise involving Brussels and all EU member states. One of the main lessons of the exercise, the first of its kind in the EU, was the need for stronger civil–military coordination.

The transatlantic capabilities debate and the Prague Summit

Both the US and NATO international staffs have encouraged the Europeans to develop their military capabilities. The reaction in most European capitals has, however, been lukewarm. For most European governments, increasing defence expenditures or signing on to expensive procurement projects that do not benefit domestic employment or growth is not an option. Moreover, while the US may have a clear conception of current threats and what they mean in terms of capabilities, most Europeans have not significantly changed their views on either since the 1990s. For the US, the standard is still US defence spending, US interests and US global commitments and ambitions. The problem is that, whatever initiatives the US comes up with for its NATO allies, defence spending and national procurement are determined by parliaments, governments and the shape of domestic politics within individual countries. It is nonetheless true, as NATO Secretary-General Lord Robertson argues, that the Europeans are still spending enormous amounts of money on capabilities that the US and NATO believe they do not need. It is also true that Europeans hesitate to buy US products in areas such as strategic airlift, communications and precision-guided munitions because this offers little benefit to European defence industries, even if these US alternatives are often cheaper, more advanced and readily available 'off-the-shelf'.

For many Europeans, the normal NATO defence planning process, as opposed to fast-track initiatives *à la* the DCI, appear sufficient as a mechanism for developing interoperability and new capabilities. In this context, the ESDP's role in defence planning has been difficult to grasp. The EU's review mechanism, the Capability Development Mechanism (CDM), the collective name for the permanent process that sets in once a political Headline Goal is set, mirrors NATO's process. It is geared towards identifying required capabilities, getting member states to commit to them, and then monitoring progress and addressing shortfalls. A working interface between EU and NATO activities in this area is essential if unnecessary and unhelpful duplication is to be avoided. However, some Europeans hope that, by using EU defence planning through the CDM and the ECAP, US involvement and pressure can be kept to a minimum. Certain EU governments have been more comfortable discussing procurement and capabilities development in this forum, rather than in NATO. Some European governments have stressed their preference to look beyond traditional military capabilities and take a more comprehensive view of security and the projection of security to crisis regions, to encompass elements such as aid, confidence-building, state-building and police or *gendarmerie* operations. This approach is in part based on experiences in the Balkans, and also reflects deep differences with the US over the threat posed by terrorism, ballistic-missile attacks and weapons of mass destruction, as well as the nature of relations with countries such as Libya, Iran and Iraq.

In this context, it is worth noting what the Europeans have signed up to in NATO. In a Statement on Capabilities, agreed by NATO defence ministers in June 2002, member states acknowledged that the capacity of the alliance to carry out the full range of its missions will depend largely on its ability to 'increase substantially' the proportion of combat and support forces available for out-of-area deployment, or where there is little or no host-nation support. Future capabilities should focus on defending against chemical, biological, radiological and nuclear attacks, secure command communications and information superiority, interoperability and the rapid deployment and sustainment of combat forces. NATO states also agreed to encourage 'the pooling of military capabilities, increasing role specialisation, cooperative acquisition of equipment and multinational funding'.[31] Change is, however, likely to be slow, and it will be several years before the impact is felt on NATO force planning.

NATO's Prague Summit in November 2002 seemed set to follow past patterns. The Prague Capabilities Commitment, launched by the US and the NATO Secretary General, set out the following aims:

- to equip all deployable NATO forces, with 30 days' or higher readiness, with chemical, biological, radiological and nuclear defence;
- to complete, by 2004, the design and development phase of NATO airborne Ground Surveillance (reconnaissance and targeting support);
- to develop a full set of deployable and secure command, control and communications capabilities for deployable HQs;
- to increase the number of precision-guided munitions by 30% by 2005;
- to increase SEAD capabilities by 50% by 2005;
- to increase the alliance's strategic airlift and air-tanker capabilities by 50% by 2004; and
- to increase deployable logistics and combat-service support capabilities by 25% by 2005.[32]

Although many of the above increases are substantial in relative terms, one must remember the real starting point which is often less impressive. Significantly, the process generated two new formulas that should be applauded, whatever the institutional label. The first is a pool of jointly-owned and operated support jamming pods for electronic warfare, an air-to-air refuelling fleet and UAVs. The second idea is for Europe to lease 10–12 US C-17 aircraft (or equivalents) until the delivery of the Airbus A400M by the end of the decade. Obviously, this 'wish list' will not materialise in full, even if the new formulas were accepted by European states. It all costs money, which most European defence budgets do not have.

At the summit, the US also launched a new NATO Response Force (NRF). The idea is that NATO needs a multinational joint force for primarily out-of-area operations, with immediate readiness (5–30 days).[33] The force is to be operational by 2006. Tasks are similar to the EU Headline Goal, and include non-combatant evacuation operations, proactive force projection and serving as an initial entry force for a large-scale operation. The US emphasis is however on joint high-intensity combat outside Europe. According to the proposal, the force is to comprise around 20,000 soldiers, with a brigade-sized land component. In its expeditionary nature, there are similarities between the new US Interim Brigade Combat Team (which is under development) and the NRF's land component. The Combined Joint Task Force (CJTF) HQs would be suitable for the NRF. The idea is that the NRF would set a new standard for European military capabilities. The need for strategic airlift, air refuelling, secure command and control and precision-guided munitions for the European elements of the NRF would be clear and European governments would be challenged to set the necessary priorities. The side benefit would be a new US–European project, with increased military cooperation and interoperability.[34]

The sum of the initiatives

According to US Senator Jesse Helms, former Chairman of the Senate Committee on Foreign Relations, the EU 'could not fight its way out of a wet paper bag'.[35] Former British Prime Minister Margaret Thatcher has called the Headline Goal a 'monumental folly' designed to 'satisfy political vanity', with 'no military sense at all'.[36]

Europe's capabilities are not quite that bad, and the EU Headline Goal and enhanced crisis-management capabilities are reasonable and logical from the point of view of almost all Western governments. Both for Europe and for future military and security cooperation between the EU and the US, not to mention Western conflict prevention, many benefits could be derived from a successful ESDP and EU/NATO capabilities initiatives pursued with determination. After having identified the capability gaps, and after having declared that Europe will be able to do more, Europe has little choice but to deliver. By late 2002, key structures were in place and the stage was set for measurable improvements. Significant challenges still remain, but there is little doubt that Europeans will eventually adjust and increase their military and non-military crisis-management capabilities. When, by how much and against which threats remain to be seen.

Chapter 2

Developing the EU's Instruments for Managing International Crises

This chapter analyses the Headline Goal and the EU's development of scenarios for the forces committed to it, as well as other elements of crisis management such as decision-making, planning and intelligence capabilities, and civilian capabilities. Together, these components constitute the current palette of EU assets and capabilities for conflict prevention and crisis management; in essence, this is the EU's contribution to the security dimension of Europe's strategic partnership with the US.

Assessing the Headline Goal

Like many ESDP initiatives, the Headline Goal is essentially a compromise between the UK and France. This does not make it less important, although it does help to explain the sometimes ambiguous and challenging formulations it uses. Although the Goal is set for the end of 2003, it reflects the priorities of 1999, the lessons and frustrations that followed the Kosovo crisis and the challenges Europe faced in deploying yet another large formation to the Balkans. The quantitative goal also reflects the Balkans experience. It is set at corps level (60,000 troops or up to 15 brigades), plus air and naval elements.

Size is not the major problem. The challenges relating to the Headline Goal concern sustainability (specified at one year), readiness (set at 60 days), combat intensity and complexity and self-sustainability. The Headline Goal was not formulated for major high-intensity warfare with a whole corps plus naval and air capabilities on the other side of the globe. The level of ambition is much more modest and, given existing capabilities, more realistic.

One-year sustainability

Depending on the other commitments of nations contributing to the European military operation, the availability and rotation of troops will be challenging. Sustaining 60,000 soldiers for one year engages at least 120,000 troops on the ground *plus* air and naval elements.[1] Depending on the specific mission and the amount of air and naval assets required, the total EU commitment for a one-year operation could engage perhaps 180,000–240,000 men and women in uniform. Moreover, for each half-year rotation, units are 'booked' for 18 months, and cannot be used for other operations.[2]

For an operation longer than one year, the total number of ground forces required for sustaining a corps-size operation would probably be at least 240,000. This is a four-to-one ratio for ground forces, but recent UN and NATO operations, and more than ten years of Balkan peace-support operations for most European armed forces, suggest that even this is insufficient for longer-term sustainment. Again, significant air and naval elements must be added, giving a total sum of perhaps around 350,000 European soldiers, airmen and sailors needed to sustain a joint operation more than one year. It is easy to forget that deployed soldiers are not mere statistics, but individuals with families, military careers and opportunities outside the military. Most units also have duties at home and training requirements for operations other than EU crisis management. In short, the Headline Goal is no small commitment, and will involve a substantial portion of Europe's assets and military capabilities.

As in most cases of crisis management, sustainability is more or less a question of national priorities. Without drawing down existing military crisis-management commitments, and based on the availability of non-engaged rapid-reaction forces in Europe throughout the 1990s, few EU members apart from the UK and France will be able to produce more than a minor, perhaps even a symbolic, additional mid to long term commitment in the next five years or so. Particularly challenging will be the sustainability of forces that are already in short supply, such as logistics, engineers, medical services, helicopter crews and other specialists. Should the operation take place in a climate zone such as a desert or tropical environment, availability would be even more constricted, whatever the formal Headline Goal commitment. Finnish, Danish, Dutch or Hungarian taxpayers would hardly accept keeping a significant portion of their armed forces trained and equipped for desert or jungle warfare.

Sixty-day readiness[3]

The stated high-end commitment is that the EU will be able to deploy up to 60,000 troops in theatre, beyond Europe, within 60 days from an EU Council order to deploy. It took longer than 60 days for NATO, with the full support of US strategic lift, to deploy a corps-sized formation to Albania and Macedonia in 1999; 1,751 airlift missions were involved, together with the movement of 78,000 tonnes of supplies and 42,380 passengers by air and sea.[4]

If there is little warning and the bulk of European forces are engaged in major international operations or have important duties at home, EU member states will most likely not be able to field a large contingent at such short notice, unless it is merely a question of relabelling an already-established force. Should commercial air- and sealift be inappropriate or unavailable, and US airlift not wanted or not available, EU member states will have difficulty quickly deploying forces several thousand kilometres away. Although with a couple of months' warning many of these deployment challenges can be managed. Besides, not all crises will be conveniently located near main airports or harbours.

The mechanisms and arrangements for deploying a major force, and transforming individual national contributions into a combined and joint fighting force, do not yet exist, nor will they be developed overnight. In other words, getting forces from A to B in time is one thing; achieving an effective and coordinated multinational fighting force in such a short time is another.

Combat intensity and complexity

The Headline Goal states that forces will be capable of the full range of Petersberg tasks. Although the scope of these tasks is open to debate, as of 2002 the most demanding is peace enforcement in a non-permissive environment. This means that Europe should be capable of using force on a par with the Anglo-French Rapid Reaction Force in August–September 1995 in central Bosnia during *Operation Deliberate Force*, but on a larger scale and against two parties at the same time. On the other hand, it does not mean that a European operation would necessarily adopt a similar operational tempo, targeting policy or risk level as NATO's *Operation Allied Force* or other US-led military operations.[5] For European forces, combat intensity up to and including peace-enforcement scenarios is not a problem. Most European forces, mainly thanks to a decade of crisis management in the Balkans, are also well prepared for complex situations, ranging from shifting tension levels, civil–military interaction and multinationality down to the lower tactical level.

Self-sustainability

The Headline Goal force should be 'militarily self-sustaining with the necessary command, control and intelligence capabilities, logistics [and] other combat support services'.[6] In other words, it must be self-sufficient and have all the intelligence, transport and command-and-control capabilities it needs for peace-enforcement operations. Today there are serious flaws in these areas. Questions arise over what individual European governments and their armed forces will demand as the minimum level of these capabilities for a high-end, high-risk operation.

Summary of the Headline Goal

The Headline Goal is primarily a political project; at least at this early stage in the ESDP, it is as much the result of political frustration, the dynamics of integration and national defence-industrial interests as it is an expression of the wish to enhance member states' crisis-management capability *per se*. There is an understanding within the EU and in individual member states that the Headline Goal will be realised, whatever assets and capabilities Europeans possess when they are faced with a crisis. The decision to focus on the Petersberg tasks reflects the lowest common denominator among the EU member states, and most European governments have their own domestic interpretation of what the Headline Goal is, how it should be developed and towards what long-term political goal. On the other hand, setting a target and then moving towards it, not an uncommon method in the EU, has proved a successful way of developing the Union. The Headline Goal will probably be updated as the ESDP and European requirements evolve.

US support and access to NATO assets and capabilities

There is an assumption that, in the event of a crisis that demands European action, the US or others may support some European states bilaterally. Faced with a crisis that Europe cannot effectively manage, the European states would then either accept US support bilaterally or through arrangements in NATO, or would redefine 'European' interests, policies and operational ambitions downwards. The Europeans have little choice but to be pragmatic and realistic when it comes to an actual military engagement. However, for all high-end and militarily difficult tasks, or for tasks that clearly lie beyond the Petersberg spectrum, there is a general assumption in European capitals that NATO or a US-led coalition will be the natural choice.

Counting on US engagement, or EU–US cooperation, would save the EU from exposing its immediate capability flaws, and allow the Europeans more time to enhance their capabilities. The basic argument is that the general imperatives of US influence and NATO's *raison d'être* will ensure US engagement in any major crisis in the European area. In most global crisis management, and particularly in crises where even the Europeans are prepared to go to war, it is assumed that both Europe (or at least a selection of Europeans) and the US share common interests. The problem with this assumption is that a strong-minded European NATO member, for reasons relating to the EU or for the sake of national prestige, could block NATO from taking the lead, or lending collective assets. Alternatively, the US might choose not to be involved in European crisis management because of other geographical or political priorities, including homeland defence. Another possibility is that EU states may simply choose not to engage under the EU banner, after rephrasing their collective interests in the given case, as happened in the African Great Lakes contingency in 1996 and 1997. Besides, coalitions-of-the-willing will always remain an option.

In 1996, the NAC agreed to what came to be known as the 'Berlin package'. To develop the European Security and Defence Identity (ESDI) within NATO, using the formula 'separable but not separate capabilities', NATO would support the WEU with planning and command arrangements and other assets and capabilities.[7] The 1999 NATO summit expanded the Berlin package into 'Berlin plus', which gave 'assured EU access to NATO planning capabilities' and ensured the 'presumption of availability to the EU of pre-identified NATO capabilities and common assets'. It also developed the role of the Deputy Supreme Allied Commander Europe (DSACEUR) in order to support European command options.[8]

There were four main motives behind Berlin plus. First, the Europeans asked for access. This reflected their acceptance that their operational capabilities were insufficient, and that they therefore had to borrow from the alliance. At the EU summit in Nice in 2000, the EU requested access only to 'collective' NATO assets and capabilities. Second, it was an effort to enhance direct EU–NATO cooperation. For the US, this would prevent the creation of a separate European SHAPE, and ensured that EU operations were conducted in accordance with NATO doctrine.[9] Third, there was recognition in Europe of the US argument that establishing separate EU planning assets would damage NATO. Fourth, it was a way for the US, Turkey and other non-EU NATO members to ensure that they were not sidelined in any EU operation – not least in the political deliberations ahead of and during an operation. By maintaining control over NATO assets and capabilities, non-EU states could still have influence and a role. Such EU–NATO arrangements are, however, controversial, and highly politicised.

In the 'Berlin-plus' arrangement, where the EU would be assured of access to NATO assets and capabilities, access was highly probable, but not guaranteed. This issue was widely debated within NATO. France, for reasons of EU autonomy and for fear of institutionalising what is seen as the EU's dependence on NATO and the US, raised objections to giving the EU guaranteed access to NATO planning capabilities. NATO's International Staff argued that the alliance could only promise 'assured access' because planning staff might become overloaded with requests from the EU, as well as from NATO. Turkey, as a non-EU European member of NATO, has been trying to translate 'assured access' into a guarantee of Turkish involvement in ESDP operations. Despite a diplomatic formula brokered by the US and UK in late 2001, this issue continued to block full implementation of the assured-access approach because Greece, which is in both the EU and NATO, made its agreement conditional on Turkish concessions regarding Cyprus, and is adamantly against increased Turkish influence in the EU. From the viewpoint of the US and most European governments, NATO's guarantee of operational-planning support to the EU is essential for preventing an EU attempt to create its own capabilities outside the NATO framework.

NATO planning

NATO defence planning coordinates national forces and capabilities to attain common goals. The planning cycle includes Ministerial Guidance (strategic goals), Force Proposals (force targets, essentially formulated by NATO military staff in consultation with individual member states), Force Goals (proposals adopted by individual members) and a mechanism for peer review and progress assessment of the national goals.[10] Although this process has been important in setting common goals and in building confidence among NATO members, it is slow and cumbersome. There is poor coordination between the various functions and capabilities, no guarantee that nations will fulfil their commitments and there is room for reform. In reality, few states are prepared to have their priorities dictated externally, and national defence ministries are keen to ensure that force goals match what they planned to do anyway – and maybe even manage to get some NATO support for the project.

One component of the Berlin-plus formula was that NATO's defence-planning system should incorporate forces for EU-led operations. However, perceptions among NATO states as to what this means clearly diverge. Some argue that it is a question of including EU 'defence planning' in NATO defence planning, while others see this as an opportunity for NATO to modify its outdated and less-than-effective planning process. If NATO defence planning had been truly effective in the past, there would not have been the need for initiatives such as the DCI and the Prague Capabilities Commitment. Moreover, in Europe there would be less duplication of national assets in areas such as air-defence fighters, main battle tanks, submarines and operational staff. Defence planning continues to reflect national political priorities, not collective needs or rational cooperation. Even with future initiatives to reenergise or rationalise NATO defence planning, the priorities of national governments, and ultimately the taxpayers, are likely to prevail.

Operational planning within NATO (as opposed to defence planning) consists of contingency operations plans (COPs), concepts of operations (CONOPS) and operations plans (OPLANS). As of 2002 the Combined Joint Planning Staff (CJPS), SACEUR and the Supreme Allied Commander Atlantic (SACLANT) produced these plans at the strategic level. NATO's International Staff and International Military Staff also contribute to elements of operational planning. There is extensive expertise at NATO headquarters in planning European military crisis-management operations.[11] The Combined Joint Planning Staff has been the key developer of ESDI-related concepts and has done a significant amount of work on the CJTFs and in support of the WEU. It has a formal role to provide support for ESDI/WEU operational planning.

During 2000 and 2001, the DSACEUR, Rupert Smith, and SHAPE took extraordinary steps to open NATO operational and defence planning to the EU. NATO International Staff and the US advocated a far-reaching EU–NATO collaborative defence-planning process, including all EU and NATO member states. There were also plans to open up SHAPE to all EU states. The official reason for this was to minimise duplication, but the underlying purpose was US and NATO concern that the alternative would pave the way for a separate EU defence-planning process, and separate EU operational planning, which could split NATO. The Combined Joint Planning Staff would play a complementary role as the prime operational planner for European military crisis management, including EU-led operations without any operational support from NATO.

There are essentially four options for EU–NATO operational cooperation. The first is for the EU to rely on NATO operational planning and command structures using DSACEUR and/or a CJTF headquarters, and perhaps other capabilities such as AWACS. This option, where the EU would only provide political leadership and strategic direction, would probably be the most effective from a war-fighting and command-and-control perspective. A second option would be to employ NATO operational planning and some NATO capabilities, while using a European operational headquarters and a non-NATO chain of command. This combination could create considerable difficulties if, for instance, US support for the EU operation was placed under the operational command of a French force commander and operational headquarters. The third option is for the EU to rely on NATO operational planning without using NATO structures or capabilities in the operation. This would demand close coordination between, for example, the Combined Joint Planning Staff and the European operational headquarters. There is also the option of EU autonomous engagement, whereby the EU does not rely on NATO operational planning or military capabilities. The UK and France and their national joint operational planning HQs would play lead roles here.

Collective NATO assets

For all the debate and posturing within NATO and the EU over providing NATO assets and capabilities, the alliance actually has relatively few collective assets, and not all of them can be categorised as capabilities for crisis-management operations. In 2002, the alliance collectively had 18 AWACS, 20 stationary headquarters, two not-yet-fully operational CJTF headquarters, a research ship and a pipeline system (mainly for jet fuel). Individual member states owned all the other assets assigned or linked to NATO. SHAPE, together with the Combined Joint Planning Staff, would probably be classified as a capability that could assist an EU operation, not an asset that could be placed under EU command.

Of these collective assets and capabilities, the AWACS and staff elements from established headquarters are of most interest for EU-led military crisis management. The CJTF headquarters have become large, heavy and US-dominated, and seem to be less attractive as lead elements for EU-led operations. NATO has no deployable land or maritime component headquarters or strategic and tactical intelligence capabilities – requirements that EU states say they need for EU operations. For operations in 2003 and 2004, NATO as such has little to offer the EU in terms of operational capabilities. It is a myth that the EU and its member states are dependant on NATO assets and capabilities; these are useful, rather than essential, as individual European states already have much of what is needed, including AWACS, deployable headquarters and intelligence capabilities.

Inside NATO, the 'presumption of availability' of pre-identified capabilities and assets does not constitute a binding commitment, and decisions will be made by the NAC on a case-by-case basis. This is a weak link that may well be exploited by an opponent. With regard to national assets and capabilities, it is up to the EU, or more likely individual EU member states, to conclude bilateral agreements for loan, lease or support. Here, cooperation with the US naturally plays a central role.

What if the definition of NATO assets and capabilities expanded to include NATO formations such as the standing naval forces, the Allied Command Europe Rapid Reaction Corps (ARRC), the NATO Response Force or *ad hoc* formations? Every government of participating forces in such a formation would still have to approve any participation, naturally on a case-by-case basis. A NATO force could however be coordinated inside the NATO framework and collectively offered to the EU. The 'NATO label' *per se* would have little or no operational significance – although the political signal could be substantial (giving headlines such as 'NATO airlift task force supports the EU Operation' or 'EU force evacuated by NATO special forces'). It is most likely that a 'NATO label' would be used by the US in order to spread the political and operational risk, accentuate the role and vitality of NATO, and strengthen EU–NATO links.

Once there is agreement for NATO or NATO-coordinated support for an EU operation, what happens if the alliance or individual states providing 'NATO support' change their minds in the middle of the operation, or after a long commitment? For example, what happens if an EU operation evolves in a direction that does not suit the US, which has provided intelligence and transport via NATO? Could compelling national reasons lead the US to pull officers out of NATO headquarters lent to the EU operation? The impact of this would be mostly political and in terms of alliance cohesion, but there could still be serious operational ramifications.

There is also a difficult question around who would pay for the operational use of NATO assets or capabilities in EU-led operations. There is no reason why the allies should collectively foot the bill – especially since the collective NATO budget is tiny.[12] Would the EU collectively pay for the NATO asset or capability, or would this be handled on a bilateral basis? Who would pay if, for example, a NATO AWACS were shot down while supporting an EU-led operation? Another issue is the potential escalation of an EU-led operation into a NATO collective-defence operation.

Should DSACEUR (a British or German officer) be designated by the EU and NATO members as the Operation Commander or Force Commander, many formal difficulties would be avoided. By being able to play both the European and NATO card, the prospects for using the best assets and capabilities from both organisations is relatively bright. However, the role of DSACEUR *vis-à-vis* EU crisis management has been politicised, and will probably remain sensitive for some time to come.

Assessing the EU's scenarios

While NATO military crisis management will take place only on a case-by-case basis, the EU has a permanent role in promoting stability through economic, political and military policies. The EU has no geographical restrictions.[13] Although EU experience is grounded in the Balkans, operations in Asia or Africa are often mentioned as examples of future EU crisis management, and there is the option of using the forces committed to the Headline Goal in international UN operations. In addition, both the EU and NATO can lend support to international coalitions outside the formal EU or NATO framework.

Scenario development

The potentially wide scope of action and national interests among the key European players has complicated the process of identifying scenarios for the forces committed to the Headline Goal. As there was no agreement in the wake of the Helsinki meeting in 1999, the path of least resistance led the EU to adopt three of the WEU's Illustrated Profiles (that is, military scenarios – the same as those used in assessing the WEU Audit of Assets). The scenarios are therefore based on traditional peace-support operations of the 1990s, and are relatively conventional in nature. That does not mean that the scenarios will not be modified over time, or that new ones focusing on, for example, civil protection, civil crisis-management or counter-terrorism, will not eventually complement this traditional scope.

While the existing scenarios do not provide a sound basis for realistic operational planning or identifying needs, they do demonstrate EU member states' level of ambition and the national political interests in play. There was a strong correlation between the force requirements for the scenarios and what EU members in 1999–2002 were prepared to offer in the first place. For many, it was important that the scenarios and the subsequent force requirements reflected EU power-projection capability and/ or already identified procurement demands: the A400M transport aircraft, aircraft carriers, intelligence satellites and UAVs, cruise missiles, attack helicopters, multiple-launch rocket systems and other pet national projects. Assets had to be 'tailored' to European needs and European scenarios to safeguard the interests of European defence industries. Buying American assets, or depending on US capabilities, was not seen as an option in many EU capitals. Some states argued that the scenarios should be small and manageable, in order not to challenge NATO's primacy, the US role in Europe and/or national defence budgets. Others saw the scenarios as a way of pressing ahead with radical defence restructuring, increasing military capabilities, maximising national defence industrial interests or increasing defence expenditure. Even within EU states, national defence, finance and foreign ministries had very different ambitions with regard to the scenarios.

On the one hand, the US supported ambitious EU goals in order to force Europeans to fulfil the DCI, assume more of the burden in Europe and enhance Europe's ability to cooperate with the US in safeguarding mutual interests beyond the continent. On the other hand, the US did not want to encourage the ESDP and competition with NATO. US defence industrial interests were also at work. France also wanted more ambitious objectives, but to reinforce European autonomy; there was, for instance, heated debate on how many combat aircraft the EU needed for the most demanding scenario, with the French calling for a force comparable with *Operation Allied Force*, and the US and more cautious European states arguing for around half that.

On several occasions, NATO operational planners (who largely developed the EU scenarios and calculated which capabilities were needed) came up with results that EU capitals did not like. For instance, one scenario called for more forces or longer deployment times than permitted by the Headline Goal. In response, the parameters were simply changed: harbours were enlarged (the tiny port of Durrës grew to Rotterdam-like size), the quality of roads improved (dirt roads became multi-lane highways), or the level of hostilities reduced to fit member states' interests and policies.[14] This resulted in the development of scenarios that were less than realistic, and of limited value as a basis for operational planning.

The 'Assistance to Civilians' scenario

The 'Assistance to Civilians' scenario dealt with refugee flows, humanitarian aid and the evacuation of EU nationals at a distance of 10,000 km from Brussels. The environment was largely permissive, but enforcement measures could be required. The reaction time would be short. The scenario resembled *Operation Alba* in 1997 or a small UNPROFOR, and tasks included area security and ensuring freedom of movement, information operations, humanitarian assistance and providing support for international agencies and evacuation operations.

The land component would require a divisional force of up to 9,000 troops (with a pool of 60,000 should the need arise), and would include armoured troops, mechanised infantry, air-mobile and armoured cavalry, artillery, special forces and psychological-operations troops. The air component would call for defensive counter-air, SEAD and close air support. Supporting air assets would include AWACS aircraft, air-to-air refuelling and combat search and rescue. Electronic intelligence, signals intelligence and airborne command, control and communications (ABCCC) and electronic-warfare forces would also be required. Maritime assets would range from carrier battle groups and amphibious shipping to submarines.

The 'Conflict Prevention/Preventive Deployment' scenario

The 'Conflict Prevention/Preventive Deployment' scenario called for expeditious and firm enforcement of a peace settlement. The scenario put the crisis at 4,000 km from Brussels. The environment was again permissive, but the force had to be capable of enforcement and securing the region. Police and civilian support would complement the corps-sized military element. This scenario implied that the EU should control a crisis area, thus paving the way for a peace process and the return of displaced people and refugees. The scenario could be compared with IFOR/SFOR, or KFOR after 1999. The forces required included a military police brigade, eight combat brigades, carrier battle groups and amphibious groups, UAVs, electronic intelligence and a considerable strategic reserve.

The 'Separation of Parties by Force' scenario

This was the most demanding scenario.[15] It required the EU to occupy a region 4,000 km from Brussels, and force two warring parties to accept a dictated peace. The environment was non-permissive and the risk high. The war-like situation precluded civil–military cooperation. Although *Operation Deliberate Force* in Bosnia in August–September 1995 was not as complex, dangerous or large, it gives an impression of the EU scenario.[16] The scenario is thus more demanding than the IFOR entry operation in autumn 1995, or the KFOR entry operation in June 1999.

The corps-level land force (60,000 troops plus 3,400 for an emergency evacuation operation) would include some 17 brigades, nine of which would be manoeuvre brigades (plus artillery, air-defence and support brigades). The force would also have attack helicopters. Although the scenario was 'land-heavy', the air component would be extensive, requiring up to 300 aircraft. It would be offensive in nature, and include all-weather strike capabilities, SEAD, offensive air and close air support, electronic warfare and ABCCC elements. The maritime component, requiring some 75 ships, would be diverse in order to deal with sea control, maritime embargo and air support for amphibious forces. The scenario called for substantial strategic reserves.

There were discrepancies between the NATO input and the proposed Force Requirements and those adopted by the EU ahead of the Capabilities Commitment Conference. NATO's technical advice did not call for intelligence or communication satellites. This may indicate that NATO staff or the US did not want to provide clear support for French and/or German satellite developments that would decrease European dependence on the US. The size and weight of the forces needed for the high-end scenario imply that Europe would be dependent on the US for several assets, such as heavy strategic airlift capable of transporting tanks. Furthermore, Europe will not own ABCCC or major combat search and rescue capabilities, or sufficient SEAD, precision-guided munitions and air-to-air refuelling for a large operation on a par with US/NATO speed and risk levels by 2003. It would be in the United States' and NATO's interest to persuade the Europeans to acquire such assets and capabilities.

EU decision-making, planning and intelligence capabilities

The EU's assets and capabilities for autonomous strategic decision-making, planning and intelligence are scarce. This is a limiting factor in conflict prevention, crisis management and cooperation with the US.[17] Although the EU has a well-established strategic decision-making capability for elements of the First Pillar (EU relations within the CFSP framework), effective decision-making for inter-governmental crisis management is unproven. Processes are still being put in place, and there is unlikely to be a true strategic decision-making capability for crisis management until the EU has engaged in one or two major crises. The role of the EU's

ESDP structures *vis-à-vis* national capitals, and how effective coordination will be between member states, will depend not only on the crisis in question and the varying national interests involved, but also on what added value the common ESDP structures can offer. In relation to the US, effective EU decision-making in the CFSP and ESDP framework is essential. If the EU cannot speak with one voice, and act quickly with cohesion and efficiency in coordinating economic, diplomatic and military elements, it will be a less attractive partner to the US.

For EU-led operations using NATO assets and capabilities, the EU Summit in Nice stated that operational planning would be carried out by NATO (SHAPE and the Combined Joint Planning Staff). In practice, this means that the EU would formally lead the operation, but that NATO would handle all the planning and command arrangements (probably through DSACEUR). US influence would be substantial as long as US and NATO assets were used, and EU autonomy would be nil. Such an arrangement may not be a problem in EU–US or EU–NATO cooperation, but it would be an issue if the EU member states must, or want to, act on their own.

For autonomous EU operations, the EU Military Staff would be tasked with setting the operational parameters at the strategic level.[18] Europe should accordingly develop a capability to plan for the whole spectrum of Petersberg tasks, an objective that will take several years to realise.[19] For any operational planning, the EU Military Staff will have to duplicate substantial parts of the planning elements of SHAPE and the Combined Joint Planning Staff. The EU would rely heavily on British and French operational joint planning capabilities. To manage an EU operation, the EU Military Staff will have to develop structures to link the SG/HR and Political and Security Committee, and indirectly the EU Commission and the member states, to the Operations Commander.[20] Multinationality, where all participating member states have representation at all levels, is not easy and not always especially effective – albeit necessary in EU or alliance operations. For small and relatively simple operations, a tactical headquarters such as the Allied Command Europe Rapid Reaction Corps (ARRC), under the EU flag, or a EUROCORPS augmented with joint expertise and liaison officers, could also play a lead role in operational planning.

Intelligence poses a major challenge. For the foreseeable future, the EU as an institution will not have credible intelligence input or output for strategic decision-making, operational assessments or operational command. Assets and capabilities are essentially limited to the small Joint Situation Centre, the EU Military Staff and the Satellite Centre (with most raw input coming from commercial satellites and the French–Spanish–Italian *Helios I* reconnaissance satellites). Even with the addition of national capabilities, the geographical scope of intelligence gathering and the likely depth of EU-wide assessments will not match the ambitions of the CFSP or the Headline Goal scenarios. Although there is extensive bilateral intelligence cooperation across the Atlantic, and also within Europe, the prospects of US or bilateral intelligence being made directly available to the EU seem remote. EU member states will continue to rely on US intelligence and little will be available at the EU level. EU CFSP/ESDP structures will be dependent on national assessments that have been 'washed' for EU consumption, delivered sporadically and voluntarily. Significant national intelligence is generally only released in the case of a specific threat or crisis, and little is channelled to the EU for more forward-looking pre-crisis conflict prevention, or for potential threats such as terrorism. Thus, current structures and processes are not a basis for strategic decision-making and operational control.

Only when European trust and cooperation enables genuine intelligence sharing among all member states will the EU be able to compete with, and manage relatively well without, US technical assistance for traditional crisis management. In practice, European states have yet to achieve equally close relations with their neighbours in the intelligence field as they have with the US. On the technical side, the small number of European higher-end intelligence sensors, such as satellites, comprise only a fraction of what the EU needs in order to plan and to take decisions autonomously.

European conflict prevention and civilian crisis management

The EU's most influential tools for affecting international stability are non-military, most notably economic measures backed by diplomacy. The EU accounts for 20% of global trade and 30% of the world's industrial production, provides 50% of all humanitarian aid and accounts for 60% of worldwide development aid. When national assets and capabilities are added, the EU has a potentially huge array of tools for projecting stability.[21]

Even before a crisis occurs, the EU can use economic instruments such as trade, tariffs and subsidies, loan policies, foreign aid, refugee management and immigration policy to exert influence. Democracy and human-rights support, arms control, de-mining and state-building are all important. Police missions, diplomatic contacts, defence diplomacy, observer missions, sharing intelligence and promoting the rule of law are also instruments of preventive diplomacy and conflict prevention. Together with other institutions such as the UN and NATO, the combined and coordinated effort of the EU's member states could have a considerable impact. In the case of counter-terrorism in the wake of 11 September, for instance, the EU's broad palette of economic and diplomatic instruments has proved useful and relevant, both for short-term initiatives and for long-term prevention efforts. This does not compete or challenge the US or NATO, or diminish the role of states and bilateral ties.

Emergency relief or civil protection in the wake of natural or man-made disasters is another tool of EU crisis management, which can be applied either within the EU itself, or globally. This element should include both non-military and military capabilities, which should be closely coordinated. Apart from counter-terrorism, threats or challenges such as international crime, drug-trafficking, people-smuggling, the illegal flow of money, goods and people and issues such as technology transfers also demand collective approaches as part of a common foreign and security policy. Many elements of civilian crisis management are equally relevant for internal and external security.

Principal challenges

There are five principal challenges facing EU civilian crisis management. All are manageable, though some will probably only be dealt with in the face of an acute crisis. Although it is too early to be certain, the events of 11 September may constitute such an event. The EU Convention may also add unexpected momentum in this field.

The first challenge is structural, and relates to the internal rivalry between the European Council, the SG/HR and the European Commission. As in any large organisation, personalities and turf battles have a significant impact on practical cooperation.

The second challenge concerns the functional coordination of the vast array of CFSP/ESDP components across the three EU pillars and the various directorates, secretariats and power-centres. Since some elements, such as counter-terrorism or civil protection, are equally relevant for internal and external security, this could complicate coordination. Furthermore, decision-making procedures and the respective roles of member states and EU organs differ between the EU's various pillars.

Third, few member states have a deep-seated interest in multinational civilian crisis management, and few have a defined policy in this area. Often, civilian crisis management is not high-profile and rarely makes for spectacular headlines. Its success is difficult to measure, and a conflict prevented is essentially a non-event in the eyes of the media and the general public. In relation to other categories of crisis management, conflict prevention will always compete for interest and resources.[22] Above all, there is little domestic support for sending scarce resources such as police officers, doctors, judges, prosecutors, engineers and money elsewhere. An added complication for national coordination is the fact that the assets belong to different ministries, individual federal states, counties and cities. Even with the EU Rapid Reaction Mechanism for financing civilian crisis management, long-term financing would be challenging for most governments. Developing such capabilities is hampered by difficulties in signing contracts with civilians, as there are challenging national training requirements, on-call arrangements and insurance issues. International interoperability and training is yet another problem, and it is often much easier to let non-governmental organisations do the job.

Fourth, there is a general reluctance to link military and civilian assets. Although the WEU made some headway on this point, many European armed forces fear that their professionalism and war-fighting expertise are threatened by further civilian cooperation. Conversely, civilians are sometimes concerned that they will be 'tainted' by involvement with uniformed personnel/combatants. Finally, there is no culture of EU preventive engagement, and the function will remain embryonic for some time.

Chapter 3

A New EU–US Strategic Partnership and Future EU–NATO Relations

The new transatlantic agenda

Between them, the EU and the US are home to 650m people, have a combined gross domestic product (GDP) of over $18,000 billion, representing 58% of world GDP, and account for more than 40% of the international trade in goods and services. In many, perhaps most, aspects of security and defence, including crisis management, the interests of Europeans and Americans coincide, even if policies, values, approaches and priorities may differ.[1]

Formal cooperation between the EU and the US is based on the Transatlantic Declaration of 1990. The New Transatlantic Agenda was adopted in 1995, and a follow-up is in preparation. Points of contact range from summit meetings and senior-level groups to working groups and meetings of experts. Since 1995, the dialogue has developed from consultations towards cooperation and joint action plans. Although a significant portion of the dialogue is on trade, the agenda has for several years included issues like the ESDP, non-proliferation and counter-terrorism, as well as the global challenges of energy, the environment and HIV/AIDS. In all probability, EU–US forums and points of contact will develop into an even closer relationship – particularly where interests and threat perceptions converge.

The US reaction to the ESDP

The US has generally viewed the ESDP and European relations through the lens of NATO.[2] The ESDP has been seen as controversial, and as posing a threat to NATO and US influence in Europe. The debate became particularly lively with the launch of the Headline Goal.[3] EU statements of 'autonomy' and 'self-sustainability', and individual states' talk of European 'first choice', 'emancipation', 'independence' and 'Western bi-polarity', reflected ambitions and visions that could be seen as threatening to the Cold War institutional setting, or as paving the way for a new transatlantic security arrangement. Whatever happens in Europe, for political and economic reasons the US does not have the option of retreating from European affairs.[4] At the same time, its reservations about the ESDP will continue for some time to come.[5]

As most Western European states are members of both NATO and the EU (giving these states a *de facto* 'double veto'), they can remain Atlanticists while also being staunchly European.[6] This initially unsettled and puzzled the US.[7] As Nicole Gnesotto observes, the US has a problem with Europe becoming too parasitic, and also with it becoming too equal.[8] It is a matter of perspective whether the US or the Europeans have most at stake in NATO.[9]

Nonetheless, the EU and the US seem to have reached a new level in their relations. The change comes from two directions. The first is the fact that the ESDP has fundamentally altered the institutional setting, and the shape of the transatlantic link. The second is that it suits the US for the Europeans to take increasing responsibility for their own security, while the US focuses on new priorities such as homeland defence.[10] This does not mean that the US does not care about Europe, that NATO is obsolete or that transatlantic ties are cut. But it does signal a new transatlantic relationship, where the US and Europe cooperate foremost on a global level, fighting common threats and defending common interests. The ESDP and the US focuses on homeland defence are not about strategic disengagement, nor are they a question of choosing between NATO and the ESDP. Rather, they mean developing new relations outside of the traditional transatlantic link, based on trade, shared strategic interests and common objectives in conflict prevention and stability.

Arguably, the autonomous decision-making capabilities that the EU is developing are no more dramatic or damaging to NATO than US decision-making autonomy. EU autonomy will make the

European pillar within NATO stronger, and autonomy is a normal part of a strategic partnership of equals. In reality, Europe will not stand alone any more than the US will, and cooperation will thrive as long as it benefits both partners. Almost nobody wants NATO to dissolve, and almost all the European states genuinely want a strong alliance, a strong CFSP/ESDP and healthy links with the US. Squaring this circle will at times be challenging, but far from impossible. There are some real differences, over trade, multilateralism, arms control, the role of the UN, the pre-emptive use of force, the death penalty, or multilateral initiatives such as the Kyoto Protocol or the International Criminal Court (ICC). The challenge lies in managing these disputes without allowing individual issues to taint the core of cooperative responsibilities and shared interests.

One of the key challenges concerns how the US perceives burden-sharing. The ESDP represents a new form of burden-sharing, rendering the traditional debate on this question obsolete.[11] The US has traditionally focused on persuading the Europeans to increase their defence spending and fulfil the DCI, rather than encouraging restructuring, reform or multinational coordination.[12] In 2001, the US DoD argued that 'unresponsive defense budgets pose a risk of stagnating or, even worse, eroding Alliance capabilities'.[13] This exemplifies the generally narrow perspective on this question in the US.[14] If the US continues to measure burden-sharing by the standards of European defence budgets, the DCI, alignment with JV 2010/2020, a US-defined RMA/transformation or Congressional demands, transatlantic squabbling will continue.

In place of traditional aspects of security and defence, tomorrow's strategic partnership should, and probably will, be dominated by trade, international politics, global crisis management, safeguarding common interests and commodities, arms control, non-proliferation and export-control regimes, counter-terrorism, international crime and strategic defences.[15] Traditional military capabilities will play a minor role.[16] The NATO-centric view is no longer relevant, and it will be in Washington's interests to have a broader and more multifaceted perception of, and relationship with, the ESDP, CFSP and European security arrangements. For all elements but European collective defence and high-end peace enforcement in Europe, the EU will be a more interesting partner in global crisis management than the European pillar within NATO. The new transatlantic strategic partnership will be a blend of respect, prestige, competition and cooperation in almost all fields. Developing this new partnership will not resolve the debates on European priorities, procurement budgets, NATO–EU relations and how best to address global threats – but these questions will be dealt with differently, and hopefully in a more constructive way.

For some time to come, the EU will remain a union of independent states, with their own interests and priorities.[17] Europe wants to be treated as the equal of the US, while maintaining national agendas and close bilateral contacts – which, from an outsider's perspective, is perhaps not a logical position. The challenge is for Europe to take steps towards greater coherence and to prove its worth as a strategic partner in global security. Conversely, it may be in Washington's interest to prove to the EU and the European states that the US provides a multifaceted security-projecting capability, and has more to offer than military might.

The challenges of EU–NATO cooperation

The question is not whether the ESDP should or could replace NATO, but how to bring about effective cooperation and coordination. Both the EU and NATO are mere institutions to enhance their member states' policies and assets, and facilitate cooperation and coordination between members. It is up to the members, particularly the major players with membership in both, to develop sound institutional working relationships.

Although the higher goals of the EU and NATO are the same and their membership broadly similar, there are fundamental differences. Their histories differ, as do their approaches to defence and crisis management, their expertise and their mandates. Other points of difference are size, budget, decision-making processes and command-and-control capabilities. The role of individual states within the two organisations – not least the US – is not equal, nor is the level of national sovereignty.

A strict division of labour between NATO and the EU would not be good for Europe, the US or the institutional development of either organisation. Above all, no European state wants two separate force structures. As the ESDP's formal focus is the Petersberg spectrum, there is a risk that NATO will be relegated to collective defence.[18] The alternative is to accept duplication and to continue to focus on commonalities, coordination and cooperation in military crisis management.[19] Even in the longer term, duplication will be good for NATO's vitality, European capabilities and the transatlantic strategic partnership as a whole.

NATO's status as the sole Western security structure has fundamentally changed with the ESDP, and it is probable, as Stephen Walt argued back in 1998, that the high-water mark of transatlantic security cooperation has passed. Transatlantic security cooperation has entered a new phase.[20] NATO's comparative advantages include the direct involvement of the US in European defence through US security guarantees to its allies; its role as a security forum and a forum for interoperability and common military standards; access to US force transformation; and its function as a structure to provide transatlantic cooperation in times of need. The pan-European nature of NATO and its partnerships, the stabilising effect it has had on Central and South-Eastern Europe and its role in European crisis management since 1992 are all valuable for European security. NATO will remain an important organisation and will retain its relevance, even in a transformed strategic partnership. Relations between the EU and NATO should be developed as long as NATO continues to play an important role in security and the EU–US relationship is embryonic, and until such time as the EU has addressed key flaws in its crisis-management capabilities and ended its dependence on US assets and capabilities for high-end military operations.

Chapter 4

Europe's Operational Limitations

On the basis of existing capability initiatives, the planned development of EU crisis-management capabilities and an evolving EU–US strategic partnership, this chapter assesses what an autonomous EU will be able to do, in strategic and operational terms, in 2003 and at the end of the decade – and what it will not be able to do. It analyses the EU's dependence on NATO and the US, and looks at the question of EU intelligence capabilities.

What an autonomous EU can and cannot do in the military field

Western Europe can cope with almost any crisis and war, including the situations envisaged in the three scenarios outlined in Chapter 2. But this is only possible if Europe is prepared to accept higher risks for engaged forces, if speed is not critical and if there are no competing military priorities. If Western European states can accept casualties and collateral damage, and if there is time to build political consensus and to deploy forces, then Europe can do a great deal on its own. However, if US high-intensity warfare is the only standard, if risks have to be kept to a minimum and a high operational tempo is needed to maintain public support and political alliances, then Europe faces major challenges in the next decade. On the other hand, Europeans and Americans have different global ambitions and priorities, and it is probable that the EU's standard of intervention will differ from the standards expected of NATO or a US-led coalition.

Although the development of the EU's capabilities since late 1999 has been vulnerable to criticism, not least because the political nature of the effort has been so dominant, the ESDP's structures and processes have taken huge strides forward, in a very short time, in terms of qualitative and quantitative output. The integrity, professionalism and initiative of the officers and civil servants involved, and the momentum of the ESDP process, should not be underestimated. Even a decrease in top-level political interest in the ESDP and the absence of spectacular new initiatives would therefore not mean that European integration and coordination in the security field had come to a halt. On the contrary, without a phase of consolidation after such an intense period of political initiatives, the whole ESDP enterprise would risk becoming a mere flow of announcements without much implementation and substance.

Military capabilities on the drawing board or in the pipeline

Half of European NATO members increased their defence spending in real terms, albeit marginally, in 2000. Elements such as intelligence received a boost due to the war on terrorism. Nevertheless, European defence budgets are unlikely to increase significantly in the medium term. On the contrary, the overall trend in total European defence spending remains downward in real terms. In addition, the challenges of multinational coordination and procurement will not disappear, and the restructuring needed for substantial savings and for the reorientation of many European armed forces will remain difficult. Conversely, the cuts in European defence expenditure throughout much of the 1990s have obviously not been severe enough to force governments into far-reaching multinational cooperation, the pooling of assets and capabilities, role specialisation or the fundamental rationalisation of defence industries.[1]

Relatively little money is spent on force transformation, procurement and research and development. While the UK and Sweden spend more than a third of their defence budgets in these areas, and France more than a quarter, the majority of Western European countries spend less than 20%.[2] Nonetheless, a number of large procurement projects with considerable defence-industrial potential are in the pipeline. Europeans have committed themselves to producing and procuring approximately 180 Airbus A400M strategic-lift aircraft. Even if this figure is not fully attained, there will probably be a significant and specific capability increase (though it will not give the Europeans a truly heavy-load, long-distance airlift capability because the A400M carries only 50% more than the common C-130 and a fraction of the C-17 or C-5).[3] The increased coordination and pooling of existing sea and airlift, fighters and aircraft logistics could enhance overall European lift capability. However, a German proposal for a joint European air-transport command, launched in the wake of the Kosovo campaign and included as a goal in the DCI, has not made progress.[4] The idea is rational, cost-effective and technically simple, but obviously unpopular in European capitals. Perhaps the Prague Capabilities Commitment will help European governments change their minds. France and the UK are acquiring several types of cruise missile, and the French and Germans are developing reconnaissance satellites (*Helios II* and *SARLupe*). Several states are acquiring UAVs and advanced fighters (*Rafale*, *Eurofighter* and *Gripen*), enhancing their precision-strike capability and acquiring new tactical communications systems, the *Meteor* air-to-air missile, *Patriot* PAC-3 extended-air-defence systems, main battle tanks, tactical airlift (C-130Js, C-295s), theatre transport such as the NH-90 helicopter, amphibious-warfare ships (LPD and ALSL) and roll-on/roll-off sealift.

Many of the DCI 'wish-list' items are not given the same priority as these projects. In fact, some take up such a large portion of procurement budgets in certain countries that new programmes more in tune with the network-centric philosophy of the DCI cannot gain ground. It remains unlikely that NATO members will jointly acquire airborne ground-surveillance systems (Joint-STARS-type assets) or new early-warning systems such as AWACS in the medium term. Other challenges or capability gaps identified in the DCI include plans for an integrated interoperable logistics information architecture, multinational exercise programmes, operational simulation devices, full interoperability between tactical communications systems, airfield-management systems, advanced air defence, combat search-and-rescue, air-to-air refuelling, electronic counter-measures/jamming aircraft, defences against weapons of mass destruction and their means of delivery and protection against modern sea mines and torpedoes. Europe is still a long way from even contemplating moving communications, including satellite communication, to broadband capabilities, an element given high priority by the US DoD and the very essence of US military transformation. For both the US and Europe, it is not a question of physics and know-how but of investment priorities and vision. As of 2002, it looked unlikely that any European government would be prepared to scrap a major equipment project such as a new line of fighters, battle tanks or helicopters in favour of something as low profile as communications, regardless of the revolutionary potential.

In the area of NBC protection, not least in the light of terrorist threats, there are acute needs in personal equipment and in safe-guarding both military and non-military infrastructure within the area of operations and at home. Further capability gaps identified in the HPC – particularly in support, logistics, engineering and medical capabilities – are equally vital in crisis-management oper-ations. Advanced fighter aircraft, precision-guided munitions, non-lethal weapons, SEAD and day/night and all-weather air-weapon systems are all being developed, but not in sufficient numbers to significantly enhance Europe's autonomous military capabilities.[5] Moreover, the proportion of logistics and support units made available to the full range of NATO missions has not, and probably will not, increase significantly.

Many current European procurement projects constitute massive duplication on a European scale. Is it wise of Europe to develop so many different types of traditional capabilities, such as main battle tanks, infantry fighting vehicles, fighters, submarines and surface combatants? For tomorrow's challenges, does Europe really need these platforms, none of which are categorised by any of the WEU, NATO or the EU capability inventories as shortfalls?

Even if projects on the drawing board are funded (which is far from certain), it will take time for new assets to become operational capabilities. In the case of the A400M, the first aircraft will fly in 2008 at the earliest, but realistically probably later. It will be several more years before units are fully operational, and a sufficient number of aircraft exists to make a significant contribution to Europe's overall airlift capability. In the meantime, leasing US C-17s like the UK has done may be an option, if strategic airlift is being acquired for operational, rather than mainly defence-industrial, reasons. For other major procurement programmes, such as reconnaissance satellites, cruise missiles, tactical airlift and advanced fighters, quantities are relatively small, and there will be little operational impact until 2005–2010. [6] It is also questionable whether sufficient money will be spent on the less spectacular capability gaps identified by the DCI and in the HPC. High-profile pet projects with greater defence-industrial links or clear application to defending against terrorism (of which there are few in the area of conventional military procurement) may attract the lion's share of political attention in European capitals whether they are needed (from a European perspective) or not. Realistically, based on what is in the pipeline and even taking the Prague Capabilities Commitment into account, a substantial increase in Europe's overall capability to successfully engage in high-end crisis management should not be expected in the medium term.

Many allies have indicated through their commitments to DCI-related Force Goals that they are not taking DCI implementation seriously.[7] As the US DoD noted in a report to Congress in March 2001, in many respects progress towards DCI objectives has been disappointingly slow.[8] The fact that the US had to relaunch a slimmed-down capability initiative in preparation for NATO's 2002 Prague Summit is further proof of the lack of progress – at least from the US perspective and by the standards of US military transformation. The DCI capability gaps will limit the EU's capacity to engage in the most demanding Petersberg tasks, not to mention US-led coalitions. These gaps will be particularly evident should the EU choose to engage autonomously.

Equally, it is questionable whether the HPC and ECAP will make much difference. It could be argued that a considerable portion of European force modernisation would probably have happened anyway – even without the DCI and the Headline Goal. The continued investment by European governments in traditional capabilities indicates that the capability initiatives have either not been understood, or have had little or no impact on procurement priorities. Perhaps the greatest benefits of these capability initiatives are political; their 'added value' may only develop in the longer term through increasingly coordinated defence planning and the development of new capabilities for a wider spectrum of engagement.

It is also questionable whether the projects planned by Europe's defence industry are on the same technological and interoperability level as the US. US capabilities are often a generation ahead of the Europeans doctrinally and technically, which means that interoperability is likely to remain a problem.[9] The speed of the US military transformation process paves the way for even greater capability gaps. However, just as it is important for the Europeans to be interoperable with the US, so too the US must secure interoperability with the Europeans, if it wants to work in coalitions and cooperate within the NATO framework.[10] Joint and combined US and European rapid reaction forces such as the NRF could be a step in the right direction.

The EU's military operational limit in 2003

In military terms, what is Europe able to manage on its own in 2003? For corps-sized operations, the European Military Staff as currently envisaged will probably be too small for effective operational planning (although this is a view not shared by all in the EU Military Staff as it grows larger and more confident – even in the planning sphere). In times of crisis, it is likely that planning will be supported (or essentially executed) by a lead nation or lead planning headquarters, identified early on. There is no reason to doubt that the British, French and German joint operational staff could produce credible plans, ideally (but not necessarily) in coordination with, and/or with the support of, NATO operational planning staff.

The primary constraint would be the time allotted to producing the palette required, from pre-crisis contingency plans to concepts of operation and operational plans, plus the time needed for them to be cleared by all the involved structures and member states. There is a risk that the lack of linkage between member states, the ESDP structures and operational staff (and back up the chain of command) will prove a bottleneck in a crisis. There is significant political sensitivity around establishing 'EU-only' structures and processes, and creating multinational staff out of national operational staff, along with secure command, control, communications, computer and intelligence links between all the levels and parties involved, is a costly and complex process. In the meantime, either multinationality and/or effective and secure links will probably have to be sacrificed. Transmitting secure broadband data from surveillance and reconnaissance assets across national contingents is an even more distant possibility.

In terms of actual operational capability, the forces committed to the Headline Goal do not constitute a fighting force, but rather are a mere catalogue of capabilities committed on a case-by-case basis by individual states. Nevertheless, the sum of just the German, British, French, Italian and Spanish contributions represents a sizeable capability of over 60,000 soldiers and almost 300 combat aircraft for a continuous one-year operation. Europe can handle a situation like *Operation Alba*: a brigade-sized multinational operation, where combat intensity is relatively low and there is no organised resistance and therefore little need for advanced air and naval support. Logistical trails are short, and the small force can be managed even without a large logistics base or host-nation support and infrastructure. However, even in *Operation Alba* Europe had no capacity to escalate. In fact, the Combined Joint Planning Staff in NATO had prepared a contingency plan for a US-led evacuation should the need arise.[11] In 2002, while the EU was politically prepared to take over from NATO's European-led operation *Amber Fox* in Macedonia, some member states were reluctant to do so for fear of over-stretching their forces because of other peace-support commitments.

Even without external help, the 'Assistance to Civilians' scenario, including smaller evacuation operations, should not pose a major challenge for the EU. The UK, France, Spain, Italy and the Netherlands have long had such a capability and EU coordination should be manageable – particularly if there are one or two lead nations. In an acute evacuation scenario, it is also probable that the luxury of EU multinationality can be sacrificed. The 'Conflict Prevention/Preventive Deployment' scenario is also within current European capacities, though there would be some flaws in the high-end spectrum. These could perhaps be managed on a bilateral basis, or with a marginally higher tolerance for collateral damage and risk. Gradual improvements in sustainability mean that a one-year operation of up to 60,000 troops for the Conflict Prevention/Preventive Deployment scenario is not a major issue. Unless the EU merely takes over an already-established mission, the main challenges will lie in drawing down existing deployments and reducing redeployment time. Should forces need new training and equipment, or if the deployment takes place in difficult climates, sustainability could become a problem, even for the Conflict Prevention/Preventive Deployment scenario. Concurrent operations would also present problems. Certain combinations of operations, particularly taking place a good distance apart, would put greater strains on some capabilities than would be the case were the most demanding scenario occurring alone.

Strategic decision-making, operational command and control and intelligence will remain bottlenecks. Indeed, the whole process of EU decision-making and unity of command will remain underdeveloped. In intelligence, even with rapid development, French and German reconnaissance satellites will be operational at the earliest in 2004, and European sensors will remain few in number and, in most cases, at least a generation behind American assets. Intelligence cooperation among EU members and the EU's central assessment capability will remain poor. On the hardware side, Europe's ability to act autonomously in high-tempo peace-enforcement operations and its high-end projection capabilities will remain limited. Perhaps the most dangerous limitation will be Europe's poor capacity to escalate. Europe will not have additional combat-ready divisions, carrier battle groups and marine and air expeditionary forces deployable at short notice, either for escalation or for large-scale evacuations; nor will it have the means to deploy and support them.

EU members will be able to do much in military crisis management by 2003. But autonomous, high-tempo peace enforcement in a non-permissive environment will not be possible – particularly if the operation is larger than divisional, risks have to be kept low and deployment times within the Headline Goal criteria. At the high end of the spectrum, EU states will remain dependent on the US for operational, and perhaps also for political, support.

The EU's military operational limit in 2010

On the basis of what has been decided as of late 2002, significant increases in European military crisis-management capabilities are likely by 2010 – at least by European standards, as defined in 1999–2002 – even if the ESDP process slows down. It is probable that both sea and airlift will increase, although whether they do so on the scale envisaged at the beginning of the decade is less clear. Nevertheless, mobility and readiness will improve. Precision-guided munitions and cruise missiles will be more readily available, and electronic-warfare and SEAD capabilities will probably also have increased. It is, however, difficult to see significant improvements in operational command-and-control networks and support elements, including logistics, engineering and medical support.

By 2010, military reform will have been completed in France, and probably also in Germany. Most European armed forces will be geared towards military crisis management, and expeditionary capabilities will play a central role. Multinationality and interoperability will probably have further evolved. Sustainability, deployability and effective engagement will have moved forward. The EU structures, and probably also individual member states, will probably be better at strategic decision-making, intelligence-gathering and strategic (and perhaps operational) planning than they were at the beginning of the decade. By 2010, it is likely that EU states will be able to meet the 2003 Headline Goal in full. This does not, however, mean that Europe will have fulfilled every DCI objective or that the capability gap across the Atlantic will have decreased. On the contrary; the US will have made its own capability increases, particularly in high-technology areas such as command, control and communications and in the whole sphere of sensors and intelligence gathering and dissemination. Judging by the much larger investment being made in the US on network-centric warfare elements, the technical gap is bound to increase. The question is whether the doctrinal and operational gap will be even greater.

Much will depend on the level of US–European cooperation in combined experimentation and force development.

Defence planning

EU defence planning, particularly if non-military and military capabilities are linked, can play an important role in increasing European capabilities. The EU Capabilities Development Mechanism will probably be geared not only to updating commitments and filling gaps, but also to formulating political goals, setting operational targets, managing national commitments and future capabilities enhancements, linking lessons learnt to planned needs and introducing peer pressure to the review phase. Key aspects are the implementation of crisis-management mechanisms and capabilities, the quality validation of those mechanisms and capabilities, and the establishment of truly operational capabilities for joint and multinational war-fighting.

However, by 2010 the Headline Goal is bound to have changed in line with changes in EU cohesion, integration and perceived threats. Where yesterday's goals are directed towards conventional military crisis management, tomorrow's may focus on other challenges, ranging from territorial defence and counter-terrorism to cyber-attacks and CBRNE weapons. The EU's goals may develop along the lines of its comparative advantages, and non-military crisis management and conflict prevention may be seen as more important than the military components.

Beyond 2010, European processes, procedures, doctrines and modes of operation may have developed in such a way that they do not fully correlate to US and NATO standards, although a certain level of interoperability would most likely be maintained. In the longer term, depending on the involvement of the UK in the development of the EU's operational capability and cooperation between Germany, France, Italy and the Benelux countries, it should not be taken for granted that Anglo-Saxon methods and procedures will remain the natural choice in all areas of European cooperation. There is thus a risk that this may add to further interoperability challenges with the US.

Legal and political considerations

The EU sees itself as a sophisticated international player with high moral standards and values. As a result, a number of factors could limit its operational capability. Although the Headline Goal is not bound by a formal UN mandate, high standards will be set for EU intervention.[12] The intervention must be 'just', a concept which, aside from self-defence, has historically included punishing an aggressor or intervening on behalf of victims of aggression.[13] The intervention must be morally justified and must be a last resort, to be used only when diplomatic and non-violent means have failed. Thus, few EU military crisis-management engagements will be initiated without considerable international debate and the lengthy exploration of non-violent alternatives. Surprise and pre-emptive force are unlikely.

Given the heterogeneous nature of the EU's composition, the fact that many member states would want a UN mandate before any military intervention and the need for close consultation with NATO, there is little reason to believe that securing legal justification for action will be any quicker in the EU than it is in UN peace-support operations – unless clear interests are threatened, as was the case with *Operation Alba* in 1997 or after the terrorist strikes in the US in 2001. (Less adversarial forms of military crisis management, such as naval patrols, as well as operations in response to acute situations, such as evacuations, can of course be performed nationally, or collectively under the EU, without any formal mandate or lengthy debate.) There may also be competition between the EU and NATO. EU bilateral dialogue with all NATO member states and Russia, and perhaps coordination and cooperation, is another potentially complicating factor – particularly if key players want to delay an operation, or prefer a different institutional slant.

Two further factors may also be important. The first is proportionality, which demands certain capabilities, like detailed intelligence and precision-guided munitions. 'Dumb bombs' are not politically acceptable unless vital or existential interests are at stake.[14] Second, there must be a reasonable chance of success (and again raises the issue of escalation). The need to define proportionality throughout a crisis, and with it to set targeting criteria and operational tempos, together with continuous assessment of the likelihood of success, could lead to debate among EU members.

Target selection by consensus does not sound easy, or militarily decisive. As long as all EU states must give their consent to military action under an EU flag, decision-making is likely to be complicated.

Before leaving his post in mid-2000, SACEUR Wesley Clark suggested that the gradualist approach to combat that NATO had demonstrated over Kosovo might not succeed the next time the alliance used force.[15] If NATO (with the full support and dominance of the US) tends to behave this way, how cohesive and decisive can the EU hope to be in crisis management? For operations or threats that demand a more proactive or pre-emptive approach, or where speed is important, national intervention by one or more allies or other *ad hoc* arrangements under a lead nation might be more appropriate, with or without a symbolic blessing from the EU and/or NATO member states. If vital interests are at stake or if a broadly-recognised case could be made for self-defence, NATO or a coalition of the willing with NATO's political support will for the foreseeable future remain the natural choice.

Europe's intelligence capability

Whatever CFSP or ESDP activity takes place, be it in the pre-crisis or the crisis phase, intelligence for strategic decision-making is paramount. Along with operational self-sustainability, autonomous decision-making is a formal EU goal. Whether an engagement demands EU–NATO and EU–US coordination, or if it is an autonomous EU operation, EU bodies and member states must be capable of taking decisions based on their own assessments. Given that intelligence cooperation in NATO has been non-existent, why should cooperation be any more effective within the EU? The difference is that the autonomous strategic decision-making capability is already a political goal; in the near future, there will be a political and operational demand for EU intelligence.

There are two purposes for EU intelligence. The first relates to long-term conflict prevention and the EU's position as an international actor. Pre-crisis intelligence can help the EU to use its economic, diplomatic and military conflict-prevention means more effectively. The second intelligence element is related to operational engagement in times of crisis. Although each demands very different kinds of analysis and capabilities, both are essential for strategic decision-making.

Current processes are not satisfactory because they are based on the principle that all intelligence, with the exception of the EU's Satellite Centre, is channelled from member states; the ESDP structures, including the Joint Situation Centre, should be happy with whatever they get. As a consequence, the EU's assessment capability is confined to a tiny Joint Situation Centre in Brussels, and there is little capacity either to check the validity of national intelligence or to compile broader intelligence assessments where national military intelligence is only one part of the equation. Little national intelligence is tailored to the needs of the ESDP structures, or put in the CFSP and ESDP context. For quick and effective strategic decision-making, current processes are not good enough.

A comprehensive joint European intelligence-assessment capability could prove an invaluable step towards more effective EU strategic decision-making for both conflict prevention and crisis management. Such an intelligence capability, within the intergovernmental Second Pillar of the EU, could also function as an intelligence coordinator in fields such as terrorism and unconventional threats. In the HHC of 2000, EU states identified the need for a facility for intelligence fusion, analysis, storage and dissemination, and for an EU Military Staff Intelligence Division.[16] Although the latter already exists, it falls short of the comprehensive intelligence function required by the EU.[17] Equally, the SG/HR Policy Unit, albeit highly capable, is too small and not geared towards intelligence analysis or coordination. The Policy Unit would be better able to serve the SG/HR and the Political and Security Committee with assessments and option proposals if it were supported by an intelligence-analysis capability. Other functions, such as the Director-General for External Affairs (primarily DGE VIII), would also benefit.

The EU's envisaged intelligence function would provide common assessments of political and operational relevance. Although any structure would spend much time comparing and compiling national assessments, the function would have to be able to produce its own analyses and assessments, both short- and long-term. This would demand a sizeable capability. EU member states would not only have full access to EU assessments, but would also be obliged to contribute raw and processed data. The intelligence function would be one element in an over-arching European network of bilateral and multilateral intelligence cooperation.

Using capabilities that already exist, the Satellite Centre could become the hub for the interpretation of satellite intelligence and imagery from European commercial and military assets. The key for the EU, via the centre, is to have increased access to French and German military satellites, including in some cases resolution codes and algorithms. For this to be a European project, full access should be provided to all EU member states, unless they choose to opt out. Sharing operating costs, and perhaps research and development costs, would have to be agreed between all the states that would benefit from the imagery, or that are involved in the EU intelligence function.

EU intelligence cooperation should also be developed at the tactical level. Experience from peace-support operations in the Balkans shows that, although intelligence remains a jealously-guarded national commodity, tactical-level cooperation is possible. The National Intelligence Cell network in SFOR and KFOR headquarters is a useful and proven model for EU-led peace-support operations.

In terms of data input, most capability assessments stress the need for high-end technical platforms such as satellites. Although defence-industrial interests, technology transfer and national prestige are significant issues, it is important to recognise that expensive platforms are no panacea.[18] High-tech assets might be spectacular and costly, but they are relatively useless unless the data they produce are properly received, assessed, contextualised and disseminated to the relevant bodies or individuals – and all in time to be useful. Real-time intelligence calls for huge resources in order to direct the satellites, receive the data, interpret them and forward them to the relevant platform or decision-maker. The ESDP structures will not have the capacity for quick interpretation, dissemination and input to policy channels in the short to medium term, let alone a real-time capability. Furthermore, for decent coverage, several different types and more than a handful of satellites are needed; however, their provision is unlikely within the next decade. Besides, almost all threat/intelligence assessments need to be based on multiple sources – not just technical data.

On the other hand, if the main function of the satellites is to give sporadic input on global flashpoints, or to provide Europe with collateral information against which to verify US intelligence, Europe could probably manage with a handful of French and German military satellites. With clear commitment and financing, such a capability could be realised in the medium term, perhaps by 2005. This would still be a clear case of duplication, just as for most military assets that exist on both sides of the Atlantic. Such a limited European capability would not make the EU self-sufficient in intelligence (as called for in the Headline Goal), and the EU and its members would still remain largely dependent on US intelligence capabilities.[19]

As well as developing satellites for a limited autonomous capability, there must also be operational alternatives. Much can be done through modifying existing platforms, using the whole palette of intelligence sources and through international coordination and cooperation. Europe's wide array of signals and human intelligence, coupled with existing satellite and air assets, could provide much strategic and operational intelligence for conflict prevention and crisis management if cooperation increased. For these combined assets to be effective, they must be coordinated at the strategic EU level, and fully integrated at the operational level.

Operationally, a combination of top-end special forces (such as the UK's Special Air Service (SAS) or France's Commando Parachute Group), advanced signals-intelligence capabilities (such as those provided by Sweden in Bosnia and Kosovo), UAVs and aerial photo and radar reconnaissance can, in most operational situations, provide more relevant intelligence at a fraction of the investment and operating cost than satellite imagery and US Joint-STAR input.

Challenges for EU conflict prevention and crisis management

The two greatest threats facing the ESDP are failure to act successfully and disengagement by a key European player. In the pre-crisis phase, Europeans are likely to have trouble deciding if a crisis is developing, what sort of crisis it is and how best to deal with it. National policies, prestige and ambition may collide, and nationally-slanted intelligence may further diminish the chances of achieving a common view. Atlanticists would probably disagree with advocates of a European approach, while others would perhaps opt out altogether. As long as vital interests are not at stake, issues of internal EU and US–EU coordination and links to multilateral bodies like the UN and the Organisation for Security and Cooperation in Europe (OSCE) would probably further complicate decision-making. Economic, diplomatic and military instruments may not be properly coordinated or used to their full potential.

Should the EU decide to mount a military operation, this would obviously mean that conflict prevention had failed. Even with a military operation under way (with at least the political support of all member states), any perceived shortcomings would damage the credibility of the EU and the ESDP. Challenges would include ensuring political cohesion among the members and other contributors, making sure that strategic decision-making did not falter and coping with military capability flaws and poor means of military escalation. The US could also choose not to support the operation – even if asked to do so; however, any perceived lack of support would affect NATO solidarity. A divided and frustrated Europe will not produce a stronger alliance or a credible strategic partner for the US.

On the other hand, even a perceived operational failure, or an embarrassing bail-out by the US or NATO, would probably not halt the CFSP or ESDP. Finger-pointing would temporarily damage European cohesion and leave a bitter after-taste, but the CFSP and ESDP are much larger phenomena than a one-off military operation. As Alyson Bailes argues, greater operational experience will make the CFSP more 'street-wise' and effective. Engagement will gradually increase the level of non-military and military coordination, and will enhance EU effectiveness. It is probable that the EU will also learn lessons from, and be influenced by, non-EU engagements.

Should decision-making at the EU level prove impossible for a prolonged period, perhaps several years, or if a series of crisis-management efforts are seen as failures, alternatives to the CFSP and ESDP may well develop. There will always be European states willing to cooperate outside international organisations, if these bodies are not functioning adequately. On the other hand, even if institutional cooperation succeeds but the mission fails – based on the experience of UN and NATO operations – the EU as an institution will probably be a useful scapegoat.

The second threat – disengagement by one of the key European players – would potentially have more serious and longer-term consequences than failure. Should the UK, France or Germany turn their back on the common EU foreign and defence policy or actively obstruct the EU, the ESDP project would swiftly stall.[20] Any long-term stagnation would be damaging for European integration as a whole and for relations among European states, particularly if the US at the same time gave priority to homeland defence, leaving Europe fragmented and lonely, and without the ability to act as a strategic partner with Washington. Large-scale recession, a collapse in the value of the euro or mass unemployment could quickly shift political attention away from secondary issues like the ESDP. Such serious developments could affect defence budgets, capability-building and most aspects of crisis management. Policies may turn inwards, towards protectionism and re-nationalisation. In the words of Helmut Schmidt, the EU is still a very young and fragile creature, and can be destroyed by national egotism as well as by international upheavals.[21]

Until effective European strategic decision-making structures are in place, and until the EU can effectively coordinate economic, diplomatic and military elements, Europe as a coherent defence entity will carry little weight or credibility, its operational limitations evident for all to see. As of late 2003, and with the Headline Goal deadline, the ESDP will be fair game for international criticism. The EU will have functioning structures at the higher level and a considerable number of capabilities in place, but they will not be fully efficient, effective or potent in conflict prevention and crisis management.

This vulnerability cannot be blamed on NATO, on the US or on new threats. The US and NATO have offered their support and cooperation. Although close cooperation is rational and logical, the US or NATO as an institution cannot enhance the EU's crisis-management capabilities, military, non-military or bureau-cratic. It is up to the Europeans, and above all the UK, France and Germany, to rationalise, coordinate, cooperate and produce better capabilities. Only by increasing its capabilities by innovative and proactive measures can Europe reduce its vulnerability and lay the foundations for credible crisis management.

Chapter 5

Practical Steps To Increase European Capabilities

The prospects for increasing European capabilities for conflict prevention and the management of international crises are good. The question is how significant the increase will be, in what time-frame it will be effected and which focus further capability initiatives will have.

Despite good intentions and a legion of NATO and EU military capability initiatives, progress is slow. Over the next five years or so, it is unlikely that the increase in capabilities will be anything more than marginal. It takes time to build platforms and equipment, to train personnel and to build a military capability – regardless of increases in defence expenditure. Only marginal capability increases are in the procurement pipeline, and a significant increase in Europe's defence expenditure is not feasible under current political conditions. On the contrary, defence expenditure will continue to decrease in many European states. For many voters and governments, it makes sense to take money away from defence and spend it on the police (for counter-terrorism and international operations), foreign aid, domestic civil protection against natural disasters, or even healthcare. The opportunities for greater and more relevant output lie in the field of national reprioritisation and European coordination.

The sum of the capabilities committed to the Headline Goal catalogue is substantial, and Europe will be able to do much on its own. However, because member states lack a handful of capabilities they say they need for the most demanding or geographically distant scenarios, the full Headline Goal ambitions will not be met by late 2003, or indeed for much of the decade. On the other hand, EU members have set their own goals, interpreted them and developed scenarios, and then identified which assets and capabilities would be needed to meet the most challenging situations. The flaws in military capabilities add an incentive for national defence procurement – particularly for those EU member states that have retained major defence-industrial capacities.

The outlook is more promising for the non-military elements of crisis management. Given the EU's low starting point, any increase is bound to be significant. The potential for development in this field is huge. The EU's goals, ranging from police capacity and state-building to civil protection and elements of conflict prevention, will probably be met by late 2003.

These outcomes are not, however, pre-determined, and Europe could substantially increase its capacities even in the medium term, and could do so at little expense. The greatest potential for significantly increasing Europe's capabilities lies in the following areas: enhanced strategic decision-making; intelligence coordination; the development of Europe's conventional military capabilities through increased coordination; national and functional coordination within the Union; and pragmatic EU–NATO and EU–US cooperation.

Enhancing European strategic decision-making

The EU's conflict-prevention and crisis-management capabilities would be significantly increased if its strategic decision-making were enhanced. To achieve this calls for centralised EU coordination of the economic, diplomatic and military and non-military elements of conflict prevention and crisis management, and a single European voice. Realistically, there will not be a common foreign and security policy on every issue in international relations, but there may be room for a common European approach in many, if not most, cases. Even so, centralised EU coordination will not and cannot replace bilateral ties between states within the EU, and across the Atlantic. Strategic EU coordination would be a complement, but not a substitute, for existing ties.

Ideally, one body should coordinate all elements of the ESDP and external relations with states and regions in potential areas of crisis. Only when trade, diplomatic initiatives, loan policies, national and EU threat-reduction schemes, national NGO initiatives and regional relations and crisis-management tools are dynamically linked can conflict prevention be successful – whatever the challenge. Furthermore, this body should coordinate crisis management and intelligence, including monitoring potential and ongoing crises, bilateral military cooperation, non-proliferation, counter-terrorism and arms and technology transfers. Such a body must grasp long-term capability development, defence-industrial cooperation and policy coordination and development within the EU. Only when these elements are tied together can the EU's capability in conflict prevention and crisis management reach its full potential.

Enhanced strategic decision-making is not just needed in times of crisis. Coordination should be the day-to-day norm in order to contribute to stability projection in the pre-crisis phase. There is much to recommend the Political and Security Committee, complemented by relevant Commission and Third Pillar representatives, as this key coordination structure – a European Security Council with joint national and functional representation. (The actual name of this council is not important, but the function is.) The SG/HR, representing competence and continuity, would be a natural chair for such a body.[1] The challenge is to secure the support of the Commission and the SG/HR and General Secretariat of the Council, and to persuade national capitals, particularly London, Paris and Berlin, to hand such an important task to a body in distant Brussels.

A wider body than the current Political and Security Committee is needed because many of the threats and challenges that the EU will face will demand the involvement of the Commission and the EU's legal/police elements. Effective counter-terrorism demands that policies relating to border control are linked with police coordination. At the same time, trade, loans and sanctions can encourage third countries to cooperate. These efforts may be coupled with military threat assessments from the General Secretariat of the Council and member states, and with military and civilian crisis-management elements that deal with terrorism outside the EU. Regional instability in the Middle East or North Africa, for instance, would call for sophisticated and complex management, using all conflict-prevention and crisis-management elements at the disposal of the EU and its members. One crisis may initially be dealt with in the Second Pillar, and then involve the First and then the Third; another may first involve the Commission, then the CFSP and military and civilian crisis-management elements as it develops.

The boundaries between military and civilian security and internal and external security are more fluid and institutions and states must develop new structures and processes to meet this reality. A joint Security Council where the Political and Security Committee is in the lead and the other two pillars are represented could be a cost-effective, useful instrument for increased security.[2] The only rational alternative to increased coordination across the pillars is to amalgamate the EU pillars altogether.

Practical steps

In terms of the technicalities, the decision-*making* Committee of Permanent Representatives (COREPER) would hand over much of its decision-*shaping* and coordination function in conflict prevention and crisis management to the Political and Security Committee. In the long term, the EU would benefit from having just one body, thus giving a joint cross-pillar Security Council improved decision-making powers. The national representatives on the Political and Security Committee should be given stronger mandates by their governments for quicker decision-making. The question of who is to have what vote in a future EU Security Council is sensitive. The CFSP remains inter-governmental, though a voice, and perhaps a vote, should be given to the other two pillars. The fact that a Security Council would be large, particularly after further EU enlargement, makes consensus-building challenging, and much will depend on the chairman and his staff. On the other hand, the large number of countries represented, plus the weight of the other two pillars, would give the Security Council significant international legitimacy and clout.

The Political and Security Committee will need to develop a more effective support staff. To an extent, such mechanisms and structures already exist in the General Secretariat of the Council, not least in the tiny but important Policy Unit and Joint Situation

Centre. These need to be enhanced, as does the role of the SG/HR. Developing policy input for the Political and Security Committee should be a major focus. The SG/HR and General Secretariat of the Council should produce political contingency plans for all conceivable areas of activity, and should support national representatives on the Political and Security Committee in achieving consensus among member states. Key functions include early warning, situation assessment and strategic planning for medium- to long-term conflict prevention and crisis management, including preventive diplomacy and deployments. The SG/HR and the Political and Security Committee/EU Security Council should spend considerable time looking at latent crises, and challenges that may develop into crises months or years ahead. Long-term conflict prevention is rarely glamorous and always difficult to sell politically, but rational and financially sound. More time and effort should be spent by the Political and Security Committee and the SG/HR (and in the future the proposed EU Security Council) on developing democracy, trade, tolerance and the rule of law, expanding contacts through defence diplomacy and supporting regional security and military cooperation and peacekeeping capabilities in areas of concern beyond the EU.

Expanding international points of contact

The Political and Security Committee and the SG/HR should also broaden their international points of contact. Direct ties through liaison offices and exchanges should be established with major international organisations such as the UN, the OSCE, the World Bank, the International Monetary Fund (IMF) and the International Committee of the Red Cross (ICRC).[3] In principle, these organisations should be informed of all CFSP and ESDP matters, and they should have the opportunity to make contributions.

The relationship between the EU and the US should be given priority, and the input of the US welcomed in matters relating to the CFSP and decision-*shaping* processes. Transatlantic dialogue, including the New Transatlantic Agenda, should be complemented by bilateral ties (liaison personnel and exchanges) with the Political and Security Committee and the SG/HR and staff elements, primarily the Policy Unity, DGE VIII, the Military Staff and the

Military Committee. Although priorities and principles may vary, EU member states should have nothing to hide from the US, and vice-versa. On the contrary, the EU must actively seek coordination and dialogue with the US in all international pre-crisis and crisis matters, ranging from areas of concern and ongoing operations to managing common threats. General coordination of long-term stability projection, plus trade and aid, is particularly important. Again, counter-terrorism and conflict prevention have enormous potential if the EU and the US can develop assessments, share ideas and form compatible policies. Although the US has no formal voice in the EU, just as the EU has none in Washington, ideas should flow freely between them as a matter of course. In addition, EU candidate states and Russia should have liaison officers tied to the General Secretariat of the Council, and via their capitals, and should be invited to contribute ideas and to coordinate with the EU.[4]

This does not mean that the EU should become a chaotic forum in which all international organisations, NGOs and states voice their grievances and concerns, thereby paralysing EU decision-making. But it does mean that the EU CFSP/ESDP structures should listen to other players and, where consistent with the policy of EU members, seek policy coordination and practical cooperation. In practical terms, the Political and Security Committee and the SG/HR could establish hearings and selected working groups in order to channel external input and support coordination.

Initiatives like these call for an enlarged SG/HR Policy Unit, an increased Military and CFSP/ESDP staff and more effective coordination mechanisms with the Commission and national representatives in Brussels. The cost of these enhanced support functions, divided by the number of EU members, is a small price to pay.[5] Establishing these processes can be quickly arranged if there is agreement in London, Paris and Berlin. Although it would take several years before the processes became truly effective, they would significantly increase the EU's capability. The price would lie in loss of national prestige and the option to 'go it alone' – particularly among the more influential EU states.

Establishing EU intelligence coordination

EU intelligence is needed at two levels – the strategic decision-making level and the operational level – and for two purposes – long-term conflict prevention and active crisis management. In the near future, Europe will need a comprehensive intelligence function for strategic decision-making. With hindsight, such a function could have played an important role in the wake of the September 2001 attacks in the US and the subsequent counter-terrorism campaign. The capability will be paramount in addressing instability and future change in the Middle East. There is a demand for intelligence by the SG/HR (and the Policy Unit), the EU Council (and its Political and Security Committee) and the European Commission. The HHC contains a 'requirement' for an intelligence division under the Military Staff – but this is not of the right calibre.

There is a need for an intelligence unit at the political level, preferably directly under the chairman of the Political and Security Committee and the SG/HR, and closely linked with the Policy Unit.[6] An embryonic capability exists in the Joint Situation Centre, but it is questionable whether this is developing quickly enough, or is sufficiently ambitious. Ideally, the EU intelligence function, in both size and role, should be modelled on the UK's Joint Intelligence Committee.

It is important that EU central intelligence is civilian-led, that it has a multifaceted analysis capability, that it is focused on pre-crisis conflict prevention and has direct access to policy makers. Its task would be to support the ESDP structures and the Political and Security Committee (or a future EU Security Council) in order to increase the coordination and output of the wide palette of EU tools for conflict prevention. Without such an analysis capability the ESDP structures, including the Political and Security Committee, depend on national intelligence assessments alone.

Apart from traditional military intelligence (which should be a minor function), the EU intelligence function would have a wider scope, and include humanitarian, economic and political elements and related assessments, ranging from cyber-threats, terrorism and organised crime to weapons' proliferation. Since risk perceptions differ across the Atlantic, it is important for Europe to produce its own risk assessments.

For both the pre-crisis and crisis phases, input would be channelled via member states' own intelligence and diplomatic services, EU Military Committee representatives and the Satellite Centre. Valuable input pertaining to political, economic, industrial and legal circumstances in states with relations with the EU can also be gleaned from the relevant commission directorates. Open-source intelligence and assessments from independent think-tanks would complement these sources. The key is for the EU to have a sizeable and autonomous analysis body that can produce original and relevant assessments. Security is a concern, but if the top secret standard can be maintained in SHAPE and the NATO Combined Joint Planning Staff, there is no reason why such standards could not be maintained among professionals working with EU intelligence.

The EU intelligence function should also act as a forum for temporary or extraordinary cooperation among national experts. Whether it be a crisis in Macedonia, unrest in a North African state, pre-crisis long-term stability projection or counter-terrorism, national intelligence experts could be pooled at the EU level. These experts should be pre-identified, and should function as informal working groups, together with the EU's permanent intelligence staff. This would allow *ad hoc* intelligence coordination and networking among member states and between national and EU experts, and would also contribute intelligence to the EU national representatives and the ESDP structures.

Increased intelligence coordination is also necessary for reasons of operational safety. Member states' intelligence has to be channelled to the EU during an operation; it would be disastrous if soldiers from a member state were killed, and it later transpired that intelligence which could have avoided the casualties had been withheld by another member state.[7]

As Charles Grant argues, there is no reason why the EU, via an EU intelligence function, could not develop a bilateral relationship with the US.[8] This would make the US feel included, dispel rumours, and pave the way for a flow of intelligence assessments where there are common interests and, at the least, compatible policies. Such cooperation would be a natural part of any strategic partnership.

An EU intelligence function would be rational and potentially highly effective. Much intelligence relating to the Balkans, for instance, is endlessly circulated in European capitals. There is a risk that intelligence coming from the same source (often American) is modified each time it changes hands. The more outdated information becomes, the greater the damage if it proves inaccurate. Today there is massive duplication of European national intelligence capabilities, not least in areas where national interests are less than vital. If the Europeans could share a portion of basic intelligence relating to areas of potential crises, resources could be channelled towards deeper and more focused assessments.

The sensitive issue of intelligence cooperation, the danger of national interpretations and slants, differing national agendas and interests and their effect on national and EU assessments – all will mean that an EU intelligence function, let alone EU–US cooperation, will be challenging. In some ways, a relatively autonomous EU intelligence function under the Political and Security Committee/Security Council will compete with national intelligence services, and the 'ownership' of intelligence and sources could become tricky. Few intelligence services wish to give more attention to European cooperation if this drains resources from their relationship with the US. However, greater openness within an EU framework and increased competition in producing original and relevant data will, in the long term, improve the quality of European intelligence services and European security overall. Meetings among EU member states' directors of military intelligence are a step in the right direction, though the real experts also need to meet and exchange views. It is up to governments to force intelligence services to cooperate and contribute more directly to the CFSP and ESDP.

For an EU intelligence function to be effective and relevant, it would have to have authority, integrity and the respect of the other EU institutions and member states. Its staff would have to be community-funded and recruited directly by the General Secretariat of the Council. Intelligence services would most likely require liaison officers to convey (and translate) sensitive information to those producing the assessments – not dissimilar from the process developed for military intelligence conveyed to the EU Military Staff. To produce new and uniquely relevant intelligence, an EU intelligence body would probably require a minimum of around

100 intelligence experts, excluding national liaison officers and support staff. A clear political directive by EU member states will be vital to the running of the intelligence function, the formulation of intelligence requirements and the national fulfilment of intelligence commitments.

On the hardware side, the EU should also develop its strategic reconnaissance capability. At least a handful of satellites is needed in order to have the ability to verify US intelligence, add a modest autonomous capability and contribute to transatlantic intelligence-gathering in both the conflict-prevention and crisis-management phases. The development of coordinated human intelligence, UAVs, aerial reconnaissance, European air-based ground-surveillance radar, special forces and signals intelligence would give the EU a better operational intelligence capability. Individual EU members and the EU as an institution must have processed and unprocessed intelligence, as well as analysis and assessments, to trade with the US.

Even with the political will to create an EU intelligence function and the establishment of security arrangements, operational cooperation and trust would still take time to develop. Even under favourable conditions, perhaps generated by an acute need for cooperation during a crisis such as the counter-terrorist campaign in 2001 and 2002, it would probably take 5–10 years for EU intelligence coordination to become effective. The development of US–EU cooperation is therefore important, not only for the benefit of European security and the transatlantic link, but also because there is little option in the short to medium term. It is, however, important to note that the development of a relatively autonomous EU intelligence analysis capability is a contribution to transatlantic burden-sharing (both old and new), and does not diminish existing bilateral intelligence cooperation across the Atlantic.

The capability initiatives and the future of European integration

The quest is for greater and more relevant output. The institutional label of the initiatives or forces is less important.

In the military field, it will be important to maintain the momentum of the DCI, the Prague Capabilities Commitment, and the Headline Goal towards deployability, sustainability, effective engagement, survivability, command-and-control systems and interoperability. Whatever the initiative, military forces should become more flexible, potent and better supported for crisis management than they are today. Improvement will not be spectacular or quick, but it will gradually enhance the EU, NATO and the transatlantic strategic partnership. It is also important that Europe acquires the assets and capabilities it needs – not what the US would like Europe to develop. European taxpayers and governments alone decide what is value for money.

The greatest 'new' output will come from those countries that have so far failed to move beyond the old concept of stationary territorial defence, and from those countries that have yet to form deployable, effective and sustainable capabilities for crisis-management operations. Forces must have dual roles [EU/national/homeland]: Security and defence *and* international crisis management. Once reforms are complete, the armed forces in Spain, Italy, Poland and Germany will produce significantly increased capabilities for the EU, and will reduce the reliance on France and the UK.

EU coordination in armaments development and procurement should, at least in theory, be one of the best ways to build new capabilities. Under the ESDP, the EU's national armaments directors meet regularly and the institutionalisation of this format, a European Armaments Agency, makes sense. Cooperation is further developed within the ECAP framework. However, this element of the ESDP has at the same time been one of its least rewarding aspects. National prestige, industry concerns and the need to preserve jobs mean that this is a highly political issue. Coordination within the EU challenges other established defence-cooperation forums (WEAG, OCCAR and the separate defence-industrial cooperation under the 'letter-of-intent' process among the EU's six largest defence producers).

Intensified defence-industrial cooperation is nonetheless essential to the ESDP, and crucial if Europe is to increase its military capabilities. There is massive duplication and over-capacity in Europe's defence industries, and quality is frequently lower than in the US. Only through further consolidation, greater competition and more standardised products can Europe hope to increase not only quantitative capability levels, but also qualitative levels. This is also a prerequisite for healthy transatlantic defence procurement.[9] Only when Europe is competitive is the US likely to take it seriously in both the security and defence-industrial arenas.

François Heisbourg has observed that deficiencies in European capabilities are not due to inadequate overall defence spending.[10] EU member states spent 173.5bn euros ($156bn) on defence in 2001.[11] Heisbourg argues that Europeans can improve the *efficiency* of their defence spending by defining force goals, improving budget structures and input criteria (for example, convergence criteria) and the pooling of key capabilities.[12] Given that force planning boils down to national interests, policies and priorities, there is little reason to believe that EU defence planning will significantly better NATO's in realising capabilities. Nevertheless, a 'Europeanisation' of defence planning and force goals is bound to occur, and could lead to a more coordinated approach to European capabilities development.

Europe has huge arsenals of assets; EU member states have almost 9,000 main battle tanks, for instance (this number more than doubles if Turkey and EU-candidate countries are included), more than 50 conventional submarines and more than 3,000 combat aircraft, but only a fraction of these assets could be categorised as capabilities for real crisis-management operations. There is thus massive duplication. The problem is that European states, most of which declare that they have moved on from the concept of conventional territorial defence, continue to invest in traditional equipment without looking at what they really need for crisis-management operations. As pooling and functional coordination is practically non-existent, any improvement through defence planning, dialogue and cooperation would be a step in the right direction.

Joint requirements and joint procurement can result in additional and cheaper assets, hopefully of a high technological standard. Above all, pooling key national capabilities could significantly increase European capabilities. It does not make sense that almost every European state has its own C-130 and/or C-160 airlift assets and full logistic support and training, however small the force. The German idea of a joint EU transport command is sound and should be developed, as should the NATO Prague Capabilities Commitment of November 2002 which called for the pooling and joint ownership of support jamming pods, air-to-air refuelling and UAVs. Leasing or buying US strategic airlift also makes sense. Pooling would also be relevant for sealift, some aircraft logistics (for the F-16, *Mirage, Tornado, Eurofighter* and an array of helicopters), military medical services, air and maritime control and submarine search and rescue.[13] Functions such as naval and air patrols could also be coordinated, at least in sub-regions. As the protection of external borders is increasingly seen as a common mission, a standing European naval force and coast guard tasked with defence and border control may emerge.

Pooling higher military education and specialist training, and the consequent closing down of some national facilities, can save money and increase quality and interoperability. Similarly, it could be possible to merge national defence-research establishments. Although the gradual consolidation of Europe's defence industries will generate more multinational research and development, governments must seek European cooperation in research beyond multinational procurement programmes.[14]

Role specialisation may *de facto* occur in all European armed forces, but few states are prepared to develop a formal policy. Coordination and the sharing of tasks with trusted neighbours, with Benelux cooperation as a model, is a more palatable option until further European integration permits bolder steps. Sub-regional cooperation – as in EUROCORPS, EUROMARFOR, ARRC and the Nordic Brigade – adds multinational capabilities that are interoperable and relevant, while enhancing commonality and spreading political risk and cost. The NRF may prove a useful instrument not only for the rational coordination of high-readiness capabilities, but also for NATO cohesion, transatlantic interoperability and European insight into US force transformation.

Increased attention is also being paid to doctrinal, operational and technical interoperability. The development of doctrines for military crisis management is done better and more economically in a multinational framework. In general, exercises and training should increasingly be multinational – even at relatively low tactical levels. National 'jointness', an area in which a majority of

EU member states still face enormous challenges, should develop towards multinational European 'jointness'. NATO standardisation is, for now, the key instrument of this process, although EU operations will demand interoperability and 'jointness' at lower levels than are called for in traditional NATO deployments. The NRF may come to play a role even in this sense. Interoperability efforts within the alliance and Europe must be accelerated; one aspect of this is increased quality control and the tactical evaluation of capabilities committed to EU and NATO service.

Exercises may seem an obvious step towards interoperability. Although there is an EU policy in this area, it engages only EU and NATO strategic-level structures, not operational and tactical capabilities and live exercises. Military units committed to the Headline Goal, including non-NATO headquarters, should exercise together. Cooperation in the Balkans helps, but only when units exercise together can they function together immediately on deployment. This calls for specific forces and units to be assigned to the Headline Goal, not just the commitment of a force whose specific composition and field partner is decided on a case-by-case basis.[15] This is an area where healthy EU–NATO cooperation can be developed in practice.

In the civilian crisis-management field, it is equally important to follow through on capability initiatives. Further steps will demand increased cooperation and coordination. Police officers for crisis-management operations are the spearhead of this cooperation, and common principles, concepts and training are being applied. Nevertheless, there is work to be done. The EU's police catalogue must differentiate between different kinds of police for different deployments. Common concepts are also being developed for rule-of-law elements. Cooperation is embryonic in EU civilian crisis management, but the potential for development is limited only by the imagination, and issues of national prestige and cost. Cooperation in the wake of national disasters in Europe has highlighted the need for coordination among neighbours, and demonstrated that some of the capabilities needed for out-of-area crisis management are equally relevant at home.

Conceptually and in practice, progress has been impressive in just a few short years. In the area of border control, the idea of a

European corps of border guards is already being debated.[16] Developing *gendarmerie*-type forces, and increasing European cooperation among them, could add an important counter-terrorism capability and a capability much in demand in peace-support operations. Capabilities cannot easily be tailored either for domestic purposes or for out-of-area operations since operational needs tend to override such definitions. Increased coordination and cooperation between border guards, coast guards, area surveillance, *gendarmerie* forces and the police makes sense, and prepares Europe for challenges both within and outside the Union.

Capability initiatives, both regional and pan-European alike, are also affected by EU enlargement. To give an example, the Baltic Sea region will be fundamentally transformed with the enlargement of the EU so that all states except Russia are members. Cooperation and coordination in what will become an 'EU lake' will in time probably affect police cooperation, border control, military environmental issues, sea and air surveillance (civilian and military), intelligence coordination, the joint monitoring of threats from organised crime and terrorists, search and rescue and practical interoperability for all elements involved. There are also significant financial and political gains to be derived from such regional coordination, not to mention advantages in European integration. As internal and external security become difficult to separate, so the need for national and regional coordination between such elements as police services, coast guards, navies and customs will increase. Just as security cooperation between Belgium, the Netherlands and Luxembourg has developed since the Second World War, so this is gradually spreading across Europe. In all probability, we have seen only the beginning. New security-related areas of cooperation are bound to emerge.

Developing joint non-military and military crisis management capabilities

The EU also faces the challenge of linking non-military and military crisis management and developing joint capabilities in order to broaden the range of tools for managing crises. There is a need to link military and non-military crisis-management capabilities at both the strategic and the operational level. Whether or not the

Political and Security Committee evolves into a EU Security Council, it must coordinate all elements of crisis management, including non-military components. The two elements should be inseparable in conceptual work, planning and operational command-and-control.[17] Currently, the EU lacks any kind of command-and-control arrangement for non-military operations. Unity of command, from the political level down to the field operators, must be established across the whole crisis-management spectrum.

EU states should identify and catalogue the relevant civilian capabilities as has been done for military capabilities. Within the various categories, a minimum of standardisation and interoperability should be established between national capabilities, and between multinational capabilities. Joint training and exercises are also necessary, as is the development of day-to-day coordination mechanisms among states and between states and the EU non-military crisis-management structure.

Taking the Headline Goal idea one step further, EU civil protection and crisis management would benefit from the establishment of 'Reaction Packages'. For example, readily-available Packages should be tailored to emergency relief in the wake of natural or man-made disasters, both within the EU and externally. This may involve linking national and international NGOs and relief agencies with civilian and military medical support, military engineering, search-and-rescue capabilities and military transport. Some Packages could be based on modular rapid-reaction police forces, while others could focus on civil emergencies, medical or search-and-rescue (non-military and military) operations. Pre-crisis state-building elements should also be available in 'Package' form. Another niche could be threat-reduction teams for detection and monitoring, or joint teams dealing with radiological, biological or chemical terrorist attacks. Post-crisis detoxification and sanitisation is another field. Fact-finding teams and several of the Reaction Packages must be capable of reacting immediately.

At the higher end of the crisis spectrum, there should be Reaction Packages for initial deployments of humanitarian missions, evacuation operations, peace-support operations and post-conflict state-building. The scenarios for such contingencies exist, but not the pre-identification of capabilities earmarked for them.

Some Reaction Packages would contain mainly conventional military capabilities, while others would focus on unconventional warfare, including special forces (both military and police) for counter-terrorism operations or countering asymmetrical threats. Naturally some capabilities or functions can be earmarked for more than one Package, at least to a certain extent and as long as a level of interoperability is guaranteed.

Size and readiness would naturally vary. Large combat-capable Reaction Packages, perhaps of divisional size, could resemble NATO's joint response force or the Standing Naval Forces, although they would contain a broader range of capabilities (including non-military elements) and standards for interoperability (because of multinationality at lower levels), and pre-readiness training would need to be higher. Another such Reaction Package could be small and highly specialised, more comparable to existing US and UK special-forces cooperation or amphibious-forces cooperation between the UK and the Netherlands. Unity of command, interoperability and the sustainability of non-military and military capabilities are vital, as these would represent the EU's initial engagement forces. If modes of cooperation are established through exercises and dialogue in peacetime, the operational phase is likely to be more effective.

Establishing Reaction Packages cannot happen overnight, and there are significant costs involved as soon as the aim is high readiness. However, most of the assets and capabilities already exist, and many of the components are committed to the Helsinki Headline Goal or could be assembled with existing national capabilities. However, there needs to be more coordination. Since many threats are commonly shared, this could be best achieved in a pan-European or EU forum. Starting off with a couple of Reaction Packages would be a realistic step, and could be a suitable follow-on Headline Goal.

It may be relatively easy to generate the political will for such coordination at the central EU level. The real challenge lies with individual member states. Each government needs to ask itself whether it is prepared to go beyond the current EU commitments, commit to training and maintain in a state of readiness, deal with legal and procedural obstacles to taking quick decisions. Is there a real interest in sending non-military assets abroad and developing the capability to contribute to quick and effective decision-making in Brussels on conflict prevention and crisis management? Some governments may fear the misguided label of 'EU Army' that could be applied to these pre-identified, pre-trained and interoperable Reaction Packages. On the other hand, many of the challenges described above are as important within the Union as they are globally, and in most cases multinational cooperation is essential for effective engagement. The institutional label is less important than the development of coordinated European capabilities. For now, the EU looks to be the most suitable forum for such coordination, though the EU should also seek broader international cooperation. Coordination with any NATO response force or operational capability is inevitable and should be encouraged. In civil emergencies, there is every reason to build on NATO's experience in Kosovo and Macedonia. In counter-terrorism, cooperation with the US should be a priority.

A practical approach to EU–NATO cooperation

A close and effective institutional working relationship between the EU and NATO would be sensible and logical. However, this will not materialise unless it is in the interests of all member states.[18] EU–NATO cooperation requires not only formal agreement on the political front, but also strategic compatibility and practical arrangements, for which the identification of common strategic objectives,[19] compatible procedures and over-arching priorities is key. This should be done at the highest political level.[20]

In an ideal world, the joint EU–NATO forum should be broadened to include all levels of cooperation, from groups of experts and ambassadors to foreign and defence ministers and heads of state and government. In areas of common interest, and where there is broad Western consensus, the joint forum should also have decision-making powers.[21] The bottom line is that the EU and NATO member states should be flexible, and use whatever institution, forum or group is relevant for the issue at hand. The major drawbacks with such a forum are that it would limit 'constructive ambiguity' between the two institutions, for states belonging to both organisations to present only one point of view (rather than different positions for each group), and add yet another layer of decision-making. However, even if the only result is dialogue, confidence-building, institutional coordination and decision-shaping between the two institutions, European security would still benefit.[22]

The alternative to a close EU–NATO relationship lies in accentuated bilateral ties – first and foremost the EU–US relationship. This could be supported, for example, by augmenting the suggested EU Security Council with an American representative on a case-by-case or functional basis. Points of contact between the EU and EU-candidate countries are also important. In time – and depending on EU cohesion post enlargement, the follow-on to the ESDP, a new form of burden-sharing across the Atlantic and cooperation on issues of common concern – the EU–US relationship may become the core not only of European, but also Western, security cooperation. The EU, because of the wide spectrum of security-projecting elements at its disposal, may become a more important dialogue partner for the US than the more narrowly focused European pillar in NATO. Nevertheless, the functions and capabilities should be in focus, not institutional labels. Over the next decade or so, the wisest course is to develop both close EU–NATO and close EU–US relations, with the aim of sustaining NATO as an organisation and exploiting the many useful elements of cooperation, including the benefits of engaging non-EU NATO members in European and EU crisis management.

EU–NATO cooperation in defence and operational planning

The EU will need to develop its own defence-planning process. Called the Capabilities Development Mechanism, this will largely mirror NATO's defence-planning process. Just as in NATO, there is a need within the EU to link collective goals and scenarios to force catalogues, procurement and operationalising capabilities, and progress reviews. Three challenges should be addressed.

First, while it will be difficult to merge the two defence-planning processes or integrate EU defence planning into NATO's, it would nonetheless make sense if both the EU and NATO member states could at least identify compatible political goals (NATO

Ministerial Guidance and EU Headline Goals), directions and priorities. Differences relating to strategic and operational needs (for example, different requirements for strategic intelligence and deployment range and different roles in territorial defence) and different linkages to defence-industrial policies and national agendas ought to be manageable as long as the aim is compatibility, not trying to make the two processes identical or one and the same. At the very least, the two defence-planning cycles should be synchronised and the processes should be parallel. When it comes to EU and NATO defence planning, there should be nothing to hide between the two organisations and, although non-member decision-shaping in defence planning may be limited, transparency and compatibility should be complete.

Just as has been the case for NATO, the EU process must permit opt-outs, without individual states being able to obstruct cooperation among the majority. In the case of obstruction by a minority, an alternative for those states that want to cooperate is to create a defence-planning process which is formally separate from the EU and NATO, but which uses the same mechanism and processes.

Second, in practical crisis management contacts between the EU and NATO should be developed at all levels and in all possible forums – particularly between military staff and the decision-making bodies. The alternative, should individual states obstruct such dialogue, is to create *ad hoc* arrangements outside the EU or NATO, or to use bilateral and multilateral contacts. Although this would damage institutional cohesion, it would also permit pragmatic and sensible cooperation.

Third, it is the responsibility of the individual member states, not the institutions, to produce the capabilities required. Although institutional staff can coordinate national defence planning and provide collective processes, every state will remain loyal to its own national interests and domestic agendas. As each state has only one defence-planning process, one set of forces and one procurement budget, it is up to individual nations to ensure that the substance of the two defence-planning processes remains the same, even though the two processes may cater to different roles and goals.

At the operational level, once the political decision has been made to initiate planning and to invite non-members to participate, all states engaged in an operation should be involved. This could mean troop contributors from non-NATO EU members participating in NATO planning, or non-EU NATO member states in EU planning. To safeguard NATO's valuable capability in operational planning, SHAPE and the Combined Joint Planning Staff should be opened up to non-NATO EU members, which should enjoy a status similar to that of the French, with national representatives in Mons. Differing transatlantic operational agendas and intelligence assessments may prove a challenge, but increased European intelligence capabilities and US–EU intelligence cooperation should minimise the problem.

Ideally, NATO and EU operational planning should be amalgamated and a formula found to ensure that no one member state can stop the others from cooperating. European operational planning could be produced by NATO staff – as long as the staff can also produce autonomous EU operational alternatives and credibly serve the EU without a US/NATO political slant. Effective contacts should be established between the EU Military Staff, the Combined Joint Planning Staff and the prime European operational headquarters. The principle of reciprocity is important. Just as the EU can rely on NATO assets and capabilities, so NATO must be able to count on EU assets and capabilities. Special arrangements would have to be made for NATO's Article 5 and nuclear planning.

This paper does not advocate the development of a European joint-operations headquarters akin to SHAPE in its calibre and role. As long as there is guaranteed access by the EU and all its member states to SHAPE, the Combined Joint Planning Staff and related capabilities, there is little reason for duplication. However, if that is not the case, a 'Euro-SHAPE' may well be developed in the longer term. The advantage would be not having to rely on the veto of non-EU NATO members; and within the union, not to have to rely on a UK-, French- or German-dominated national operational headquarters. A European HQ should be able to handle both civilian and military crisis-management capabilities, a point that will become increasingly important the more military and civilian crisis-management capabilities are coordinated at the strategic and operational level. If such a European HQ was purely military, it would compete with SHAPE and only complicate common operational perceptions and planning transparency. The main challenge with a European HQ would lie in operational cooperation with the US. US cooperation through both SHAPE and a European HQ sounds complicated, but may be manageable.

EU–NATO cooperation is not technically or practically difficult – the obstacles are purely political. Theoretically, if there is the political will, then effective EU–NATO cooperation could be established, even in the short term.

Conclusion

Policy coordination in the CFSP and ESDP has developed since 1999 and today the EU is a net exporter of security. The Union is well placed to link a wide palette of economic, diplomatic and military means in the fight against multifaceted threats and challenges. It is a unique forum for coordination and consultation across nations, borders, sectors and institutions. The EU has the potential to become a global force in conflict prevention and crisis management. While the EU may not manage potential or active crises in the same way, or using the same instruments, as the US or a US-led coalition, it may potentially become a valued strategic partner where common values and interests are at stake. However, without the development of more relevant capabilities, and increased European coordination Europe will be limited to yesterday's tools for tomorrow's challenges.

Currently, the military capabilities of EU member states fall short of their declared ambitions, and will do so for years to come. Relying on current institutions, processes, defence-budget levels and defence planning, Europe will, at best, see only marginal increases in its military capabilities over the next five years. The picture is brighter regarding non-military/civilian crisis-management capabilities. However, significant political obstacles complicate efforts to enhance the EU's overall capabilities, both in the civilian and military fields.

The US and NATO have offered their support and cooperation. It is now up to the UK, France, Germany and the other EU member states to improve and better coordinate their efforts to produce enhanced capabilities and, ultimately, achieve an increase in the substantive level of European contributions to regional and worldwide security fully commensurate with the role, interests and resources of the EU and its members. It would help if the debate on increasing European crisis-management capabilities focused less on institutional labelling, fanciful notions of European global power projection, a 'European Army' or supposed challenges to the US and NATO, and instead identified how European states can realistically increase their capacity for effective conflict prevention and crisis management. Most of all, Europe needs better mechanisms and processes for coordinating national capabilities.

Despite slow progress in implementing the NATO Defence Capabilities Initiative and the EU Helsinki Headline Goal, the Europeans will in 2003 possess a large, albeit traditionally-structured, force reservoir. The EU member states will essentially be capable of performing all the military tasks that fall explicitly within the Petersberg spectrum, including peace enforcement. For complex operations demanding a high operational tempo, reduced risks to EU forces and minimum collateral damage, Europe will, for the rest of the decade, still depend on US assets. Strategic sea and airlift, intelligence assets and all-weather precision-strike capabilities are further prerequisites for major high-tempo operations.

Over the next few years, quantitative and qualitative improvements in reconnaissance, communications, strategic lift, air-to-air refuelling, tactical mobility, force protection, combat search and rescue, electronic counter-measures, theatre-missile defence, UAVs, precision-guided munitions, NBC protection and logistics will indicate how far the NATO and EU capabilities initiatives have succeeded, and to what extent the prospects of EU operational autonomy for larger combat operations are going to be realised. In any case, several years will normally elapse between the appropriation of funds and the availability of new operational capabilities. So far, the impact of the DCI and the Headline Goal on European force modernisation has been limited. It remains to be seen if the November 2002 NATO Prague Capabilities Commitment will generate more than a marginal additional increase.

Real increases in European military capabilities will derive not only from the acquisition of new assets, but also from innovative organisational approaches. There is great potential in the pooling of assets and capabilities, rationalisation and multinational cooperation in military education and training, doctrinal development, logistical support and defence-industrial consolidation. Joint procurement and production and far-reaching pooling initiatives – from air transport, electronic warfare, maintenance and logistics to defence-research establishments – will save money and produce more interoperable and flexible capabilities. It takes several years for multinational formations to become truly effective and operational. Action must be taken soon, or the opportunity to increase European capabilities in this decade will be lost. The price for such action will be paid mainly in national prestige, as the desire for national ownership of defence assets and industries dies hard. Unilateral engagement against the will of partners and allies will also become more difficult once multinational development, procurement and pooling are the norm.

'Jointness' and interoperability within NATO remain key challenges. The transatlantic technological and doctrinal gap will not close given the rapid pace at which the US is acquiring new high-tech assets. The European focus on crisis management and peace support is in stark contrast to the US attention to high-tech warfare and homeland defence. Of course, the responsibility for keeping forces interoperable and enabling them to reap the benefits of 'jointness' rests on both sides. This is likely to be an issue of transatlantic debate and finger-pointing. The standards of US-led war-fighting coalitions and NATO peace enforcement will not necessarily be the same as those for EU-led operations. The new NATO Response Force may bridge part of the gap. European interest and European access to US transformational technology and doctrine will determine the level of success.

The EU's dependence on NATO (as opposed to US) assets and capabilities is actually marginal. Although NATO's UK-led rapid-reaction corps is the most effective corps headquarters in Europe, the only collective NATO capability upon which the EU depends is the operational planning capacity in SHAPE's Combined Joint Planning Staff. National planning and command-and-control capabilities exist in the UK, France and Germany. This means that the EU is in fact not vitally dependent on NATO's collective assets. Even 'SHAPE-like' multinational planning capabilities could if necessary be duplicated within the EU.

Nevertheless, NATO's established military-integration structures provide an indispensable framework for the transition to enhanced European forces capable of full-spectrum operations. NATO is likely to remain relevant to the EU even after its dependence on US forces becomes less pronounced than today. In the interest of reaching the EU's declared capability goals, practical contacts between the EU and NATO must be developed at all levels, particularly between military staff and decision-makers. There is value in working towards synchronised defence planning in parallel in NATO and the EU. The EU would greatly benefit from live exercises to develop its operational and tactical capabilities.

European capability-building efforts must be evaluated on their own merits, and in their own timeframe. The EU's comparative advantage lies not in high-intensity warfare, but in conflict prevention through the coordinated use of diplomatic and economic measures, and crisis management with civilian and military means. It would be a mistake to judge the EU's military capabilities in isolation from its other crisis-prevention and conflict-management capabilities. For many scenarios, improvements in decision-making and the determined application of the economic, diplomatic and civilian elements of crisis management could prove just as important, if not more so, than war-fighting capabilities. Increasingly, the capabilities needed for such operations are just as relevant for many internal challenges, such as civil emergency support, man-made and natural disasters and the fight against terrorism.

The development of crisis management in the spheres of civil protection and conflict prevention is particularly important. Significant progress has already been made in the EU, but there is vast potential for additional measures to strengthen the EU's ability to deal with disasters, build coordinated European police and *gendarmerie* capabilities, promote the rule of law in areas of instability, conduct observer missions and defence diplomacy and share intelligence on threats and risks from terrorism, critical-infrastructure attacks and weapons of mass destruction. In combining such capabilities with its diplomatic, economic, financial and military potential, Europe has much to offer. Close coordination between the civilian and military elements of crisis management, including establishing pre-trained, interoperable and high-readiness Reaction Packages, would further enhance Europe's ability to employ its widely-defined power to the benefit of international peace and security.

The core challenge is to develop the EU's political cohesion and strategic decision-making capability, linking the various elements together in common long-term policies. Only when trade, diplomatic initiatives, loan policies, national NGO initiatives and regional relations are combined can conflict prevention succeed. It would also make sense to coordinate issues such as defence-industrial cooperation, technology transfer and intelligence at the strategic EU level. Today's EU lacks a command and control establishment even for civilian operations. To turn the EU as a whole into a strategic actor, unity of command would first have to be assured across the crisis-management spectrum, from the political level down to field operations. In the complex relationship between member states and community institutions across the EU's three pillars, the question of who is in command must be resolved.

Eventually, one body needs to be coordinating all civilian and military elements of the ESDP and the EU's external relations. Such an 'EU Security Council' would go a long way to overcoming the well-known shortcomings that have prevented the EU from being seen as a strategic actor: insufficient coordination between the three pillars, inadequate civil–military integration, ill-defined interests and policies, insufficient efforts to build public support and a failure to actively seek wide coordination and dialogue with other governments and international organisations – above all the US – in early, proactive engagement, initiative, risk-taking and leadership.

Autonomous strategic decision-making and military self-sustainability in intelligence – both declared goals of the EU – also call for proper EU intelligence capabilities, including CFSP ESDP-specific assessments and analysis. Effective conflict prevention in the pre-crisis phase demands high-quality and multifaceted intelligence. Further operational intelligence is necessary for any crisis-management engagement. There is a growing need for a centrally-coordinated EU intelligence function modelled on the UK's Joint Intelligence Committee, and a fundamental reassessment of intelligence cooperation requirements in Europe.

Capabilities development is not about autonomy, national posturing or grand visions of power projection. Mere quantities of assets and institutional labels are of little use. What it is really about is rational coordination within Europe, pragmatic cooperation between the EU and NATO and between the EU and the US, and the development of a combined ability to project security internally and externally. The outcome will depend, more than anything else, on the quality of political relations between the EU and the US. European capabilities, both civilian and military, are likely to advance faster and with more success if transatlantic relations focus on generating improved abilities to act jointly in preventing crises, countering threats, managing conflicts, supporting stability and enhancing international peace and security.

Appendix

Table 1 Selected military ESDP capabilities (as committed in 2002)

	Land forces	Aircraft	Ships	Other
EU member states				
Austria	1 mechanised infantry battalion 1 light-infantry battalion 1 NBC defence/SAR unit 1 transport company 1 CIMIC unit 1 humanitarian assistance package 100 observers	1 medical/transport helicopter squadron		
Belgium	1 mechanised infantry brigade	1 squadron (12) F-16s 8 C-130s 2 Airbus	2 frigates 6 mine-countermeasure vessels (MCMV) 1 command/support ship	
Denmark	None	None	None	None
Finland	HQ component 1 mechanised infantry battalion 1 engineer battalion 1 transport company 1 civil-military cooperation (CIMIC) group Logistics/support Military observers		1 mine-countermeasures command/support ship	
France	1 light-infantry brigade 1 armoured brigade	75 combat aircraft 24 carrier-based combat aircraft	1 nuclear-powered attack submarine	Various headquarters C4ISR

(Continued to p. 114)

	Land forces	Aircraft	Ships	Other
France continued	1 airborne brigade 1 amphibious brigade Special forces NBC defence support Multiple-launch rocket system (MLRS) Electronic-warfare support Reconnaissance systems	2 carrier-based reconnaissance aircraft 2 AWACS aircraft 8 tanker aircraft 3 long-range transport aircraft 24 mid-range transport aircraft SAR helicopters 3 maritime patrol aircraft	1 aircraft carrier 2 large amphibious ships 4 frigates (1 air defence) 3 support ships Ship-borne medical support	Satellite imagery
Germany	7 combat battalions 8 air-defence squadrons 1 CIMIC unit 2 signals-intelligence units 1 information-operations unit Reconnaissance/surveillance systems Support elements 2 field hospitals	7 squadrons combat aircraft (1 naval) Air transport Sea surveillance	13 combat vessels 1 ship-borne hospital	Various headquarters
Greece	1 HQ 1 mechanised infantry brigade 1 light-infantry battalion 1 *Patriot* air-defence battalion 1 MLRS battalion 1 short-range air-defence (SHORAD) squadron	1 combat helicopter company 1 transport helicopter company 42 combat aircraft 4 transport aircraft 1 maritime patrol aircraft	8 combat vessels 2 amphibious ships 2 auxiliary ships	
Ireland	1 light infantry battalion Special-forces group			

	Land forces	Aircraft	Ships	Other
Italy	2 mechanised brigades (with mountain option) 1 airmobile brigade 1 amphibious infantry battalion 1 engineering battalion 1 NBC defence company 1 CIMIC group Special forces 2 SHORAD units Military police units	6 carrier-based AV8B combat aircraft 8 carrier-based helicopters 8 amphibious support helicopters 26 *Tornado* and AMX combat aircraft 6 combat SAR helicopters 9 transport aircraft 2 tanker aircraft 3 maritime patrol aircraft	1 aircraft carrier 1 destroyer 3 frigates 4 patrol vessels/corvettes 1 submarine 4 MCMVs 1 mine-countermeasures command/support ship 2 amphibious ships 1 support ship 1 oceanographic vessel 2 coast guard vessels	Various headquarters C3I
Luxembourg	1 light reconnaissance unit			
Netherlands	Headquarters component 1 mechanised infantry/airmobile brigade 1 amphibious battalion Air defence	3 squadrons F-16s Transport aircraft	1 landing platform dock Frigates (air-defence, command, multipurpose)	
Portugal	1 infantry brigade 1 marine battalion Military observers	1 squadron (12) F-16s 4 C-130s 16 C-130/C-212s 3 maritime patrol aircraft 4 SA/330 helicopters	1 frigate 1 submarine 1 patrol boat 1 support ship 1 survey ship	Tactical air control
Sweden	1 mechanised infantry battalion 1 engineer company	1 squadron (4) reconnaissance aircraft	2 corvettes 2 command/support vessels	

	Land forces	Aircraft	Ships	Other
Sweden continued	1 military police company Military observers	4 C-130s 1 electronic warfare/signals-intelligence aircraft	1 submarine 2 MCMVs	Various headquarters
Spain	1 mechanised brigade 1 marine brigade 1 mountain battalion 1 light-infantry battalion 1 special-forces battalion	2 squadrons (24) F-1/F-18 combat aircraft 1 naval air unit 1 squadron (9) CN-235s reconnaissance aircraft tanker aircraft medical-evacuation aircraft electronic-warfare aircraft	1 aircraft carrier 4 amphibious vessels 2 frigates 1 support vessel	
UK	1 armoured/mechanised/airborne brigade 1 amphibious brigade Artillery SHORAD Logistics/support 1 field hospital	72 combat aircraft 58 strategic transport aircraft *Chinook/Merlin* transport helicopters attack helicopters	1 aircraft carrier 2 nuclear-powered submarines 4 destroyers/frigates 1 helicopter carrier 6 ro-ro support vessels 2 landing platform docks	1 mobile joint headquarters Mobile communications

	Land forces	Aircraft	Ships	Other
Non-EU European NATO member states				
Czech Republic	1 mechanised infantry battalion 1 special-forces company 1 field hospital 1 humanitarian/rescue operations centre	1 transport helicopter unit		
Hungary	1 mechanised infantry battalion 1 SHORAD platoon			
Iceland	Up to 50 civilian personnel			
Norway	3,500 troops			
Poland	Framework brigade (HQ elements 1 infantry battalion Engineering company Military police section)	SAR elements 1 An-28 transport aircraft	2 MCMVs	
Turkey	1 mechanised brigade	2 F-16 squadrons 2 C-130/C-160s	2 frigates 1 submarine 1 support vessel 1 amphibious ship 1 MCMV	

	Land forces	Aircraft	Ships	Other
Others				
Bulgaria	1 mechanised battalion 1 NBC defence company 1 reconnaissance company 1 military field hospital 1 humanitarian refugee centre	1 helicopter squadron		Infrastructure in Cyprus
Cyprus	1 transport company	1 medium-altitude reconnaissance and surveillance system		
Estonia	Component of the Baltic battalion 1 infantry battalion 1 military police group 1 explosive ordnance disposal unit CIMIC personnel		2 MCMVs 1 support ship	
Latvia	Component of the Baltic battalion 1 infantry battalion 1 explosive-ordnance disposal unit 1 medical team 1 military police unit		1 MCMV	
Lithuania	Component of the Baltic battalion Component of the Lithuanian-Polish battalion 1 mechanised infantry battalion	1 helicopter 2 aircraft	2 MCMVs 2 vessels	

	Land forces	Aircraft	Ships	Other
Romania	1 mechanised battalion 1 engineering battalion 1 military-police company 1 mountain-infantry company Special forces (1 diving team)		4 vessels	
Slovakia	1 mechanised company 1 engineering unit 1 military-police unit 1 field hospital	4 Mi-17 transport helicopters		
Slovenia	1 mechanised company 1 military-police unit 1 medical unit	1 transport helicopter		

Sources: IISS, *The Military Balance 2002–2003* (Oxford: Oxford University Press for the IISS, 2002); national press releases; *Atlantic News*, 21 November 2001; *Jane's Defence Weekly*, 12 December 2001.

Notes

Acknowledgements

The author would like to thank Klaus Becher, Helmut Schmidt Senior Fellow for European Security at the IISS. For valuable input and comments on drafts, thanks also to Alyson Bailes, Giles Baldwin, Hans Binnendijk, Lawrence Freedman, Nils Gyldén, François Heisbourg, Björn Müller-Wille, Alessandro Politi, Sven Rudberg, Lars Wedin and Erik Windmar. Mats Berdal, Katarina Engberg and Bo Huldt have also been greatly supportive.

Introduction

[1] For historical background on the European Security and Defence Policy (ESDP) and initial debate around it, see: François Heisbourg, *European Defence: Making It Work*, Chaillot Paper 42 (Paris: WEU Institute for Security Studies, 2000); Jolyon Howorth, *European Integration and Defence: The Ultimate Challenge?*, Chaillot Paper 43 (Paris: WEU Institute for Security Studies, 2000); Alyson Bailes, 'NATO's European Pillar: The European Security and Defense Identity', *Defense Analysis*, vol. 15, no. 3, 1999; Strobe Talbott 'Transatlantic Ties', *Newsweek*, 18 October 1999; Charles Grant, *European Defence Post Kosovo?* (London: Centre for European Reform, 1999); James Thomas, *The Military Challenges of Transatlantic Coalitions*, Adelphi Paper 333 (Oxford: Oxford University Press for the IISS, 2000).

[2] Where NATO provides assets and capabilities to the EU, political sensitivities have added further facets to these two terms. Here, 'capabilities' describes a function or service, such as information, airborne early warning or access to communications. For EU-led operations, NATO would not transfer capabilities to the EU; NATO would remain in command of its own capabilities even while they are used to support an EU operation. An asset (HQ, units, personnel, specific equipment) could, however, be temporarily transferred to the EU and placed under its control and command for the task at hand. This paper will however use the more generally accepted definitions of capabilities and assets as described in the text.

3 'Military crisis management' encompasses traditional peace-support operations, from preventive deployment and peacekeeping to armed intervention and peace enforcement. It also includes humanitarian and evacuation operations, civil-protection tasks that use mainly military instruments and proactive engagement against weapons of mass destruction and counter-terrorism. Examples include UNPROFOR, embargo operations in the Adriatic, the Sierra Leone operation and military counter-terrorism strikes. Civilian crisis management, as defined by the EU Summit at Feira in June 2000, comprises four areas: police, the rule of law, civil administration and civil protection. The first three are sometimes referred to as 'state-building' activities. Civil protection is essentially humanitarian support in times of crisis, and can include military components such as airlift, medical support and logistics. 'Conflict prevention' is a formal term used officially by the EU. It is defined as the use of primarily non-military means to stabilise a state or a region in the pre-crisis phase (i.e. before the use of force). Initiatives include preventive diplomacy, defence diplomacy, observer missions, the sharing of intelligence and promoting human rights and democracy. Confidence- and security-building measures, arms control and non-proliferation initiatives may also be included.

4 Should vital interests be at stake, states tend to either redefine those interests or go to war, whatever the legal, institutional or multinational context. This paper defines 'vital' interests as interests that are of overriding importance to the survival, safety and vitality of a state.

Chapter 1

1 US aircrews flew just over half of the Kosovo campaign's 10,484 strike missions, delivered 80% of munitions and conducted 70% of support missions. Of the 38,004 sorties flown, Italy accounted for 3%, the UK 4% and France roughly 10%. France and the UK dropped just 4% each of the 23,614 air munitions released by NATO aircraft. Of the 4,397 Suppression of Enemy Air Defence (SEAD) sorties flown, the UK carried out less than half a dozen, and France none. Only the US had long-endurance unmanned aerial vehicles (UAVs), advanced radar-jamming aircraft, strategic bombers, stealth capabilities and battlefield ground surveillance, in the form of the Joint-Surveillance Target Attack Radar System (Joint-STARS). There were, however, gaps in US capabilities as well, particularly in 'jointness', readiness, interoperability, logistics and infrastructure support; several of the above mentioned assets were severely stretched. See Linda Krzaryn, 'Cohen Calls On Allies To Share the Load', *American Forces Press Service*, 8 July 1999; *Report on Allied Contributions to the Common Defense*, A Report to the United States Congress by the Secretary of Defense (Washington DC: Department of Defense, March 2000), pp. II–10; *Kosovo – Lessons from the Crisis* (London: Ministry of Defence, June 2000), Annex F; and *Les Enseignements du Kosovo*, Ministère de la Dèfense; Jeffrey Lewis, *Preliminary Lessons From Operation Allied Force*

(through June 1, 1999) (Washington DC: CSIS, 1999); Dick Diamond *et al.*, *Raytheon Kosovo Lessons Learned Study*, Raytheon Systems Company, 9 September 1999; and *Kosovo Air Operations: Need to Maintain Alliance Cohesion Resulted in Doctrinal Departures*, US General Accounting Office Report GAO-01-784 (Washington DC: USGAO, July 2001).

2   Strategic lift was a major bottleneck. Even the UK's request for airlift support from the US was turned down because of a lack of US assets. The Europeans could not rely on strategic airlift or sealift assets owned by states not sympathetic to the NATO operation, such as Russia and Ukraine.

3   The UK's after-action report noted shortfalls in precision all-weather strike capabilities, strategic lift, intelligence, surveillance and reconnaissance, SEAD, electronic warfare and air-to-air refuelling. The French assessment focused on pet projects such as conventional cruise missiles, electronic counter-measures, UAVs, intelligence satellites and satellites for global positioning. *Kosovo/Operation Allied Force After-Action Report*, p. 25; Sharon Hobson, 'NATO Allies Agree Need To Upgrade Capability', *Jane's Defence Weekly*, 29 September 1999; *Kosovo – Lessons from the Crisis*, chapter 5; Joseph Fitchett, 'Allies Emphasize Need To Prepare for Kosovo-Style Air Wars', *International Herald Tribune*, 12 November 1999.

4   Elinor Sloan, 'DCI: Responding to the US-led Revolution in Military Affairs', *NATO Review*, Spring/Summer 2000.

5   The flaws exposed during *Operation Allied Force* and set out in the DCI, as well as US criticism of European capabilities, were balanced by a report to the US Senate from the US General Accounting Office. The report, issued in September 1999, concluded that, during the 1990s, the allies had made their armed forces more mobile and deployable. The majority of European NATO states had increased their air and sealift, in-flight refuelling, interoperability and precision-strike capabilities. The GAO report concluded that the Europeans had done what they had agreed to do in the 1991 NATO Strategic Concept. *NATO: Progress Toward More Mobile and Deployable Forces*, Report to the Chairman and Ranking Minority Member, Subcommittee on Defense, Committee on Appropriations, US Senate (GAO/NSIAD-99–299 NATO), September 1999. Since then, however, institutional ambition and peer pressure have both increased.

6   NATO's Supreme Headquarters Allied Powers Europe (SHAPE) produced over 200 recommendations some months after the Kosovo campaign, and not surprisingly gave added support to the DCI. According to SHAPE, major flaws lay in nations contributing strike aircraft lacking the full spectrum of targeting capabilities, targeting training, battle-damage-assessment capabilities and intelligence data-processing systems. The North Atlantic Council (NAC)'s procedure for approving targets was criticised as too complicated and slow. Member states' national operational planning was not fully integrated with NATO's, and there was no comprehensive campaign plan. SHAPE also noted the need for a NATO information-operations doctrine, and for more

legal advisers at NATO headquarters.

[7] See Susan Ellis, 'NATO Prepared for New Multi-threat Security Environment', USIA, 16 April 1999; Hans-Christian Hagman, *NATOs Strategiska Koncept 1999*, MUST EXO 5/99, J2 (Stockholm: Swedish Armed Forces HQ, 1999), chapter 3.2; and Hans-Christian Hagman, *Europeiska Militära Krishanteringsförmågor*, EXO 11/99, 10433:74782, J2 (Stockholm: Swedish Armed Forces HQ, 13 December 1999), chapter 3.3.

[8] See Hagman, *Europeiska Militära Krishanteringsförmågor*; Sloan, 'DCI: Responding to the US-led Revolution in Military Affairs'.

[9] Colin Clark and Luke Hill, 'NATO Extends Defense Capabilities Initiative to Partners', *Defense News*, 10 January 2000.

[10] See *Report on Allied Contributions to the Common Defense*.

[11] *Kosovo/Operation Allied Force After-Action Report*, pp. 25–26.

[12] See Lawrence Freedman, *The Revolution in Strategic Affairs*, Adelphi Paper 318 (Oxford: Oxford University Press for the IISS, 1998); Yves Boyer, 'Joint Vision 2010 and the Allies: When Conventional Wisdom Meets Strategic Issues', *RUSI Journal*, April 2000; Michael Codner, 'Some European Concerns About Joint Vision 2010', *ibid.*, April 2000.

[13] Luke Hill, 'TMD: NATO Starts the Countdown', *Jane's Defence Weekly*, 3 January 2001.

[14] See *Report on Allied Contributions to the Common Defense*.

[15] According to the Petersberg Declaration of 1992, and later the Treaty on the European Union, these would include 'humanitarian and rescue tasks; peacekeeping tasks; [and] tasks of combat forces in crisis management, including

peacemaking'.

[16] See *WEU Council of Ministers Audit of Assets and Capabilities for European Crisis Management Operations*, Luxembourg, 23 November 1999. For a more detailed assessment of this and other capabilities reviews, see Hagman, *Europeiska Militära Krishanteringsförmågor*.

[17] As some states had reported entire orders of battle, the WEU staff had to make a 'realistic', albeit subjective, assessment of what could really be committed for Petersberg operations.

[18] Until Helsinki, the collective term for European defence- and security-related initiatives had been the European Security and Defence Identity (ESDI). In 2000, 'Identity' was replaced by 'Policy', and ESDP became the accepted acronym for these EU initiatives.

[19] Annex IV, Presidency Reports to the Helsinki European Council on 'Strengthening the Common European Policy of Security and Defence' and on 'Non-Military Crisis Management of the European Union', Nice, 11–12 December 1999.

[20] See the European Council Declaration on Strengthening the Common European Policy on Security and Defence, Cologne, 4 June 1999, paragraph 1.

[21] Presidency Report on the European Security and Defence Policy, Presidency Conclusion, European Council, Nice, 7–9 December 2000. The UK-originated formula came from the St. Malo declaration, and was also used at the NATO summit in Washington in April 1999. In Cologne, France argued that this formula gave NATO first choice. The word 'where' in the formula 'where NATO as a whole is not engaged' can mean both a geographical limitation (the

Euro-Atlantic area) and a reference to time; the latter is more generally accepted. This double interpretation may in the future limit NATO in relation to the EU in crisis-management operations.

22 Annex IV, Presidency Reports to the Helsinki European Council on 'Strengthening the Common European Policy of Security and Defence' and on 'Non-Military Crisis Management of the European Union'. See Peter Norman, 'Plans for EU Military Force Agreed', *Financial Times*, 7 December 1999.

23 IISS, *The Military Balance 2000/2001* (Oxford: Oxford University Press for the IISS, 2000).

24 For an official point of view, see *EU Military Structures: Military Capabilities Commitment Declaration*, http://ue.eu.int/pesc/military/en/CCC.htm.

25 Presidency Conclusions, European Council, Helsinki, 10 and 11 December 1999.

26 Presidency Conclusions, European Council, Santa Maria da Feira, 19 and 20 June 2000.

27 See Carlo Jean, *An Integrated Civil Police Force for the European Union: Tasks, Profile and Doctrine* (Brussels: Centre for European Policy Studies, 2002).

28 See Graham Messervy-Whiting, 'The European Union's Nascent Military Staff', *RUSI Journal*, December 2000.

29 Presidency Report to the Gothenburg European Council on European Security and Defence Policy, Brussels, 11 June 2001.

30 See the French EU Presidency Report on European Security and Defence Policy, 4 December 2000.

31 Statement on Capabilities, issued at the Meeting of the North Atlantic Council in Defence Ministers Session, June 6, 2002, NATO Press Release (2002)074.

32 See Prague Summit Declaration, Press Release (2002) 127, NATO, November 21, 2002, and Joseph Fitchett, 'U.S. Urges NATO Allies in Prague to Update Forces', *International Herald Tribune*, 21 November 2002.

33 See initial thoughts from Hans Binnendijk, 'A European Spearhead Force Would Bridge the Gap', *International Herald Tribune*, 21 October 2002; and Hans Binnendijk and Richard Kugler, 'Transforming European Forces', *Survival*, vol. 44, no. 3, Autumn 2002.

34 See Charles Grant, 'What role for NATO', Centre for European Reform, November 2002.

35 'Quote/Unquote', *International Herald Tribune*, 29 April 1998.

36 'Britain's Thatcher Attacks EU Force as Folly', *Reuters*, 22 November 2000.

Chapter 2

1 Operating combat aircraft, air- and sealift, carrier battle groups and surface combatants for a year – even for the less-demanding missions – would engage tens of thousands of airmen and sailors. The more demanding missions call for 300 aircraft and 75 surface combatants, requiring a massive support structure.

2 For a half-year deployment (the norm for most contingents), the military unit cannot be used for other missions for 18 months as it must have stand-by readiness and tailored pre-deployment training, time for the operational engagement itself and post-deployment reconstitution and retraining.

3 The Helsinki Headline Goal Task Force (HTF) used NATO definitions for readiness. The same five categories are used by the EU.

4 Statement by General Wesley Clark, Commander-in-Chief US European Command, before the Senate Armed Services Committee, 29 February 2000.

5 No NATO pilots were killed in action, while some 500 Yugoslav civilians were killed as a result of NATO air strikes. Less than 1% of missions led to unintended fatalities (collateral damage). *Kosovo – Lessons from the Crisis*, chapter 7.

6 Presidency Reports to the Helsinki European Council, Annex IV, paragraph 7.

7 Final Communiqué, Ministerial Meeting of the North Atlantic Council, Berlin, 3 June 1996, paragraphs 5–8.

8 Washington Summit Communiqué, 24 April 1999, paragraph 10. Throughout 2000 and 2001, there were lengthy debates within NATO over what had been agreed to in the Berlin-plus package. Often, the term 'asset' was defined as personnel, HQs, units or equipment, which could be temporarily placed under EU control. 'Capabilities' such as sealift, operational planning, intelligence, communications and airborne early warning are thus functions or complete services provided to the EU. These definitions are politicised, and relevant only in the EU–NATO/Berlin-plus context.

9 *Report on Allied Contributions to the Common Defense*, p. II-3.

10 See Frank Boland, 'Force Planning in the New NATO', *NATO Review*, vol. 46, no. 3, Autumn 1998.

11 SHAPE/ARFPS planning for a possible ground engagement in Bosnia began in mid-1992. Since then, a vast array of Balkans-related plans has emerged. See Hagman, *UN–NATO Operational Cooperation in Peacekeeping 1992–1995*, University of London PhD, 1997, chapter 7.

12 The NATO budget in 1999 was $1.6 billion, composed of the civilian budget ($164m), the military budget ($720m) and the NATO Security Investment Program ($734m).

13 The fact that EU scenarios have a geographical limitation is only relevant for generic planning. It could be noted that NATO's Article 5 was related to direct support for US territorial defence. The fact that NATO gave the US political support for its counter-terrorist engagements in Asia did not mean that those operations were NATO operations, or that they reflected a collective response by NATO.

14 For operational force planners such as those in NATO, who did most of the number crunching in order to produce credible force requirements, the level of manipulation was frustrating.

15 By late November 2000, this scenario contained two sub-levels: Separation of Parties by Force; and a case where the mission was to maintain the separation of parties in a 'Stable State' setting. The latter would require only some 20,000 troops.

16 *Operation Deliberate Force* had the support of a warring faction, and the Rapid Reaction Force was deployed on non-hostile territory.

17 'Strategic decision-making' describes processes related to decision-making at the highest level. In the EU, the strategic level is the EU Council, COREPER (with decision-shaping from the Political and Security Committee and the SG/HR), and the European Commission. In NATO, strategic decision-making is the domain of the NAC. Strategic planning, on the other hand, is done by the highest-level

planning staff at the military strategic level, which in NATO means SACEUR. As of 2002, the only EU strategic planning capability lies with the EU Military Staff.

18 See *EU Presidency Report on the European Security and Defence Policy*. Realistically, the parameters would have been set in London, Paris and Berlin before there was EU agreement to act collectively.

19 See Messervy-Whiting, 'The European Union's Nascent Military Staff'.

20 The envisaged command structure would be: Council/EUMC, Operational HQ, Force HQ, tactical HQs/component commands and forces.

21 See 'Designing an EU Conflict Prevention Capability', summary of the EU–NGO CFSP Contact Group meeting, European Parliament, 19 September 2000.

22 Lars Wedin, Chief Concepts Branch, EU Military Staff, interview with the author, 2 March 2001.

Chapter 3

1 Alyson Bailes notes that converging interests do not necessarily and automatically produce joint action or joint approaches. See 'National Interests vs. European Approaches to Crisis Management: A View from Brussels', paper presented at the Swedish Institute of International Affairs Conference 'Making the CFSP Work', Stockholm, 30 September 1999.

2 Opening Statement before the US Senate Committee on Foreign Relations, 17 January 2001.

3 See Julian Lindley-French, 'Terms of Engagement', Chaillot Paper 52 (Paris: EU Institute for Security Studies, 2002) and William Drozdiak, 'US Seems Increasingly Uncomfortable With EU Defense Plan', *International Herald Tribune*, 6 March 2000.

4 Two-way trade was valued at $507bn in 1999. EU investment in the US totalled more than $480bn, and US investment in the EU more than $430bn. See *Strengthening Transatlantic Security – A US Strategy for the 21st Century* (Washington DC: DoD, December 2000); and Ed Gunning, *The Common European Security and Defense Policy (ESDP)* (Washington DC: Atlantic Council of the United States, 10 May 2000).

5 See Stanley Sloan, *The United States and European Defence*, Chaillot Paper 39 (Paris: WEU Institute for Security Studies, 2000); and then Secretary of State Madeleine Albright's warnings of 'decoupling', 'duplication' and 'discrimination', in Drozdiak, 'US Seems Increasingly Uncomfortable'. See also François Heisbourg, 'European Defence Takes a Leap Forward', *NATO Review*, Spring/Summer 2000; Stafano Silvestri and Andrzej Karkoszka, 'The EU–NATO Connection'; and Nicole Gnesotto and Karl Kaiser, 'European–American Interaction', in Heisbourg, *European Defence: Making It Work*.

6 See Willem Van Eekelen, *EU, WEU, and NATO: Towards a European Security and Defence Identity*, Defence and Security Committee, North Atlantic Assembly, 22 April 1999, paragraphs 29–30.

7 See Henry Kissinger, 'The End of NATO as We Know It?', *Los Angeles Times*, 15 August 1999. In December 2000, Cohen warned that NATO could become 'a relic of the past' if the Europeans opted for increased autonomy.

See William Drozdiak, 'NATO Allies Grow Edgy as Security Choices Loom', *International Herald Tribune*, 15 December 2000; and Jim Garamone, 'Cohen Says Allies Must Invest or NATO Could Become "Relic" ', *American Forces Press Service*, 5 December 2000. See also Kissinger, 'The End of NATO?'.

8 Nicole Gnesotto, 'Transatlantic Debates', *Newsletter*, WEU Institute for Security Studies, no. 29, April 2000. See also 'Excerpts from Secretary of State Madeleine Albright's Interview With the International Herald Tribune', *International Herald Tribune*, 15 January 2001. For expressions of US concern, see Charles Babington, 'A "Strong Europe" Can Depend Less On US Power, Clinton Declares', *ibid.*, 3 June 2000; and then US Ambassador to NATO Alexander Vershbow's comments in Drozdiak, 'US Seems Increasingly Uncomfortable'.

9 As argued by William Pfaff, 'NATO's Europeans Could Say "No" ', *International Herald Tribune*, 25 July 2002; see also 'If Forced To Choose, Europe Will Ditch NATO', *ibid.*, 17 August 2002. See also Klaus Becher, 'Organizing NATO for the Future', in Christina V. Balis (ed.), *Beyond the NATO Prague Summit*, CSIS Conference Report, Washington DC, September 2002, pp. 65–73.

10 See the US DoD *Quadrennial Defense Review Report*, 30 September 2001.

11 Strobe Talbott, 'Transatlantic Ties', *Newsweek*, 18 October 1999.

12 William Cohen, 'Preserving History's Greatest Alliance', *Washington Post*, 8 January 2001; 'Cohen on NATO–US–EU Partnership, Joint Defense Planning', *Washington File*, US Department of State, 6 December

2000; and the 2000 *Report on Allied Contributions to the Common Defense*.

13 *Ibid.*, p. II-2.

14 In 1997, the US Congress took it upon itself to set targets for its allies. Allies should increase the proportion of their GDP spent on defence by 10% over the previous year, or to a level commensurate with the US; they should increase military assets contributed or pledged to multinational military activities; offsets for US stationing costs should increase to 75%; foreign assistance should increase by 10% over the previous year (or to a level equal to at least 1% of GDP). *Ibid.*, p. F-1. Canada, Luxembourg, Netherlands and the UK failed to achieve these targets in all four categories. All but Greece and Turkey failed to meet the targets on defence spending, and no NATO ally met the cost-sharing target.

15 See *Strengthening Transatlantic Security – A US Strategy for the 21st Century*, US DoD, December 2000, part VI.

16 For a different view, see Charles Kupchan, 'In Defence of European Defence: An American Perspective', *Survival*, vol. 42, no. 2, Summer 2000.

17 Van Eekelen, *EU, WEU, and NATO*, paragraph 37.

18 Peter Schmidt, 'ESDI: Separable But Not Separate', *NATO Review*, Spring/Summer 2000.

19 Not all duplication is bad, as argued by Kori Schake, *Constructive Duplication: Reducing EU Reliance on US Military Assets*, CER Working Paper, January 2002; and 'EU Should Duplicate NATO Assets', *CER Bulletin*, Issues 18, June–July 2001.

20 Stephen Walt, 'The Ties That Fray', *The National Interest*, no. 54,

Winter 1998/1999; and Charles Grant, 'NATO's New Role', *Financial Times*, 7 August 2002.

Chapter 4

1 See Hagman, Europeiska Militära Krishanteringsförmågor, pp. 31–37.
2 Report on Allied Contributions to the Common Defense, p. III-24.
3 A conventional C-130 takes some 90 combat soldiers compared to the A400M's 120 soldiers. The C-130J-30, the extended version, takes more troops but slightly fewer cargo pallets and tons in comparison to the A400M. According to the UK, during Operation Essential Harvest in Macedonia in 2001 the C-17 took as much as four C-130 loads.
4 Haig Simonian and Ralph Atkins, 'Scharping Urges Joint Air Command', *Financial Times*, 1 November 1999.
5 The Netherlands, Norway, Denmark, Belgium and Portugal are increasing their day/night and all-weather strike capabilities, and upgrading their F-16s. This is a step in the right direction, but the upgrade is long overdue, the numbers are small and the added value is marginal. However, should the above states procure substantial numbers of PGMs such as JDAM, the increase would be significant.
6 Report on Allied Contributions to the Common Defense, p. II-2.
7 As correctly noted in Strengthening Transatlantic Security – A US Strategy for the 21st Century, US DoD, December 2000, part III.
8 Report on Allied Contributions to the Common Defense, p. II-2.
9 See Burkard Schmitt (ed.), Between Cooperation and Competition: The Transatlantic Defence Market, Chaillot Paper 44

(Paris: WEU Institute for Security Studies, January 2001).
10 See Hans Binnendijk, 'A Trans-Atlantic Division of Labor Could Undermine NATO', *International Herald Tribune*, 7 April 2001.
11 Several thousand US Marines, plus US air assets, were on call in the area should the European operation have required them. The ARFPS, later the CJPS, has experience of evacuation plans for non-NATO operations dating back to UNPROFOR and AFSOUTH OP 40104, 1992–95.
12 Annex IV Presidency Reports to the Helsinki European Council.
13 See J. P. H. Wathen, The Justification of Humanitarian Intervention Operations, unpublished paper, St. John's College, University of Cambridge, 17 July 2000.
14 The UK MoD conceded in its Kosovo after-action report that cluster bombs, because of the negative public perception, will be a less attractive alternative to precision-guided munitions and missiles such as the Maverick. Depleted-uranium armour-piercing ammunition, used by the US, will probably also fall into the same 'unsuitable' category. See Kosovo – Lessons from the Crisis, chapter 7. In humanitarian interventions and smaller-scale contingencies precision-guided munitions are a prerequisite for low collateral damage. Roberg Holzer, 'Military Trends Demand More Complex Weapons', *Defense News*, 25 October 1999.
15 Joseph Fitchett, 'Clark Recalls "Lessons" of Kosovo', *International Herald Tribune*, 3 May 2000.
16 Both the UK and France committed this capability to the EU in November 2000. France committed a capability to the

Capability Commitment Conference in November 2000 that matched this label. The EU Military Staff Intelligence Division is composed of three branches: Policy, Requirements and Production. Each member state has its own intelligence cell. The linking of national intelligence data is primarily done in the Joint Situation Centre. However, the staffing of the Intelligence Division is small, and there are no formal plans to develop it into a multi-functional and effective intelligence function.

[17] The Military Staff Intelligence Division does not have civilian analysis functions or civilian leadership. It is too small and too narrowly focused, as it does not cover the whole spectrum of international assessments, conflict prevention and operational intelligence functions for EU-led operations.

[18] US intelligence satellites reached 0.1m resolution in the 1980s. US-operated commercial high-resolution satellites have recently crossed the 1m resolution barrier. Helios II and the German SARLupe satellites will have resolutions of 0.8 and 0.5m respectively. 'Satellite Pictures – Private Eyes in the Sky', *The Economist*, 6 May 2000; *Charles Grant, Intimate Relations*, Centre for European Reform Working Paper, April 2000; 'European Military Satellites', *Strategic Comments*, vol. 6, no. 10, 2000; Peter de Selding, 'Three Nations Find Common Uses for Helios', *Defense News*, 13 December 1999.

[19] The commercial satellite market is dominated by the US. The close links between the US government and US satellite firms mean that commercial imagery would only be available to Europeans as and when the US wants to release it

(see 'European Military Satellites'). For the same reason, Europe should also look to military satellites for its communications, rather than using commercial sources. European reliance on US global-positioning systems (GPS) for sensors and weapon systems is growing. Furthermore, the US is developing precision-guided munitions for GPS-denied mode situations (i.e. GPS jamming). The US is thus free to switch off or encrypt the GPS network, either regionally or globally, albeit with consequences for trade, civil shipping and air transport. The Galileo European GPS satellite system may, in the distant future, increase European self-sufficiency, while enhancing related capabilities.

[20] Naturally, any EU member state could block the CFSP/ESDP, but this would not do as much damage.

[21] Helmut Schmidt, 'Don't Believe What Critics Say About the Euro', *International Herald Tribune*, 25 June 1997.

Chapter 5

[1] This paper does not advocate the creation of a 'Mr ESDP' (see Daniel Keohane, 'Time for Mr ESDP', *CER Bulletin*, no. 26, October–November 2002). In practical terms, the workload of the SG/HR is a major challenge to this coordination. There would be an advantage in giving the Deputy SG a more active role. However, there are already enough cooks in the Brussels kitchen; see David Hannay, 'EU Foreign Policy: A Necessity, Not an Optional Extra', *ibid*. See also Hans-Georg Ehrhart, 'What Model for CFSP?' Chaillot Paper 55 (Paris: EU Institute for Security Studies, 2002).

[2] See Gilles Andréani, Christophe Bertram and Charles Grant, *Europe's Military Revolution*, Centre for European Reform, London, 2001.

[3] These are contacts beyond what is managed by the European Commission's Directorate-General External Relations. In mid-2002, the EU had some 140 representatives in international organisations and states. Ideally, the pillars should be able to share international points of contact. Should this not be possible, an overlapping system may be the only realistic option.

[4] Some EU candidates are concerned that EU Headline Goal demands may conflict with NATO's criteria, and thus force them to take sides. In practice, if the DCI and NATO interoperability are seen as the guiding principles, candidates' capabilities will be equally relevant for EU crisis management.

[5] Of the 2,700 employees in the General Secretariat of the Council, some 2,200 work with translations and document distribution, and only 500 focus on the various elements of the CFSP and coordination functions.

[6] For an assessment of the plans for an intelligence division in the EUMS, see Messervy-Whiting, 'The European Union's Nascent Military Staff'. As of 2001, the EUMS had established an Intelligence Division, which was composed of national representatives (and their secure communication systems) tasked with channelling national intelligence of primarily operational nature.

[7] See Becher, 'European Intelligence Policy'.

[8] Grant, *Intimate Relations*. Grant also observes that not all national intelligence services are coordinated. This adds to the challenge of funnelling national intelligence into a central EU structure.

[9] See Björn von Sydow's prescription, in 'Sweden: Swedish Minister Urges Europe To Intensify Weapons Production Co-operation', *Reuters*, 22 January 2001. It could be argued that defence industries in Europe and the US are already intertwined; see Andrew James, 'The Prospects for a Transatlantic Defense Industry', in Schmitt (ed.), *Between Cooperation and Competition*.

[10] Heisbourg, 'European Defence Takes a Leap Forward'.

[11] IISS, *The Military Balance 2002/2003*.

[12] Heisbourg, 'European Defence Takes a Leap Forward'; and François Heisbourg, 'Europe's Strategic Ambitions: The Limits of Ambiguity', *Survival*, vol. 42, no. 2, Summer 2000. See also the recommendations in Andréani, Bertram and Grant, *Europe's Military Revolution*.

[13] See Tim Garden and John Roper, *Pooling Forces*, Centre for European Reform, December 1999, www.cer.org.uk.

[14] See Klaus Naumann, *Europe's Military Ambitions*, Centre for European Reform, June–July 2000, www.cer.org.uk.

[15] Preferably, there should be a correlation between EU and NATO rapid-reaction forces for interoperability reasons – whatever the institutional banner for an operation.

[16] See 'Communication from the Commission to the Council and the European Parliament "Towards integrated management of the external borders of the Member States of the European Union" ', Secretary-General of the

European Commission to Javier Solana, 12 May 2002 (9139/02).

[17] The current division of labour between the Director-General for external affairs (more specifically DGE VIII), which has responsibility for police operations, and the Military Staff, focused on operational military crisis management, is not satisfactory.

[18] Much institutional coordination depends on such banal factors as the cooperative nature of individuals in the two organisations, competence and time.

[19] For suggestions as to how to develop an EU White Paper, see Heisbourg, 'Europe's Strategic Ambitions'. See also John Vinocur, 'EU Defense Autonomy Lacks a Unifying Voice', *International Herald Tribune*, 9 April 2001.

[20] Nicole Gnesotto and Karl Kaiser, 'European–American Interaction', in Heisbourg (ed.), *European Defence: Making It Work*.

[21] In January 2001, it was decided that the Political and Security Committee and the NAC would meet at least three times during each EU presidency. Formally, the first PSC–NAC meeting was held on 5 February 2001. Extra *ad hoc* meetings are also arranged to discuss operational matters. The first GAC–NAC meeting was held in Budapest on 30 May 2001.

[22] The experience of the Euro-Atlantic Partnership Council, OSCE and UN, although different in scale and scope, may indicate that the main function of a joint forum is dialogue and confidence-building, rather than far reaching cooperation and decision-shaping.

Freedom Fighters

Affective Teaching of the Language Arts

Nancy Lee Cecil

California State University, Sacramento

Sheffield Publishing Company

Salem, Wisconsin

For information about this book, write or call:
Sheffield Publishing Company
P.O. Box 359
Salem, Wisconsin 53168
(414) 843-2281

DEDICATION

With love . . . and hearts and princesses and rainbows. . . to Chrissy, who is teaching me what the learning process is REALLY all about.

Contents

FREEDOM FIGHTERS:
Affective Teaching of the
Language Arts

● **Anecdotal Outline** ●

Introduction. This initial chapter explains the need for a whole language, cross-curricular program that will integrate the language arts into every facet of the learning experience. It describes the components of such a program and the underlying rationale in terms of current research and educational thought.

1   **Writing: Process and Product.** Writing is exposed in this chapter not as a "one-shot" attempt, but as the developmental process of jotting ideas down as they occur, and then editing with peers and teacher guidance, while post-writing and publishing activities are proposed to celebrate the product. Also looked at are the spelling stages that a child progresses through, highlighting the value of invented spelling for beginning writers.

2   **Dialogue Journals: Personalizing Writing.** Presented here is an avenue that provides an intimate, bonding function of writing for children, similar to the way they have already experienced the intimate bonding possible through oral language with important persons in their lives. The rationale and ways to implement the activity are included, as well as sample entries.

3   **Copy-Cat Books: Expanding Upon Children's Literature.** This chapter demonstrates some ways that children's literature can be used to inspire the writing of books with similar rhythm and rhyming patterns, and offers an opportunity for children to collaborate on classroom books. Specific suggestions are offered for applying this method to nine children's books, and a bibliography of appropriate "predictable" books is included in Appendix I.

4   **Episodic Novels: Becoming REAL Authors.** Described here is the more ambitious and self-motivating experience of writing a class-collaborative novel by following a brief outline of chapters, brainstorming each chapter as a clsss, and then breaking up into "think" groups to finish individual chapters. A sample highly-motivational, field-tested outline is provided.

5   **Other Motivators: When They Don't Know What to Write.** A panoply of story starters, story plots, and other "getting started" ideas are presented in this chapter to spur initial creative attempts. Also included is a test of creativity, and some general suggestions designed to foster creativity in *all* areas of the curriculum.

6   **Build-Me-Ups: Enhancing Self-Concept Through the Language Arts.** Explored here are a host of language activities that are specifically focused upon improving the self-images of children. Acceptance of cultural and socioeconomic differences, and valuing what is "unique" in people are highlighted in such proposed activities as "Good or Bad?" and the "You Are Special Because . . . " Circle.

7   **The Newspaper: Conduit to Our Reading Culture.** This chapter demonstrates many ways to make children feel comfortable with the newspaper through activities designed to develop their critical reading, thinking, and writing abilities. A newspaper scavenger hunt, writing headlines, and doing interviews with lottery winners are among the activities included.

8   **The Wonder of Words.** This chapter explains how to give children positive associations with the dictionary through highly-motivational games that reinforce dictionary skills, and through the creation of original, humorous dictionaries.

9   **Visualization Activities: Why the Book Was Better than the Movie.** All that most children must do to begin to write both prolifically and creatively is to learn to "tune in" to their own imaginations, or "mind pictures." This chapter includes techniques to help teachers to foster these natural abilities in their students.

10 **Role Playing: Trying Life on for Size.** There are many ways to turn "child's play" into an educational enterprise and one such technique is described here. Moral dilemmas are also portrayed in this chapter as opportunities to show children that there are a myriad of alternative solutions to common problems. Through role plays, children get to take opposite points of view, broaden their thinking, and expand their language skills.

11 **The Integrated Teaching Unit: Tying It All Together.** The "why's" and "how's" of a unit approach that best exemplifies cross-curricular language arts teaching are presented here, along with some specific guidelines. Sample units are included in Appendix II.

12 **Learning Stations: Child-Centered Language Learning.** This final chapter describes how to set up child-centered learning stations where children can go individually and in small groups to reinforce language arts skills in an enjoyable way. Sample learning stations are included in Appendix III.

Appendix I. A List of Predictable Books

Appendix II. Two Field-Tested Units

Appendix III. Sample Learning Stations

Introduction

What is the significance of language for a small child? To answer that question, one must only listen to young Anthony, who is learning all about the power that language is beginning to hold for him. Anthony is learning how to pose questions and he does so interminably. He is learning how to get his needs met and he practices endlessly. He now knows how to give commands to his dog--and even his baby brother--and he revels in the responses he can now cause. Anthony is also becoming aware of the many rituals of our language and he finds that chirping "Have a nice day!" coupled with his sunny, gap-toothed grin, may soften even the grumpiest of adults.

Language, simply put, is the systematic ability to communicate and understand the communication of others. This ability to communicate is pure, unadulterated power. But without this power a child can easily be the victim of other children, of teachers, of the school, and of virtually the whole society outside the child's home environment. A child who lacks this communication facility remains largely on the fringe of all social interaction; on the fringe of all life. Without the ability to communicate--and the tremendous FREEDOM it affords--the child is locked into a netherworld between the stimulating world of voices and print and the frustrating chains of his own powerlessness.

What is needed to best impart this important power to children is an "affective" approach to the teaching of the language arts--that is, an approach that reaches right to the *heart* of the learner. Such an approach regards communication as the most basic human need to interact with others on a very real emotional, as well as intellectual, level. Therefore, the affective teacher of language arts--the arts of reading, writing, speaking and listening--will be viewed in this book as the ultimate Freedom Fighter, sensitively preparing her students to one day participate in the twenty-first century by freeing them to communicate effectively. Such a teacher must be well aware of the unique nature of this charge, for the ability to communicate is the most personal, human, and profoundly vulnerable of the tools a child will need to succeed. It also takes much long practice, yet touches every aspect of the child's environment. By freeing the child, the affective teacher

1

allows that child to grow by following his or her own thoughts in oral or written form. The affective teacher helps the child to ". . . unlock the doors of language . . . to discover the best that human beings have thought, written and spoken" (California State Board of Education, 1987).

Unfortunately, much of what goes on in our elementary classrooms has quite the opposite effect from offering our children the freedom to communicate. For example, a perplexed teacher consulted me recently about her observation that her third-grade students seemed to dislike writing; they appeared to be producing less and less writing than they had been at the very beginning of the school year. She showed me an example of young Barbara's latest composition and it soon became quite clear what the problem was--the child's composition was awash with red marks and curt marginal admonitions. Every misspelled word, uncapitalized letter, or bit of improper grammar or punctuation had been conscientiously circled and sarcastically chastised. But the saddest thing of all was that not a mention--not *one word*--had been made of the original thoughts that Barbara had been trying to communicate! Is it any wonder that this child's creative juices were "drying up"?

Similarly, I observed a "Show and Tell" session not long ago in which a very timid first-grader was trying to tell the class about her very scary adventure on Halloween. The little girl could barely finish a sentence before the teacher would pounce upon the child's grammar or word pronunciation, and then would ask the little girl to now . . . "repeat the sentence the proper way." The teacher later confided to me that her pupils seemed to have nothing to say in Show and Tell, yet they . . . "are little chatterboxes when they are supposed to be doing their workbook pages"!

The above anecdotes are unfortunate and all-too-familiar examples of well-meaning teachers who are unknowingly restricting the language powers of children when they should be freeing them by allowing them to become more fluent communicators through practicing with their own ideas. An affective teacher is, of course, also concerned with arming her students with the necessary skills involved in the language arts. Skills in grammar, capitalization, spelling, reading and listening for specific purposes, and punctuation, for example, are all mechanics, or "tools of the trade," and are vital for the pupil who is to be successful in future academic endeavors. But an affective teacher of the language arts could never interrupt a child's natural exhilaration when the creative ideas are flowing and the child's mind is racing ahead of her mouth or her pen. Instead, in an affective language arts program, skill instruction takes a subservient position to the decidedly more exciting enterprise of capturing, somehow, what one is trying to communicate. *This* is the crucial focus--this freeing of the child's thoughts--and the mechanics can surely be scrutinized and then cleaned up in a later, less emotional moment, when the child has finished creating and now wants to share her "magnum opus" with the rest of the world. Often, using this approach of "create now, edit later," the most amazing thing happens: the child feels free to express herself and begins to write unself-consciously. The more unself-conscious she becomes, the more she begins to pay more careful attention to the writing of others and the conventions (mechanics!) of our language. While I would not go so far as to say that the mechanics then take care of themselves, I *can* heartily avow that significant growth will just naturally take place in the mechanics of a youngster who writes often and joyfully.

To allow burgeoning, unself-conscious communicators to flourish to maximum fluency, the language arts program must permeate every single hour of the child's day. Language arts must not be trivialized into discrete packages of reading, writing, spelling, handwriting, literature, language, etc., but must blend and flow into every nook and cranny of the curriculum. In a truly affective, whole language program, oral language is happening all day long and might take the form of discussions, debates, drama, interviews or twenty questions. Social studies might be the vehicle through which a "rap" on current events is performed, or a writing lesson is undertaken about how a passing butterfly could have changed the events of the Boston Tea Party. In such a program, too, literature is constantly being interwoven to motivate and to personalize learning in all subjects, for to exclude it from the language arts program is to . . . "create a program that deprives children of their right to improve their language in the most honest and enjoyable way" (Coody and Nelson, 1986). In an Affective Language Arts Program, simply put, "language arts" is happening all the time so that no one segment of the school day need arbitrarily be labeled "language arts times." As an added bonus to such a joyful program, it should be noted that current research suggests that the more the language arts are carefully coordinated or correlated with each other and with other academic instruction, the greater the total achievement of the students will be!

* * * * *

The following chapters will give specific suggestions for creating an affective whole language, cross-curricular program which will free children to communicate and then give them plenty of motivational reasons to continue to do so. Of course, the key to this program, as in any sound educational program, is a knowledgeable and caring teacher who can capably model a love for language. He must be able to share the bittersweet experience of finishing a stirring book that he wished would never end; he should be able to express to his students the glee that is his when he finds just the right word to express what he wants to say; and he must desperately want to free his students by helping them to develop that same fine power to communicate effectively.

This book is for him. And for all the other Freedom Fighters in our schools today.

References

Anderson, Richard, et al. *Becoming a Nation of Readers.* 1985.

Coody, Betty and David Nelson. *Teaching Elementary Language Arts.* Prospect Heights, IL: Waveland Press, 1986.

California State Board of Education. *English-Language Arts Framework.* Sacramento, CA: California State Department of Education, 1986.

Chapter One

Writing: Process and Product

Although writing is closely linked to its "cousin" language arts--speaking, reading, and listening--a child who is able to tell a wonderfully bone-chilling story with aptly descriptive words and finely-tuned phrases may often have major problems when it comes to writing down such stories. The observers of this phenomenon are perplexed. If writing and oral language are so closely linked, as we are led to believe, then why is it that the child speaks so articulately and yet cannot write fluently?

First of all, good writing has the same general qualities whether it is the scribbled composition of the second graders or the carefully-crafted essay of the adult writer. Learning to express oneself is always a meticulous, time-consuming process--perhaps the most difficult of the communication skills, and it basically subsumes all the others: writing requires the combined ability to talk and form sentences, to read, to make letters, to spell, to punctuate, and to think clearly and logically. Also, there is the tough physical labor of getting the material down. While an animated nine-year-old may speak as many as two hundred words per minute, she will be doing well to write that many in an hour!

Secondly, the practice ratio of time spent on speaking as compared with time spent on writing in a young child's life is very much in the favor of speaking time, in all but the rarest of cases. Perhaps because conversation is not usually structured for them, children talk a *lot*. In every facet of their environment, children seem to have new opportunities to practice their oral language, but unfortunately, the same myriad of opportunities do not exist for language in written form. In many cases, the only writing practice children will have in a day will be the practice of identifying parts of speech and putting one line under the subject and two under the predicate in their "language" books!

Lastly, there is the important issue of positive reinforcement. Picture in your mind the four-year-old who stumbles and stutters over his words in youthful exuberance to tell his parents about his trip to the circus, or the preschooler who makes up a story about a "wed wabbit." Now picture the reaction of the adults as they listen to these children. Invariably, there will be a positive, even indulgent response to this immature speech. Unfortunately, no such indulgence greets the immature writer when he rushes home with his first rudimentary attempts to write. Somehow, we seem to expect children to go from being nonwriters to perfectly literate authors in one quantum leap!

The bottom line is that writing is a most difficult task requiring a good deal of varied practice, and the beginning writer's first feeble attempt at the craft must be thoughtfully accepted and encouraged from the perspective of what we now know of the developmental process of a child's written language.

Invented Spellings

This knowledge has led to increased attention placed on the value of accepting a beginning writer's "invented spellings." Invented spellings are the combinations of letters that a young child uses when he is just beginning to understand that letters represent the sounds that form words. These novel spellings that a child has created by sounding out words are not "errors," although they are not actually "correct" according to our whimsical English orthography. Rather, they are really immaturities that show the developmental stage the child is at in terms of his knowledge of the way sounds and symbols come together in our language. By allowing these invented spellings in the initial stages of writing, children become free to communicate anything they can conjure up in their fertile imaginations, while it also provides the best opportunity for them to extend their knowledge of phonics, or the way that letters and sounds correspond.

In learning to communicate in written form, a child generally goes through five basic developmental stages, although it is not uncommon for children to evidence elements of two or more of these stages in their writing at any one time.

The Precommunicative Stage

The first stage of such development is the precommunicative stage and it occurs about the time that a child learns the alphabet and makes the connection that words are composed of letters, although the child has little or no concept at the time of which letter stands for which sound. A child at this stage might compose a story about an elephant and to our eyes it will be virtually unintelligible:

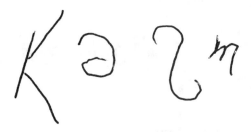

The Prephonetic Stage

The second stage of development is called the prephonetic stage and it evolves when a child begins to understand that letters have certain sounds which form words. About this time, too, children are usually beginning to become aware of the left-to-right orientation of our language. This particular writing stage might be considered analogous to the stage in a very young child's beginning speech when he will use one word to symbolize a whole concept, such as "Up!" to mean "I want you to pick me up!" Similarly, in this particular stage, one letter, which is often the most obvious sound, will be used to represent the whole word. In the previously used story about the elephant, the word elephant would merely be represented by an "l," its most salient auditory feature. The whole story might look like this:

The Phonetic Stage

The third stage, the phonetic stage, is in some ways just a refinement of the prephonetic stage, except now a letter will be used for each sound that a child can hear in each syllable. Although vowels and silent letters may often be left out, the child seems to have become aware of some of the most basic word patterns and families in our language (e.g. fab, cab, hat). Now the same story about an elephant might look like this:

I wnt to thezunDswnafnt

The Transitional Stage

The fourth developmental stage is called the transitional stage and at this phase children's writing is quite coherent, as children begin to have a repertoire of words that have been taught to them and everything need not be sounded out. At this stage, too, children have usually begun to read, so they are now more aware of the words' more visual aspects, some of which would not be detectable to the ear. Vowels begin to be placed in each syllable at this stage, and common English sequences such as the "ai" in "rain" and "pain," begin to emerge in the child's spelling. The elephant story might now become:

I went to the zou and saw an ellefent

Correct Spelling

The final stage of writing development, that of correct spelling, evolves when the child is tuned in to the idiosyncrasies of English orthography and just "knows" by sight if a word is spelled correctly. Now the child's spelling shows an understanding of contraction, affixes, silent letters, and he or she has a great many words that can be spelled as automatically as the child's own name.

Keeping these developmental stages in mind, as well as the value of a child's use of invented spellings, may help the teacher decide what level of writing might be expected from each child and may help to keep unrealistic expectations from inhibiting the writing process.

Before a child has reached the phonetic stage of development, the writing process should be kept as simple and unconstrained as possible. At this early stage, many opportunities should be provided for children to do art work and then tell stories about their creations in rough written form. This process could be varied by the child sometimes telling his story to the teacher as she transcribes it and with individual and group language experience stories. Also, much writing by children in these stages can be performed with plastic or metal letters on flannel boards or with primary typewriters to lessen the frustration of handwriting constraints. At these initial stages of writing, invented spelling is a worthwhile end in itself and little or no actual "editing" of children's writing should be attempted.

The Writing Process

When children are beginning to write freely, beginning to spell phonetically, as well as expressing a real desire to share their writing with others, it is time to begin turning them into true authors by introducing them to the hard work--and the ultimate joy--of editing their work with the intent to publish. They are ready to begin what is known as "the writing process."

The Creating Phase

The writing process begins with a creating phase and it is absolutely crucial to the free flow of ideas that both the teacher and the pupils realize that NO ONE--not even a published author--writes a perfect, error-free copy the first time through. The phrase requires the formulation of a rough draft, or "sloppy copy," and the ideas produced in this phase remain, for the moment, in the same form in which they left the author's head. In this creating phase, the teacher facilitates by reacting in a positive, interested way to the child's ideas, and nothing else. If something in the writing, a word or phrase is unclear, the teacher asks the child if she could elaborate, but does not EVER interfere with what the child has to say. As part of the writing process, children should be urged to keep on-going personal folders of their writing so that they can choose what would be worth the effort of editing, or "polishing up," for publication. The teacher should make his students aware that everything that is written is not necessarily of the same quality; thus, every piece that has been written during the year need not be selected for publication. Therefore, self-evaluation of one's writing is also an important component of this creating phase. Children should be encouraged to choose works for publication that they feel have the best ideas, the best expression of those ideas, as well as pieces that they are very proud of and wish to share by taking the time to edit them for publication.

Self-Editing

The second phase in the writing process is the self-editing phase. Now that many creative ideas have been put on paper and the child has selected among them a work that she feels is worthy of extending more effort upon, the attention can now be directed toward any spelling, punctuation, grammatical, or capitalization concerns. Children should be encouraged to read and reread their work several times at this stage, circling errors, or putting check marks in the margins where corrections need to be made. Students might then be asked to trade their work with a trusted friend who will also help to spot additional mechanical errors.

When the child has completed the self-editing phase to the best of her ability, the work is then turned in to the teacher, who thoughtfully reads the piece and may fill out an "author's evaluation form" similar to the one on page 11.

The Writing Conference

When such a form has been completed, the teacher schedules a writing conference with the child. The teacher begins this conference on a very positive note by reacting to some interesting ideas in the child's work and praises something about it. He gives the child the distinct impression that he respects the effort that has been expended thus far in the creating and editing phases, but somehow makes it clear that the joint goal of the teacher and the author is now to make this important piece of writing even better. At that point, the teacher and child discuss the piece and the points that have been brought out in the evaluation form. During the conference, the affective teacher should always be careful to:

*** Author's Evaluation Form ***

Title " The Horse Adventure "

Author Juanita Quiroz

The idea I like best is I like the idea that the horse talks to many animals and an old woman. They say funny things to each other.

I'd like to hear more about What happened when they walked down the road with the black cat?

Organization:

  Beginning Good - grabs my attention

  Middle lots of exciting adventures

  Ending Could be more interesting

Comments You have created a wonderful set of adventures for this horse! It was a very comical story.

1) be sensitive to the author's feelings;
2) tune in to ability and developmental writing stage of the author; make sure the author is able to understand the comments;
3) use only the author's words--not the teacher's;
4) be more concerned with WHAT was said, than HOW it was said;
5) make all corrections in the presence of the author;
6) ask permission to make any major revisions.

Paragraphs

When the self-editing process has been completed and the writing conference has produced a revised piece of writing, the child is ready for the next phase, which involves deciding how to group the sentences into cohesive paragraphs and how to turn bits of narrative into dialogue by the use of quotation marks. Since the essence of a paragraph is a group of sentences that support a main idea, this concept should be pointed out with stories that are read aloud to children and in stories that children read for themselves. Then, when they are producing their own writing, paragraphs are not an unfamiliar idea. Children can be asked to reread their own work to decide which sentences go together to accompany an illustration, or which group of sentences best describe an event that is taking place. When they have selected the sentences, they should be directed to draw a large circle around them, like so:

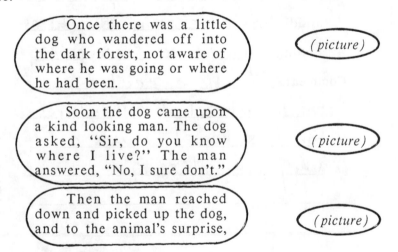

Once there was a little dog who wandered off into the dark forest, not aware of where he was going or where he had been.

(picture)

Soon the dog came upon a kind looking man. The dog asked, "Sir, do you know where I live?" The man answered, "No, I sure don't."

(picture)

Then the man reached down and picked up the dog, and to the animal's surprise,

(picture)

he took him straight to the
pound!

At this point, rough sketches may be drawn of
characters and events that accompany the paragraphs. To
determine what the actual dialogue might be like, children
should be encouraged to use balloons coming from the
characters' mouths, "cartoon style," and then they should
ask themselves, "What exactly would this dog have said
when that happened?" to find out where the quotation
marks would be.

Additionally, it is helpful here to provide scissors,
paste and sturdy cardboard so that writers can rearrange
paragraphs by cutting and pasting as they discover a more
logical sequence for their ideas.

Making a Cover

The fifth phase of the writing process, making a
cover, is strategically placed toward the end of the process
so that children can have a mental break (remember: they
have now rewritten their original work three or four
times!) and get an inspirational glimpse of what the final
product will look like. It often provides an additional
incentive to keep going with all this hard work. Now
students should be encouraged to make a picture for the
front cover that shows a salient feature from their work--a
major event or the funniest incident--so that the important
reading skill of finding the main idea is reinforced. A
wide variety of methods for designing covers should be
made available to children: tempera paints, felt-tip pens,
tissue paper, wrapping paper, and torn bits of construction
paper are all media I have seen used with excellent results.
To add interest, book covers can also be cut into different
shapes to enhance the ideas in the book. Animal shapes,
car shapes, football shapes, or banjo shapes, for example,
would provide a curious stimulation for both the writer
and the future readers. Finally, lamination (by the teacher,
art teacher or media specialist) then gives the finished
cover more substance. Of course, actual book covers should
be conspicuously on display in the writing center and
pointed out during read aloud time, so that children can
see the variety of titles and that the author's name is on
every published work.

When an original cover has been designed with the
author's name prominently in evidence on it, in most cases,
wild horses could not keep a child from now completing

the book! They are now ready to produce the "final copy," which means that previous revisions must be incorporated with the child's very best handwriting, which the child now has the highest motivation to use. Initially, lined paper may be used for the final copy of beginning authors, but eventually tracers should be provided so that children can produce books that look as close to the "real thing" as possible. Primary children might be instructed to place one paragraph on a page and leave plenty of room for the pictures, while older children may want to have more text on a page and fewer illustrations. When all the handsomely-polished print has been perfectly wedded to the page, children can attend to the final touches of elaborate illustrations and the very important title page. During this final phase, careful attention should be drawn to the variety of illustrations used in existing children's literature and the importance of the illustrator should be underscored during read aloud time, and as a child selects a book for recreational reading.

Publication

The final phase of the writing process is the publishing phase and it is the blissful time when young authors receive copious recognition for all the very important hard work they have just completed. In an Affective Language Arts Program, this phase is THE KEY to the success of the whole endeavor. The child has been laboring industriously with her whole mind, and she now reaps the emotional pay-off as she learns what it feels like to actually publish something that she created. Finished work should be ceremoniously put on display in the classroom for others to read, after profuse congratulations have been expressed by the teacher. A separate sheet of paper should be carefully clipped to the back of the book so that classmates can add their comments and extend "kudos" to the author. Parents can take part in the celebration if a brief note is sent home with the book so that the child can proudly read his "magnum opus" to the other members of the family. Finally, any other audiences that can be rounded up should be utilized. Other avenues for sharing the work might include reading it to other classes (kindergarteners are wonderful, *adoring* listeners!), reading it over the P.A. system, to the principal or librarian, presenting it at local P.T.A. meetings, nursing homes, or sharing it with a host of other interested community groups that would be thrilled to recognize the child's achievement. Additionally, an "author's chair" should be a standard feature in an affective program where much writing is going on. It is in this very special seat that deserving writers can personally share their efforts with other class members, if they so desire.

All this recognition and applause over the child's work are the positive reinforcement that make all the hard work suddenly seem quite worthwhile. Soon other, more reluctant writers in the class observe the author's success and they, too, begin to write. A creative renaissance is begun in the classroom and it can only lead to one more thing: *more* books!

Summary

Writing as a process can be tedious and very difficult for everyone, let alone the beginning writer. So to launch a writing program with the best chance of success, the affective teacher must be aware of the developmental writing stages that all children go through, so that her expectations can be appropriate to the writing ability of each of her pupils. Invented spellings should be encouraged in the early stages, until children have become confident to the degree that they are eager to write because they feel they have important things to say; they must feel free to explore print as an avenue for expressing ideas without worrying about the correctness of form. When children have reached the stage where they are able to "sound out" most words and have memorized many others, they are ready to begin the very same writing process that published authors go through.

Eventually, every child should have the freedom and the power to produce a good piece of writing that he is proud of and eager to share with the world. Such an end product takes phenomenal effort, so children must be gently guided through the writing process and encouraged to keep going when they become discouraged or frustrated with the many revisions that a good piece of writing necessarily entails. But with enough assistance along the way from an affective teacher who genuinely believes in each child and his unique ideas, a writing revolution will soon occur in such a classroom. It can be so exciting that the momentum will be self-perpetuating. As the first beautiful books are published and are met with the "oohs" and "aaahs" of classmates and admiring adults, everyone else in the class will want to write and publish and have these grand feelings of success for themselves.

References

Applegate, Mauree. *Freeing Children to Write.* New York: Harper and Row, 1963.

Cecil, Nancy L. *Teaching to the Heart: An Affective Approach to Reading Instruction.* Salem, WI: Sheffield Publishing Co., 1987.

Cowen, John E. *Teaching Reading Through the Arts.* Newark: International Reading Association, 1983.

Graves, Donald. *Breaking Ground: Teachers Relate Reading and Writing in the Elementary School.* Exeter, NH: Heinemann Educational Books, 1985.

Olson, Carol Booth, ed. *Practical Ideas for Teaching Writing as a Process.* Sacramento: California State Department of Education, 1986.

Petty, Walter T., and Patrick J. Finn, co-editors. *The Writing Processes of Students.* Buffalo: Report of the Annual Conference on Language Arts, 1975.

Weiss, Harvey. *How to Make Your Own Books.* New York: Thomas Y. Crowell, 1974.

Chapter Two

Dialogue Journals:
Personalizing Writing

Probably what most attracts children to diary writing as they are growing up is the secretive aspect of penning something very private, that no one else will see, in a diminutive, special book that contains nothing but the child's thoughts and dreams and personal events. Young children who are in what Piaget would deem the most self-absorbed stage of their lives seem to relish the opportunity to divulge, to no one in particular, all the things about themselves that perhaps no one else is really interested in. Most of us fondly remember some such self-indulgent, whimsical writing.

Until recently, there was no place for such intimate writing in school, leaving a rather large void in the writing curriculum. There has always been a time for children to engage in intimate oral communication with significant people in their lives, in school and out. But writing in school, somehow, has usually been a much more formidable task, mainly concerned with the external, observable form that the writing takes--its vocabulary, grammar, handwriting, and other issues of mechanics--rather than its function, or personal meaning to the child.

Fortunately, today's schools are experiencing a most welcome trend toward "journal writing" that is emerging to fill this need for a personal use of written language and provides much real writing practice as well. The use of a personal journal kept by each child with an allotted time set aside just for the sheer joy of writing is a step forward, to be sure, but the implementation of such writing components is taking many forms, some more beneficial to children than others.

Of the variety of journal-writing formats I have observed being used in elementary classrooms, the one that seems best suited for use in an Affective Language Arts program is the "dialogue journal." The "dialogue" part simply means that in this journal, a running dialogue is carried on between two people--the teacher and the child. The child begins by writing down anything that is of interest to him or her, and the teacher simply responds by commenting on the child's ideas, asking thoughtful questions, or sometimes merely paraphrasing what the child has said to affirm those thoughts. The teacher, and no one else (unless the child initiates sharing with someone else) reads the entries the child has written.

This chapter will explore some of the important issues involved in starting a dialogue journal writing component of an Affective Language Arts program. Such issues include: 1) What should the children write about? 2) How much should children write? 3) When should they write? 4) How should journal writing be evaluated? 5) What is the rationale for spending valuable curriculum time on such informal writing? While there are many different ways to answer such questions, all equally valid, we will focus here on each of these concerns in terms of how best to provide experiences that foster a real love for writing as an ideal avenue for personal self-expression.

What Should the Children
Write About?

I have seen many classrooms in which the question "What shall I write in my journal?" was answered by the teacher assigning a daily topic that the children were instructed to address in their journals that day. While this is certainly a well-meaning technique to get children started, "options" are the real key to success in an Affective Language Arts program. To initially launch the idea of dialogue journals, it might be helpful, instead, to write two or three questions on the blackboard, such as "If you could have any animal that you wanted as a pet, what would you choose? Why?" and "What are some of your favorite things to do on a Saturday morning?" Advising children that these questions are *only* possibilities for writing topics--not "mandates"--then frees those children who already have their own agenda to pursue their own ideas. Note, also, that the topics suggested here were real questions that would require personal, open-ended answers. Too often children are coerced into making their journals outlets for fictional "story" types of pieces, which is all right, as long as it is the child's own wish to use such a genre. My concern is that there is usually plenty of story writing already in the curriculum, so the journal should instead be a possible vehicle through which children could write their personal, first-person statements and vent their feelings and views on life.

write their personal, first-person statements and vent their feelings and views on life.

An additional possibility for getting the routine of journal writing started is to brainstorm, as a class, at the beginning of the first few writing sessions. During the brainstorming, the teacher might ask the class to decide upon a particular topic, such as music. The teacher would then ask the children to tell what words or phrases come to their minds when they think about music. Since there is no right or wrong answer, children may come up with all sorts of responses that this stimulus provokes. The teacher, then, may choose to "cluster" the responses to help the children mentally organize all the ways it is possible to think about music. For example:

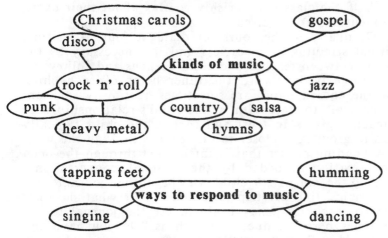

The children might go off into two or three tangents (usually, many more!) in response to the broad term "music." As one student responds "Rock 'n' Roll!" and another pipes up, "Christmas carols!" the teacher then clusters these two similar ideas together, as shown above, under the category "kinds of music," and then performs the same task for "ways we respond to music." With this rudimentary kind of brainstorming about a subject chosen by the class, every child has a chance to respond with his or her own "free association" to the subject, and all the children have begun mentally conjuring up all the different things they know about the topic. Then, keyed in to many possible ideas they could express about the subject, children can write about that topic, assisted by all the ideas on the blackboard, or feel free to pursue their thoughts on something entirely different.

For beginning writers who are often feeling constrained by lack of words that they know how to spell it is often helpful for the teacher to position herself at the blackboard during the entire journal writing session, with the offer that she is there to write down any words that the children might want to spell, but don't know how. The results of this spelling assistance by the teacher are twofold: first, the children are freed to write down whatever they are able to think up due to the immediate spelling help; and second, the children are often stimulated by the words that other children have asked to have spelled on the blackboard, quickly "borrow" them, and then start writing with gusto. Often it takes only one child to query, "How do you spell 'trapeze,' Mr. Vega?" and suddenly half the class is feverishly writing about their exciting adventures at the circus.

Gradually in the course of dialogue journal writing, a formal stimulus becomes less and less necessary as the dialogue between teacher and child deepens and follows its own unique path toward the inner being of each child. While the chosen topics are sometimes cautiously emotionally "neutral" to start with, as the child's relationship with the teacher grows in trust and caring, the child typically begins to grow even closer to the teacher through the writing. A bonding occurs that is intensified through the open communication afforded by the personal, conversational nature of the journal. A child who began her journal with "safe" topics, like her trip to Grandma's or what she likes to eat for breakfast, may begin to use the journal to ask the teacher personal questions such as "Do you have any children, Mrs. Roma?" or "Do you think my new haircut looks dumb?" At this point, when events happen in class that may be unsettling to a child, that child may begin to vent his anger through the journal. He may now use the journal to apologize to the teacher for something he did in class that he wishes he hadn't done, or he may begin to confide in the teacher about hurtful things happening to him at home or in his relationship with others at school. Some children may complain about homework in the journal; others use the journal to confess to "petty crimes" they have committed, such as having told a lie or having cheated on a test, or having taken something that did not belong to them. Too, children begin to use the journal to express feelings that are too embarrassing for them to own up to in person; in writing, they suddenly may feel free to offer their undying love and appreciation for their teacher.

How Much Should Children Write?

Exactly how much writing should be done in the journal on a daily basis is an issue that must be confronted, because it will surface almost immediately (especially with older children who are more entrenched in "the system") and will almost certainly get in the way if not laid to rest. Too often children are instructed to . . . "write a 250 word essay on . . ." or ". . . write a five page story which tells . . ." and the more fretful and hesitant writers get so caught up in counting words and pages they soon lose sight of anything they had to say. To avoid this squelching of the free flow of ideas I suggest, instead, that the teacher tell the children at the onset of the dialogue journal writing sessions that during each session *something* must be written, but that the amount is of little significance. Students may write in response to the questions placed on the board, they may take off on the brainstorming topic, or they may even write down the lyrics to a song on the radio that they liked and tell why. In some cases, they may resort to writing down, "I don't know what to write" and then try to explain how they feel about having to write when they feel they have nothing to say! Although the first several entries from the "word counter" will probably be slim pickings, the teacher who waits out the drought will soon be rewarded: as children begin to realize they are really free to write about whatever interests them; when they see that their lack of perfect mechanical prowess in the language is not pointed out; and when they begin to understand that everything that they say will get a thoughtful response from their teacher, I can testify to the fact that they *will* start writing. They may not become prolific writers in "three easy weeks," but the difference in the quantity and quality of writing produced by erstwhile reluctant writers after several months of using dialogue journals is often striking.

Ideally, children should have time set aside to write in their journals every day. It might commence as a ten minute writing block for primary children and turn into half hour sessions after several months, when children begin finding more and more to say, and look increasingly forward to reading the teacher's responses. Some children may ask to bring their journals home in order to write more in the evening as well; this is a sure sign of success and should be encouraged (but not forced) by all means. For some children with difficult home lives, the journal becomes an outlet for them to react to confusing things that may be happening to them; a sympathetic ear, or in extreme cases, a life-line.

How Should Journal Writing Be Evaluated?

The teacher's responsibility in the dialogue journal is pivotal--and time-consuming; there seems to be no easy way to make the task of writing personal responses less demanding on one's time. However, the tedious, "nit-picky" ordeal of correcting every misspelled word or sentence fragment in red pen is scrupulously avoided here. But the teacher must still read everything each child has written and make appropriate comments as deemed necessary. As the writing progresses, the teacher may be more familiar with the nature of each child's writing; several pages may need no comments or an occasional "What an interesting thought!" or "I agree!" Corrections, in the traditional sense, are **not** made, but the teacher does model, through her paraphrasing or questions, correct form in writing.

The following is an excerpt from the journal of a third-grader in which the process of teacher-modeling, as well as some basic problem-solving, has taken place:

When I grow up I have disided to be a scubba divver. I think it would be so net to swim around with all those fish. Have you ever been scubba divving, Mrs. Reed. You know what Mrs. Reed yesterday in math you said I was talking but it wasn't me. It was Lisa. She is always bothering me Mrs. Reed. Can you change are seats?

* * * * * * *

How exciting that you have decided to become a scuba diver! No, I have never been scuba diving, Ann. Will you go scuba diving when you go to Florida on vacation? I will see about changing your seat, Ann. I am so sorry you were bothered!

Yes Mrs. Reed, we are going to go scuba diving when we go to Florida Dad said. I can't wait!! Daddy said we might see some very big and colorfull fish.

In this entry, Ann has spontaneously expressed her current desire to be a "scubba divver" when she grows up. Note that the teacher sensitively responds only to the ideas Ann has, yet in her response, the teacher correctly respells "scuba diver," "decided," "diving" and models the correct punctuation for addressing someone. Note, too, that this is duly noted by the child, who does not feel at all chastised by this "subliminal" correction, but she does spell "scuba diving" correctly in her next use of the words, because it is axiomatic that every child would love to spell everything correctly, if it were just possible for them to know how to spell each word as they needed it.

Also in this entry (practically in the same breath in which she has rhapsodized about becoming a scuba diver!), Ann airs her hurt feelings about a minor altercation that occurred the previous day. While not actually taking Ann's side in the matter, the teacher assents to resolving the problem by separating the two children. The teacher's judgment in originally telling Ann to stop talking may or may not have been in error, but in a typical class of nearly thirty children, many hasty judgment calls must be made. The added perspective offered to the teacher by the dialogue journals is often invaluable.

To make the task of looking over the journals less formidable, some teachers elect to read half the journals every week. This means that all children get feedback on their entries at least every two weeks, yet the teacher's reading and responding is minimized. Often a teacher can respond sensitively to thirteen or fourteen journals within a couple of hours. To be sure, two hours a week is a hefty commitment, but the teacher's rewards in terms of seeing his students' writing become much more fluent cannot be overestimated.

Why Implement Dialogue Journal Writing?

The justification for adding dialogue journal writing to an already overloaded language arts curriculum are many, and in this age of teacher accountability, it would seem they are worth reiterating here. First of all, the improvement in attitude toward writing of children who have participated in such a program is phenomenal. As was previously mentioned, if the sessions are frequent enough (preferably once a day) and endure for the better part of a school year and include the kind of positive feedback described in this chapter, children at every grade level will be much more favorably inclined toward writing, and will write MORE.

Second, the confidence of children will increase as they begin to believe in their own writing ability and they look *forward* to the teacher's comments rather than dreading the more typical "sea of red marks." As they realize, through their teacher's comments, that their thoughts and ideas have merit, their self-concept, too, will improve.

Third, children receive important writing practice through journals and, as a result, they become more fluent writers. As in skiing, typing, or riding a bicycle, writing improves with concerted practice. Moreover, due to the modeling the teacher does, and the prodding questions that he asks, children begin to learn just what kinds of details to elaborate upon in order to make their writing effective. Additionally, through the modeling, children's spelling and other use of mechanics of our language improves markedly. The teacher is able to be there for every child's "teachable moment" of wanting to know how to spell a certain word or how to use an unfamiliar grammatical construct.

Fourth, children begin to see a new use of writing for their own purposes, rather than just completing a teacher-directed assignment. Many children begin to find that writing can be a very cathartic experience--especially when they are venting some very intense feelings and emotions. They often find, too, that writing is a great outlet offering them a way to diffuse potentially explosive situations ahead of time by being able to examine their feelings objectively *before* they act.

Finally, the effect that dialogue journal writing can have on the relationship between teacher and students is perhaps the happiest side benefit of this writing activity. With an affective teacher who does not take lightly the trust of her pupils, the dialogues can lead to a much deeper, holistic understanding of the children that she teaches as distinct individuals. As intimate details of the child's life are offered to a teacher, and that child, in return, is assured that he is indeed a valuable and worthwhile human being, a serendipitous bonding occurs that, under normal over-crowded classroom circumstances would have taken years to build. Additionally, the teacher receives some valuable feedback into the "grapevine" of the classroom culture that a teacher is not ordinarily privy to. She gets some interesting feedback about her teaching techniques, her relationship with pupils, and her handling of classroom crises as they arise. With the privilege of being able to "feel the classroom pulse," if there are any major class concerns, the teacher is one of the first to know.

Summary

The use of the dialogue journal in an Affective Language Arts program is an ideal way to ensure that children receive adequate practice in the kind of intimate, informal practice that is most meaningful to them. The journals can be the prime vehicle through which a capable teacher can gently model effective writing techniques, as well as the mechanics of our language. Such a teacher can also prod children into elaborating on what they themselves have already decided to write about. Although the journals require a commitment of time and effort on the teacher's part, their use tends to produce a greater bonding between teacher and students, and the teacher is able to get a child's-eye-view of the emotional climate of the classroom. Most of all, students who keep dialogue journals grow more confident in their ability to use written communication. With the guidance of a sensitive and affective teacher, children experience the joy of being able to express their innermost thoughts and ideas to a caring adult. Indeed, the highlight of the students' week becomes the moment when their journals are returned by their teacher, and they reread their entries with the teacher's comments to see how their youthful musings were received.
Soon the prosaic "How much do I have to write?" dies a natural death, as the young writers move on to more important questions.

References

Danielson, Kathy Everts. *Dialogue Journals: Writing as Conversation.* Bloomington, IN: Phi Delta Kappa Educational Foundation, 1988.
Gambrel, Linda B. "Dialogue Journals: Reading-Writing Interaction." *The Reading Teachers* 38 (1985): 512-15.
Kreeft, Joy. "Dialogue Writing: Bridge from Talk to Essay Writing." *Language Arts* 61 (1984): 141-50.

Lindfors, Judith W. "From 'Talking Together' to 'Being To-gether in Talk'." *Language Arts* 65, no. 2 (February 1988): 135-41.
Staton, Jana. "Writing and Counseling: Using a Dialogue Journal." *Language Arts* 57 (1980): 514-18.
Staton, Jana, R. Shay, J. Kreeft, and L. Reed. *Dialogue Journal Communication: Classroom, Linguistic, Social, and Cognitive Views.* Norwood, NJ: Ablex, 1987.

Chapter Three

Copy-cat Books: Expanding Upon Children's Literature

Mrs. Perry has just finished reading "The Three Billy Goats Gruff" to her second graders. The story is one they have heard before, and because this is so, they know what is coming and eagerly chime in, "Trip, trap, trip, trap!" at the appropriate times and spontaneously cheer and applaud when the ugly troll is sent flying over the bridge. Now Mrs. Perry has an irresistible proposition for the children: "Let's write a new story much like this one, only we can change the characters. What three animals could we have who need to get somewhere?" The class decides upon three dinosaurs--a big one, a small one, and an in-between one. She then asks her charges, "Where might the dinosaurs be heading in our new story?" Enrique offers that the dinosaurs might be on their way to the jungle to find some ferns, as these dinosaurs are of the plant-eating variety. "Who or what might stop our dinosaurs from getting to the jungle?" Mrs. Perry inquires. Lorena insists that they must swim across a deep lake, but there is a huge monster in the lake, not unlike the Loch Ness monster that she has read about. Her contribution is greeted with much appreciation and excitement; these second-graders are quite fond of monsters. The class is ready to compose. As they take turns thinking up new lines for a modified story, Mrs. Perry transcribes their ideas onto the blackboard. The children will copy their new story, and some children will be inspired to write yet another new version of "The Billy Goats Gruff" on their own. Meanwhile, Graciela, the class artist, has drawn the dinosaur family, the Loch Ness monster, a lake, and a jungle to use with the flannel board so that the class can later retell their new story, *Three Dinosaurs Daring* with the help of her felt cut-outs.

This teacher has demonstrated how certain literature can be successfully used to inspire children to adapt the existing rhyme schemes, ideas, or catchy phrases of stories they know and love. We know that great artists and writers of the past have often begun their careers by first modeling the products of esteemed artists and writers; it seems only fitting that children should be given similar opportunities to learn some techniques from the masters of children's literature. This "copy-catting" method not only reinforces the children's appreciation for the literature, but it also gradually encourages them to become authors by providing them with a tried-and-true structure that they already know will be wonderful.

The remainder of this chapter will describe how nine favorite children's books can be read to a class and then turned into new creations by allowing children to copy some part of the book. While this is only a small sample, Appendix I contains many other books that have patterns that also lend themselves to similar modeling. Hopefully, the affective teacher reading this book can soon follow many read-aloud sessions by encouraging his students to write new books.

A House Is a House For Me

Mary Ann Hoberman's enchanting book takes children from reality to fantasy while having them consider just what constitutes the concept of a "house." She starts out with obvious enough statements: "A web is a house for a spider; A coop? That's a house for a chicken," and always comes back to the phrase . . . "and a house is a house for me." Later in the book, however, the author begins to be more broad in her interpretation of what a "house" can be, and the fun begins. "A sandwich is home for some ham . . . a throat is a house for a hum . . . a mirror's a house for reflections." Children delight in these far-fetched ideas and are then ready to write a new book of their own with some original ideas that may not have been included in Hoberman's book. For additional inspiration, one class leafed through magazines, and then came up with a wonderfully imaginative book. Here's an excerpt:

> A radio is a house for music,
> The sky is a house for a rainbow,
> Heaven is home to the angels,
> And a house is a house for me.
>
> A chest is a house for a cough,
> A blizzard is a house for a snowman,
> A cup is a home for chicken noodle soup,
> And a house is a house for me.

What Do You Say, Dear?

What Do You Say, Dear? is a wonderfully tongue-in-cheek compilation of episodes in which children find themselves in rather unusual circumstances that require them to consider their repertoire of courteous phrases and select just the right one. Each episode ends with the query, "What do you say, dear?" For example, my favorite: "You have gone downtown to do some shopping. You are walking backwards because sometimes you like to, and you bump into a crocodile. What do you say, dear? --Excuse me." After the eleven hilarious episodes in the book have been read to the class, children are tuned in to the author's sense of humor and are ready to write an "etiquette" book of their own. It is helpful to first write a list of the possible courteous phrases on the blackboard or overhead. Then, after the whole class has helped to brainstorm one or two far-fetched situations that would require such courteous phrases, children can be broken up into small groups, with each group responsible for two or three more phrases. For example, one group came up with these episodes:

> You are swimming in the ocean when suddenly a great white shark appears and is about to chomp on your leg. Suddenly a skin diver appears and spears the shark. What do you say, dear? --Thank you very much.

> Michael Jackson is putting on a rock concert in your bedroom. Your mother is trying to whisper something in your ear but you can't quite hear her. What do you say, dear? --I beg your pardon?

If It Weren't For You

Charlotte Zolotow has written several books with wistful, recurring phrases with which every child can readily identify. *If It Weren't For You* is one such book. In Zolotow's story, a young boy is reflecting upon all the things that would be possible if it weren't for his little brother: "If it weren't for you I'd be an only child and I'd get all the presents. I could have the whole last slice of cake and the biggest piece of candy in the box." The child does finally concede, however, that if it weren't for his little brother . . . "I'd have to be alone with the grown-ups." Children who may not have siblings still may have similar ambivalent feelings about many people--even their parents and teacher. To use the motif of the book requires that first the whole class brainstorms some people about whom they sometimes have mixed feelings. Discuss the fact that this is true in *any* relationship; people we love can often cause us problems! Start off with the phrase "If it weren't for you . . ." and let the class express some resentments. For a final line let them think of some positive element that the person adds to their lives (the old "bait and switch"!) to end the story on a happy note. One class devised these lines about their teacher:

> If it weren't for you, Mrs. Sowa,
> I wouldn't have to wake up on a Monday morning,
> I wouldn't have to do any homework.
> I wouldn't have to stay in at recess when I've been rude.
> If it weren't for you, I'd be fishing right now!
> But it's also true, if it weren't for you,
> I wouldn't have learned as much as I know now.

Someday

Charlotte Zolotow's earlier book *Someday* has a motif of a day far in the future when the things that go predictably wrong will all of a sudden be perfect--the stuff of dreams. Every child can relate to this child's "Someday I'm going to dancing class and Miss Bird will say, 'Ellen is doing it just right. Everybody watch her,' or 'Someday I'm going to catch a high, high ball and my team will win because I did it.' " For children to adapt this book into their own wistful, "someday" projections, a brainstorming session should begin with sharing some everyday experiences that children have had that are usually quite frustrating. "Someday" perhaps these situations could be reversed, as these fifth-graders wrote:

> Someday I'm going to make blueberry pancakes and flip them high in the air and they will land just in the right place on the griddle--NOT on the floor!

> Someday my big brother will say to me, "Was there something you would prefer to watch on TV rather than football? I would be happy to change the channel for you!

Rosie's Walk

Pat Hutchins has written a book for very young children that establishes a simple pattern of prepositional phrases that children can have fun duplicating using their *own* walk--real or imaginary--as a guide. *Rosie's Walk* takes Rosie, the hen, on a walk "... across the yard, around the pond, over the haystack, ... and back in time for dinner." The story can be read aloud to primary children and then, after a brief recap about all the places that Rosie went, followed by a walk to the library or around the school yard, or even an imaginary walk with eyes closed to some far-away place. After a walk and the second reading of the book, children will want to write their own book, using Hutchin's patterns of prepositions, about their walk:

> Mrs. Najera's class went for a walk
> across the field,
> around the swings,
> over the sandbox,
> past the jungle gym,
> through the bushes
> under the slide
> and got back in time for recess.

A variation with older children might include adding descriptive adjectives to each place that was visited. One fourth grade class, for example, wrote:

> Mrs. Nakahira's class went for a walk
> Across the congested auditorium,
> Around the inviting water fountain,
> Over the well-traveled tile,
> Past the deafening lunch room,
> Through the quiet halls,
> Under the acoustic ceiling,
> And got back in time to turn in their math
> homework!

Animals Should Definitely NOT Wear Clothing

Judi Barrett's book tickles children's funny bones and inspires them to add to her ideas with their own creations. With entries such as "Animals should definitely NOT wear clothing because it could be very messy for a pig," and "... because a giraffe might look sort of silly," with amusing illustrations to match, children are ready to write. Fortunately, Barrett has used nowhere near *all* the possible animals in her book, so the next step, after reading the book aloud, is to have children brainstorm some other animals not included in the original book and for the teacher to write them on the blackboard or overhead. Next, brainstorm some possible problems that two or three of these animals might have if they were to wear clothing:

> Animals should definitely *not* wear clothing
> ... because a skunk might make them smelly;
> ... because a whale would wet them with his spout;
> ... because a cat could claw them to bits.

After the whole group effort, children can be divided into groups of four or five and given an animal from those just contributed on the blackboard. Each group then brainstorms a possible reason why their animal should *not* wear clothing because . . . Each group's phrase is then combined with the other groups to make a new class book. Groups can, of course, be encouraged to illustrate their phrases, using Barrett's hilarious drawings as a guideline.

Brown Bear, Brown Bear, What Do You See?

Bill Martin's classic *Brown Bear, Brown Bear* is a favorite with primary children because of its clever rhyming and repetition, and it lends itself to the fresh ideas of children who will like using the same pattern:

> Redbird, redbird, what do you see?
> I see a yellow duck looking at me.
> Yellow duck, yellow duck, what do you see?
> I see a blue horse looking at me.

After the children have listened to this book, they are ready to brainstorm some new creatures or objects to consider what *these* objects might see. The original brainstorming might take place orally, as a group game, after the first object has been decided upon, and might proceed like this:

> Candle stick, candle stick,
> What do you see?
> I see a matchstick

That's going to burn me!
Matchstick, matchstick
What do you see?
I see wind
That's going to blow me.

After this oral "warm up" exercise, an add-on, or cumulative, book can be written by the class. Each child individually selects a creature or object and combines it with the question, "What do you see?" This question is exchanged with another child. Each child answers the other's question with, "I see a *(rhyme)*." This exercise is repeated nine or ten times, until each child has written several questions and answers and has completed an ending line to one new book.

I Know What I Like

Part of every child's coming to terms with who he is involves sharing his opinions about what he likes and what he doesn't like. As the sum total of these likes and dislikes makes a unique individual so also the sum total of each child's likes and dislikes can create a new book that can be patterned after Norma Simon's *I Know What I Like.* Most of the "likes" in Simon's books are ones that most children will subscribe to: "I like to taste peanut butter . . . I like to see kittens . . . I like to be first in line . . .." And the dislikes equally popular: "But I don't like to taste this medicine . . . I don't like to see scary television . . . I don't like to be spanked."

Simon's book will surely inspire a discussion of likes and dislikes and the inevitable disagreements may give the affective teacher an opportunity to reinforce the idea that there is no "right" or "wrong" when it comes to opinions; it is okay to disagree with one another. The class as a whole can then brainstorm on the blackboard some things that they like to see, hear, taste, be, and try, as in Simon's book, and then, in an opposite column, make a list of some things they do *not* like to see, hear, taste, be, and try. Encourage children to then write their *own* books that describe their own personal likes and dislikes. Additionally, children may be inspired to illustrate their books by looking at Dora Leder's sometimes humorous accompanying pictures.

Alexander and the Terrible, Horrible, No-Good, Very Bad Day

Everyone has an occasional bad day now and then, and Judith Viorst makes light of this subject by introducing Alexander, who is having a day in which absolutely everything is going wrong--from waking up with bubble gum in his hair to having his Mickey Mouse night light burn out. Every unfortunate episode ends with the observation, "It was . . . a terrible, horrible, no good, very bad day," and children, as always, look forward to this repetitive phrase.

Viorst's book makes a perfect story for a copy-cat book. After reading it and reiterating all the things that went wrong for poor Alexander, children can be asked to tell about some bad days that they have had and what it was that made them that way. They can then write their own story, including their experiences, real or made-up, interspersing every two or three unhappy events with, "It was a terrible, horrible, no good, very bad day."

Conversely, some children may want to talk about a very *good* day they had and tell why. Real or imaginary events can be used to write a book that describes a perfect day. One fourth-grader, for example, decided to pen "Nicole and the Wonderful, Marvelous, Very Good, Exceptionally Fine Day."

Summary

Copy-cat books can be an excellent device to extend the positive feelings of a read-aloud experience through a session in which children use some of the same themes, ideas, phrases, or repetitive schemes in a book to write a new text--borrowing some ideas here, adding an original thought there.

In this chapter, nine children's books were selected and sample, teacher-tested ways to use their motifs to create new books were described. While every trade book may not lend itself to this wonderful reading-writing interaction, much of the available literature for young children contains the kind of repetition and predictable phrases that inspire children to write similar stories, or even to forge ahead into different directions. Appendix I offers a bibliography of many other children's books that can also be used for copy-cat sessions by an affective teacher who wants to show her students just how rewarding it can be to write books--with a little help from some of the masters of children's literature.

References

Barrett, Judi. *Animals Should Definitely NOT Wear Clothing.* New York: Atheneum, 1973.

Cloer, Thomas. *A Teacher's Handbook of Language Experience Activities.*

Hoberman, Mary Ann. *A House Is a House For Me.* New York: Viking Press, 1978.

Hutchins, Pat. *Rosie's Walk.* New York: Macmillan, 1968.

Joslyn, Sesyle. *What Do You Say, Dear?* New York: Young Scott Books, 1958.

Simon, Norma. *I Know What I Like.* Chicago: Albert Whitman & Co., 1971.

Viorst, Judith. *Alexander and the Terrible, Horrible, No Good, Very Bad Day.* New York: Atheneum, 1982.

Wertenberg, Jacque. *Helping Children Become Writers.*

Zolotow, Charlotte. *If It Weren't For You.* New York: Harper & Row, 1966.

Zolotow, Charlotte. *Someday.* New York: Harper & Row, 1965.

Chapter Four

Episodic Novels:
Becoming REAL Authors

If asked to describe one's most pleasant reading experience, most avid readers might immediately conjure up a full-length novel that was devoured recently, or perhaps many years ago. Whether it be an autobiography, a thriller, or a modern romance, there is something special--even endearing--about a multi-chaptered story that an author has carefully crafted with three-dimensional characters created in an exact time and place with a certain set of problems and resolutions. We feel it is a privilege to share the fictional lives of these characters. But it is the very length of a novel, as compared with shorter genres, that allows the reader this greater time of getting to know the characters, and thus makes the reading experience all that much more intense. Moreover, it must be admitted that the sheer volume of pages in most novels gives us a feeling of some satisfaction at having persevered and finished the tome!

As children enter the intermediate grades they, too, start to read lengthier books. Brief picture story books begin to give way to stories divided into chapters with highly sophisticated plots and, as children are reaching the period in their lives when their adult reading interests are formed, they are also introduced to the pleasures of "armchair escapism" that can be found in a protracted literary experience like reading a novel.

Although children at this age are often reading longer books, their writing assignments, while tending to become more complex, are rarely lengthening to a similar degree. Most students in the intermediate grades are still instructed to write short stories, two-page compositions, and 250-word essays, with only an occasional research paper that may stretch beyond the usual succinct expectations. Teachers often complain that they are pulling teeth to get them to write even that much!

But I have found that children who have had the experience of writing an original episodic novel--with several discrete chapters--come away with a much more

memorable feeling of accomplishment, and a fair sense of
pride at having produced a new set of characters who have
evolved with time and effort and have become real to
them. Children who write episodic novels are also under-
standably quite impressed that their creation resembles an
"adult" novel in size and scope. I am convinced that no
other writing experience can offer children such an
overwhelming sense of authorship.
    Tried and true ways to help children bridge the gap
from composition writers to episodic novelists will be
explored in the remainder of this chapter.

Story Maps

    To prepare children for the formidable-sounding
task of writing a novel, they first need practice
identifying the components of fiction--short stories as well
as novels. They need to recognize and be able to produce
these fictional elements:
    • **Character(s).** The hero or heroine of the story.
What does (s)he look like? How old is (s)he? What is
his/her personality like? What does (s)he enjoy doing?
What has his/her life been like up until now? Would we
like him/her?
    • **Setting.** Where and when will the story take place?
What does the place look like, feel like, smell like, sound
like?
    • **Episodes** (eventually, chapters). What sequence of
events will happen to the main character(s) and how will
he or she feel about what happens? Who will the
character(s) consult? How will they make decisions? What
will they do next?
    • **Consequences** (could be after each episode or all
episodes). What happens when the character(s) carry out
their plans? Do they succeed? What or who gets in their
way? How do they feel?
    • **Reactions** (ending for novel). What did the main
character(s) learn from all these episodes? How is (s)he
different from when we first met him/her? What can *we*
learn from all of this?
    The above fictional elements should be routinely
discussed with children after they have finished reading
books individually or as a group. As they become increasingly facile at identifying these components as they
encounter them in short stories and novels, it becomes very
natural for them to want to create their own.

Brainstorming

To initiate the novel-writing process, it is helpful to use the previously discussed structure to brainstorm some rudimentary novel ideas together as a class. One fourth-grade class produced the following ideas for a novel.

Characters. The hero of the story is a very kind, but timid scientist who keeps botching up his experiments. He has had nothing but bad luck in his life. His wife and children died in an automobile accident and his dog was poisoned. He is very old and bald, skinny and very nervous. He speaks very slowly (he keeps forgetting what he was going to say) and he says "hmmm" a lot.

Setting. Our scientist lives on a small island in the Pacific Ocean sometime in the future. The island is very green and smells like coconuts and salty breezes. The island is uninhabited except for a few natives and sometimes tourists whose ships get wrecked on the island.

Episodes (chapters) 1) A very evil sailor gets shipwrecked on the island. He wants the island for himself and he is afraid of the natives, so he decides to kill them (he has a gun).
2) The natives decide to go to war against the sailor. They have no weapons except spears. They're not good fighters.
3) The natives lose the war. Many of them are shot and several die. The evil sailor thinks he got rid of them forever, but he didn't. Two are still alive.
4) One of the natives asks the scientist if he will devise a potion that will make the sailor fall asleep so that they can steal his gun.
5) The scientist thinks about it for a long time, but then he says no (he is too shy). The natives are very sad.
6) Then the scientist gets very sick with a tropical disease (malaria). The natives save him by bringing him tea and herbs. He gets better.
7) The scientist is very grateful, because he realizes the natives saved his life. He decides to make the potion.
8) The natives put the potion in the drinking water of the sailor while he is cleaning his gun.

Consequences. The sailor drinks the water and falls asleep. The natives take the gun and bury it under a tree. The sailor wakes up and the natives make peace with him. They shake hands.

Reactions. The scientist decides he has been selfish his whole life and that was probably why he had such bad luck. The sailor makes friends with the scientist and helps him to do his experiments without botching them up.

Moral: If you are kind to people and use your talents wisely, people will want to help you and your luck will get better!

Small Groups

Having brainstormed some rudimentary ideas for the class episodic novel, children are now ready to break into groups of two or three writing partners to elaborate on the ideas that were contributed in the whole group session. The above brainstorming session produced twelve discrete components of the story, which would now be called episodes, or chapters. Each writing team would now select one of these chapter parts and expand the germ that was brainstormed into a more fully developed composition. The writing partners are especially helpful here, because the children can continue to bounce ideas off one another orally, as the inspiration is still fresh from the recent group brainstorming. Also, the children in each writing group can serve as editors to read and reread their group's effort for any glaring spelling or punctuation errors. As all this thinking and writing is going on, the teacher is moving from group to group, listening to each group as they are expounding their ideas to support and affirm, but also to prevent any group from radically deviating from the ideas set forth in another chapter.

Group Conferences

When each group has finished its episode and turned it in, the teacher calls conferences with each group. First she checks to see that each episode makes a logical transition from one chapter to the next, while keeping all the characters somewhat consistent in their behavior. While maintaining respect for the authors' words and ideas, the teacher may ask the authors to expand an idea or phrase, or advise them of some information they may need from other chapters written by other groups (at this stage, only the teacher is privy to the *whole* novel!). Now is also the optimal time to show each group of children how to make their descriptions more lively and realistic by using dialogue. Children who have not had this instruction will usually create lines such as, "The natives asked the scientist if he would devise a potion to make the sailor fall asleep."

Children are now open to the idea that the same idea is much more powerful like this:

"Sir, could you help us by devising a potion that would make the sailor fall asleep?" the native hopefully inquired.

The group then prepares a revised chapter.

Sharing the Novel

Using this abbreviated group writing technique, the class has just written a twelve-chapter novel, and the next step--sharing it--will ensure that each individual author will soon be ready to branch out on his or her own. With ceremonious acclaim the teacher reads the novel (so as to avoid conflicts between group members as to who should read their chapter), as well as to provide the appropriate savoir-faire!

After plenty of congratulatory behavior all around, the children can be asked to write their final finished copy with one illustration contributed by each author. Then the final product can be shared with others outside the classroom, as discussed in chapter two, and used as an inspiration for future episodic novels.

The Individually-Written Novel

After the intensive group exercise in novel writing, most children feel confident enough to attempt to write a novel of their own, while looking forward to a product that is as exciting, yet expedient, as the group effort was. Of course, the individual effort will take much longer, but the children must be reminded that the more chapters they add to their novel, the more interesting and fun it will be to write.

The teacher then provides an extensive episodic outline for each child. This outline differs from the story maps only in that specific chapter ideas are offered in episodic-size chunks. Also, outlines might focus on themes of a certain emotion, such as grief, envy, hatred, love, or hope. Or, after reading a wide variety of Greek or Roman myths, children can pick a similar hero or heroine. Using the basic story elements already described, the writer can have the hero and his actions try to explain the creation of one of our natural phenomena, such as floods, tornadoes, lightning, etc.

Because children have already had some experience with the previous shared novel in character development, as well as the need for a setting, problems, and resolution, these particular facets are woven into the novel outline, which can become increasingly complex as the children start to demand more sophisticated plots. The following is a sample episodic novel outline that works well with intermediate age children who have already had some practice writing shared episodic novels. It can be expanded as needed:

Chapter One: Invent and describe a character. Is (s)he real or pretend? What does (s)he look like? Where does (s)he live? How does (s)he behave? What things does (s)he like to do? What things are special about him/her?

Chapter Two: What is your character's family like? Describe his/her friends. Tell about some things that may have happened to him/her when (s)he was a baby and growing up.

Chapter Three: Describe one full day in the life of your character. Does (s)he work or go to school? Where and what does (s)he like to play? Who and what does (s)he play with? What does (s)he eat? What kinds of things usually happen?

Chapter Four: Your character is going on a trip. How does (s)he decide to go on this trip? How does (s)he prepare for it? How does (s)he feel about going?

Chapter Five: Just before going on the trip, someone warns your character not to go on this trip. Who or what warns your character? Should your character go? Why or why not? Describe your character's thoughts and feelings now.

Chapter Six: Your character decides to go on the trip anyway. What makes him/her decide? Describe your character's voyage there and his/her feelings on the way.

Chapter Seven: Your character has a wonderful, magical first day at his/her destination. Describe the place at which your character has arrived. Tell what made the first day so extra special.

Chapter Eight: The second day of the trip your character meets someone or something very strange. Who or what? Describe what makes this person so strange and tell about what happens at the meeting.

Chapter Nine: The strange person [or thing] asks your character to do something evil, but your character doesn't want to. The strange person says something bad will happen if your character doesn't do the evil thing. Describe the bad thing and the conversation between your character and the strange person. Tell what is supposed to happen if your character does not do what is asked of him/her.

Chapter Ten: Your character decides not to do the evil thing. Describe how (s)he reaches this decision. Your character then decides to go home early from the trip to try to escape from the strange person and the bad things that will happen. Describe his/her escape.

Chapter Eleven: The strange person spies your character just as (s)he is about to leave. The strange person chases your character all over the city. Describe the chase.

Chapter Twelve: Your character gets away from the strange person just in time and arrives home safely. Tell about your character's feelings. What did (s)he learn from the problem with the strange person? What did (s)he learn about him/herself? What is your character thinking and feeling as we leave him/her?

To initiate the writing of this individually composed episodic novel, it is helpful to introduce the outline for one episode at a time and then to brainstorm a myriad of ideas with the whole class. This time, instead of trying to develop a group composite novel, the teacher is trying to elicit as many ideas as possible, so that children can be inspired to select an idea to work up by themselves. For example, in the first episode the characters brainstormed as a class may range from a telepathic Martian to a foxy lady living out on the prairie with eight children. Most importantly, it is crucial to underscore the fact that there are no right or wrong characters here; just a great many ideas to share, each of which could be the start of an interesting novel.

After the class brainstorming session, each child selects a character that has been mentioned, or one that they have thought of but hadn't shared, and then they flesh out the chapter outline with class ideas as well as their own. Children can then be paired up with an editing partner to read each other's chapter, do some initial editing, and make some POSITIVE responses, as well as requests for more information ("can you tell me more about what happened when the angel broke her leg?").

Novel writing sessions are usually about a week apart, with revisions and teacher conferences in between. By the second session, children are enjoying getting a chance to tell even more about their character. Now, because each child has his/her individual character in mind, the class brainstorming becomes less and less important and serves more as a general prompt to writing. When children are following the outline just discussed, they very often like to offer anecdotes that were shared by their family about *their* infancy and sometimes they are incorporated into the second chapter of their novel (novels *are* often thinly-veiled autobiographies, we are told!).

By the third session, most children are usually feeling very close to their characters and are looking forward to expanding them. The teacher's job at this point is to go around to individual children who are temporarily "blocked" and affirm ideas that they come up with, urging them to relax, close their eyes, and trust their own "mind pictures."

By the fourth session, the characters in most novels have usually evolved to the point where they have lives of their own. Therefore, as the teacher introduces the chapter outline, she can encourage children to feel free to deviate from the outline if they feel their own characters are quite naturally heading in other directions. As more and more episodes are written, the outline becomes less and less important, and the bulk of ideas that have already been established becomes the positive impetus that makes children excited about working on their novels.

When the last chapter has been completed through the joint efforts of the child, the teacher, and the editorial partner (with twelve chapters, this usually takes about three months), children are actually eager to do the illustrating and laborious final editing. A title is chosen with great care, to catch the reader's attention and also to capture what the novel is mainly about. Finished novels are worthy of professional plastic ring binding, which can often be done by the media center or a PTA looking for worthwhile projects. As the final products are completed, the teacher reads them to the class during read aloud time, instead of the usual fare of children's literature, yet with the same attention to author, illustrator and preliminary predictions as to what the children think the story will be about and what they think the main character might do next. After such an extreme effort, each author's moment in the read-aloud spotlight is enough to bolster his feelings about himself as a budding author of novels, perhaps forever.

Summary

Although children enjoy reading and listening to longer stories as they reach the intermediate grades, there are often few opportunities for them to experience writing anything as lengthy and involved as a novel. By having children first become familiar with the elements in a longer story, or a novel, the teacher can help them to break down the project into smaller components that may seem less threatening and more possible for them. Brainstorming some rudimentary ideas for each story part and then assigning each part to a group is an ideal way to launch the idea of novel writing, as children quickly get to see the finished whole group project and are very proud of what they have contributed to. They are then ready, with the help of an action-promising episodic novel outline, to write their own individual novels. The teacher introduces one chapter idea for each weekly session and after some class brainstorming, allows children to proceed on their own. As the sessions go along and the characters evolve, children begin to feel very close to their creations and look forward to adding new dimensions to their characters' lives. Often, the teacher's outline becomes obsolete as the spunky characters take off on their own journeys from each child's vivid imagination.

As the novels are completed, they are read by the teacher with gusto, just as she would read any children's novel during read aloud time. In the child's perspective, it has been a long, long time from the start of the novel to its finish, but suddenly it is all worthwhile and she is already thinking about the next one.

Chapter Five

Other Motivators:
When They Don't Know What to Write

The mere presence of a blank sheet of paper causes Dana to begin writing furiously, penning her elaborate fantasies or scary whodunits with elan. On the other hand, Yolanda, in the same classroom, stubbornly resists writing and constantly complains to her teacher, "But I don't know what to write!" The harried teacher, tired of the plaintive little phrase, rationalizes that she, the teacher, could not be to blame if the Yolandas in her class do not write eagerly, for the prolific Danas are there to attest to the teacher's expertise as writing motivator--or so she would like to believe. Most affective teachers, however, are not satisfied until EVERY child is feeling joyful success at communicating his or her thoughts and ideas in written form.

Yet the sad lament, "I don't know what to write!" is too familiar in most classrooms, with some children. The goal, therefore, is always to spark that zest for writing not just in some, but in ALL children. Achieving this goal consists, in part, of piquing the imagination of children by providing exciting writing activities that they feel confident they can do because they have first participated in a group brainstorming effort. More importantly, achieving this goal also centers around providing a fertile classroom atmosphere that is most conducive to fostering creativity. By the term "creativity" what is meant here is not the usually proffered pedagogical definition: "a piece of writing that is original, clever," or simply "cute"; creativity is defined by this author in a broader sense, and includes a whole compendium of ways that children might freely express themselves, by way of a socially sensitive observation, a well-constructed practical joke, or a reflective question, for example, as well as the more traditional means of demonstrating creativity via the production of an aesthetically pleasing work of art. Just how broadly creativity is defined by the affective teacher is crucial, because far too often creative ideas are unnoticed, or worse yet, actively squelched because well-meaning teachers are adhering to an unnecessarily rigid definition of the term; for the good news is that research suggests that creativity is not necessarily inherited, but can actually be developed in the right kind of environment. If this is so, affective teachers must be committed to the notion that ALL children can be encouraged to express ideas, words, and concepts that are the personal products of their own unique experiences and fertile imaginations; every child CAN have the emotional luxury of a creative outlet.

The remainder of this chapter will include some important axioms for nurturing creativity in the classroom, and will also provide some teacher-tested ways to actively inspire creative expression for even the most reluctant of would-be writers.

Fostering Creativity in the Classroom

A researcher interested in exploring the nature of creativity once did an experiment involving a "test" of creativity. He showed several children a rock and gave them these instructions: "I want you to think of as many things as you can that could be done with this rock." To a similar group of six children he gave these slightly different instructions: "I want you to think of as many clever and unusual things as you can to do with this rock. Only think of very 'good' ideas." The results of this researcher's study, as you may have guessed, showed that the children who were not restricted and made intellectually self-conscious by having to continually monitor the quality of their ideas, the first group, came up with significantly more things to do with the rock than the other group. And, ironically, their ideas were more imaginative and original--or "creative." The study makes an important observation about what is most needed to foster creativity in the classroom: There must be a lack of self-consciousness, and children must feel free to create, without anxiety about how others might perceive their product. Following are suggestions for providing the kind of classroom environment that is most conducive to nurturing creativity in the classroom.

* *Value what is unique about each child.* Although the large number of children in most elementary classrooms makes a certain amount of group conformity necessary, the affective teacher will always make it his business to find out what is truly special about each child. He will make it clear that he values a child's personal statement, whether

it is expressed through an unusual hairstyle, an interesting manner of speech, or a unique way of looking at the world.

* *Constantly stress that there is more than one answer to most important questions.* Because the rudimentary components of learning (for example, times tables) are so often on a factual or memorization level, children may unfortunately begin to believe that there is a "correct" answer to everything--even a correct way to write out their own fantasies. Children must feel free to risk exploring alternative solutions to problems and feel comfortable considering other different ways of looking at the world. An affective teacher can foster this approach by frequently asking, "Does anyone else have a *different* idea about that?" or "Is there another way we could think about this?" while affirming a variety of thoughtful responses.

* *Ask many questions requiring critical thinking and provide adequate "think time."* An atmosphere where creativity is nurtured is also one in which children are continually stretched beyond simple "yes" and "no" answers to questions. They are provoked to think about the teacher's questions, as well as those of their classmates. The affective teacher must be comfortable with moments of silence that give each child the opportunity to carefully reflect upon why they feel the way they do.

* *Model creativity for your students in whatever way you can.* Most teachers that I have observed possess some sort of creative talents (especially if one allows a broad definition of the term), but teachers can be unduly modest. *All* creative aptitudes should be proudly displayed in the classroom! If, on the other hand, one is truly *not* creative, an avid appreciation for creativity when it is manifested in colleagues, world and national figures, as well as the students, will compensate.

* *Never assign grades to creative work.* Assigning letter or numerical grades to any piece of personal authorship, especially if the grade is less than satisfactory, is one of the surest ways to thwart all future creative attempts of reluctant writers. Besides the obvious argument that art is "subjective" and cannot be absolutely evaluated, there is the deeper concern that a low grade on a child's proud work may be profoundly harmful to that child's concept of himself as creator. Thoughtful comments that address the ideas that the author is trying to express are preferable, and the teacher's words are graciously received by the children.

* When sharing written work, never single out some as "the best" and (heaven forbid) "the worst." Again, yours is a single subjective evaluation, and children must be allowed to create in the manner that their own heart, soul, and imagination dictates. It is far better to point out some strengths in *all* pieces of writing that are read aloud and to help children learn to critically evaluate their own writing.

* *Incorporate creativity into the TOTAL program.* Creativity is sadly diminished as an entity when it is encouraged and expected only at certain specified times, such as in "creative writing time," or during art, music, and language arts. An affective teacher must believe in, and model, creative approaches to math, science and everything else in the curriculum--even a layup shot in basketball could have its creative aspect. To really free children, creativity must be encouraged and integrated into *every* phase of the school day.

**Tried and True Activities to
Inspire Creative Writing**

Even the most reluctant writers can be motivated to write if they are given a bit of a boost initially, either through a fixed writing formula, a provocative idea, or an outright "gimmick." The following ideas contain one or more of these elements, and have been used often with young writers who just have a difficult time getting started. Many practicing teachers I have worked with have proclaimed these motivators to be "just what the doctor ordered" to get the pencils burning.

* *Dear Abby.* Carefully select from an advice column some letters that pose problems that would be of interest to your class. Read several of them to the children and have them brainstorm some possible solutions to the problems that have been posed by the writers. Here is an example of the kind of letters that children cannot resist responding to:

> Dear Abby,
>   The question I want to ask is so indelicate I am having trouble putting it down on paper. Please tell me how to let a very nice gentleman know it is improper to blow one's nose at the table in a linen napkin. I don't mean wipe, Abby; I mean *honk.*
>   --Nameless

After children have orally brainstormed some possible solutions to the dilemma of "Nameless," read Abby's answer:

> Dear Nameless,
>   The next time the 'gentleman' honks, ask him if he has a handkerchief. Then explain what it is for.

The chances are excellent that your students will have come up with a solution just as good, if not better than, Abby's.

Next, read two or three other letters of concern and let children select one for which they will write individual responses.

Finally, have children divide up into partners. Encourage each child to write a letter describing a problem, real or fictitious, which solicits a solution. Then let partners exchange letters and try to solve the problem of their partners, "Dear Abby" style (for grades 4-6).

* *Animal Crackers.* Place an animal cracker on the desk of each child with instructions to look at and think about the animal, but don't eat it. Make a list on the blackboard or overhead of all the animals that are represented in the room and ask for words that describe each animal, and facts the children know about each one. Then, returning attention to the animal crackers on each desk, discuss the following questions:

> Are these animals alive?
> How do you think the animal felt about being in the box?
> How does it feel to be out of the box?
> What might your animal say right now if it could talk?
> Does your animal miss its friends from the box?
> What does your animal eat?
> Does your animal know it will soon be eaten? How does it feel about that?

Finally, have the children write a story about their animal using the discussion questions, facts, and descriptive words on the board to help them. When they are finished, allow them to eat their cracker, although some may choose to keep it as a "pet"! (Grades 1-3.)

* *Story Plots.* Introduce this activity as a "Mystery Story Telling" project. Have the children select three

numbers, each ranging between one and twelve (for example, 4, 3, and 11). The numbers will serve to identify pre-determined parts of the story, as listed below:

Character	Event	Result
1.lonesome witch	1.became invisible	1.was put in jail
2.rich hobo	2.learned to speak Chinese	2.left the country
3.mysterious taxi driver	3.discovered a new planet	3.got rich
4.toothless tiger	4.hated the sun	4.received an award
5.evil cowboy	5.got stuck in an elevator	5.got picture in paper
6.forgetful astronaut	6.got the hiccups	6.caused an earthquake
7.bashful girl	7.fell in a deep hole	7.lost all his money
8.talking monkey	8.lost his/her memory	8.joined the circus
9.overweight frog	9.caught a shark	9.got married
10.mad scientist	10.couldn't stop laughing	10.built a tepee
11.skinny football player	11.got lost in space	11.learned to read minds
12.canine detective	12.shrank to the size of an insect	12.learned to love everyone

After the three numbers have been selected-- different combinations for each child--present each child with the story plots above, or replace characters, events, or results with those of your own choosing. Have each child find her predetermined parts of the story using the numbers selected. Review the different parts of a story and stress the need for elaboration and lots of colorful description to make the story as interesting as possible. (This can be accomplished by choosing a story plot orally with children or reading a model that you or other children have written.) Finally, have children write their stories using the predetermined plot, adding plenty of details as well as an original story ending (grades 3-6).

    * *Imagine What Happens!* Select a picture story book that has much predictable dramatic intensity, such as *The King, the Cheese, and the Mice* or *The Gingerbread Rabbit*. Read the story aloud and stop at an exciting turning point in the story. Ask children to predict what might happen next using a "predictive web" on the blackboard or overhead, like so:

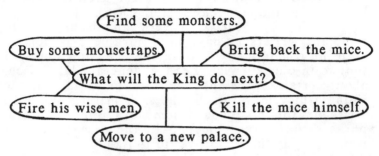

    Then let children select one of the ideas brainstormed by the class, or another of their own, and write their version of the ending of the story. Allow children to then volunteer to read their original endings. Next read the real author's ending to the story to confirm or reject the children's hypotheses about what would happen. Emphasize that there is more than one way to end a story; the chances are that they have come up with some endings that are more interesting than the original author's! (Grades 3-6.)

    * *Balloon Sensitivity.* Very beginning writers are often inspired most by concrete things that they can see, hear, and touch in the world around them. Help each child to blow up and tie a balloon. Next, divide children into groups of five. Give them a few moments to experiment with the balloon and their five senses: how does their balloon look, sound, smell, feel, and taste? Then give each child a sheet upon which is written one of the five sentence stems:

My balloon looks _____.

My balloon sounds _____.

My balloon smells _____.

My balloon feels _____.

My balloon tastes _____.

Explain that each child in a group will be responsible for *one* sensory statement about their balloon, e.g., "My balloon sounds squeaky" and will write their word on their page. The teacher should stand at the blackboard ready to write down words that need to be spelled. With individually-contributed balloon illustrations, each group now has five pages for a class book about balloons and the five senses (grades K-2).

   * *How-To Stories.* A very humorous way to get reluctant writers to have an enjoyable experience with expository material is through the "how-to" story--with a tongue-in-cheek twist. Lead a general class discussion about certain skills that we need to be taught, such as riding a bicycle, tying our shoes, or making our beds, etc. Write on the blackboard some examples of "how to" phrases that have come up in the discussion. Explain which part is the infinitive (to tie) and which part is the direct object (our shoes). Next ask children to select their favorite "how to" phrase, write it on a small piece of paper, and then carefully tear it off between the infinitive and the direct object. Example:

How to milk   a cow

Then the teacher collects the direct objects and redistributes them to the children so that each child ends up with a rather comical combination phrase, e.g., "How to milk our shoes," that will no doubt inspire him to write a short, expository paragraph explaining in detail how to do this absurd task. Finally, make a class booklet, illustrated, to proudly share the products (grades 4-6).

   * *Story Starters.* Standard classroom fare for the reluctant writer is the "story starter" and many affective teachers regard this device as invaluable for getting children to begin writing. The most effective story starters are those that provide an exciting first sentence, a provocative accompanying illustration, and a list of four or five words that might be found in the story. Typed or neatly printed on 5"x8" cards, these "ignition keys" can be simply illustrated by the teacher or a student volunteer, or appropriate pictures can be cut from magazines and pasted

onto the cards. Then the cards can be laminated, for durability, and placed in the classroom writing center to be used whenever a child needs some inspiration to start a story. Here are two examples of typical story starters (grades 2-6):

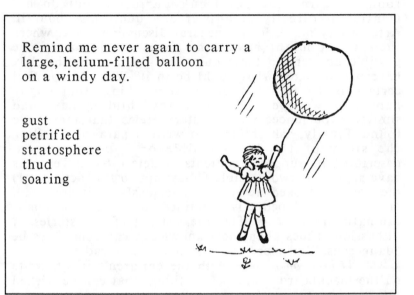

Remind me never again to carry a large, helium-filled balloon on a windy day.

gust
petrified
stratosphere
thud
soaring

It was the smallest, most adorable pony you have ever seen, and he had been hiding under my bed.

miniature
whinny
frightened
secret
shrunk

* *Mystery Boxes.* Bring in a large box upon which is painted in large block letters one or more of the following phrases: "Pandora's Box," "Spare Space Parts," "Captain Bluebeard's Treasure Chest," or "Danger! Do Not Open!" Allow the box to sit conspicuously in the room arousing the children's curiosity, but do not mention it directly or answer any questions about it. After a day or so, lead a general discussion about where such a box might have come from. Brainstorm some possible answers to these questions: Who might this box have belonged to? What might be in it? What do you feel certain is *not* in it? What are some things that might happen if we open it? Ask if any children have had similar experiences with mystery items that they have found. Finally, ask children to write a paragraph telling the story of the box--possible or impossible--and describing its supposed contents in detail. Note: Teachers have suggested two possible follow-ups to this activity: 1) the box is whisked away as mysteriously as it appeared; or 2) an encyclopedia is contained in the box, which is dramatically opened after the sharing of the stories. A discussion ensues about how knowledge can sometimes be "dangerous," but more often a "treasure" (grades 2-6).

* *Wishing on a Star.* With the children's input, write on the blackboard a number of things that can be wished upon, such as a wish bone, an eyelash, a penny thrown into a well, etc. Ask if anyone knows the poem about wishing on a star. Recite it together:

> Star light, star bright,
> First star I see tonight,
> Wish I may, wish I might
> Have the wish I wish tonight.

Encourage children to share some of the various things they have wished for. Then hand out lined ditto paper in the shape of a star and ask children to write about a time they remember when they wished upon a star (or an eyelash, or wish bone, etc.) and describe what happened after that. Did the wish come true? Did it cause the child to be happier or unhappier? Explain that their wish stories can be real or imaginary. Make a wishing bulletin board for those who want to share their products (grades 2-4).

* *What If . . . Stories.* Hypothetical situations are the kind of rich stimuli that turn the fantasizing of children into colorful stories. Every so often pose one of the following questions, or similar ones, to the class:

> What would happen if you could have three wishes?
> What if we could talk to animals?
> What if you could read peoples' minds?
> What if you could be invisible?
> What if you could fly?
> What if everyone looked exactly alike?
> What if nobody ever got old?
> What if you got younger, not older?
> What if there is life on other planets?
> What if you could always have everything you
>   wanted?

When one of these "what if . . ." situations has been introduced, let each child take a few moments to think about how life would change for her. Then, with the use of the blackboard, have children contribute a list of possible advantages and disadvantages to the hypothetical situation actually occurring. Finally, ask each child to write down her version of what life would be like if this change actually were to happen (grades 2-6).

Summary

Most affective teachers have a burning desire to open the flood gates of each and every one of their students so that each can experience the joy of self-expression through a satisfying creative outlet. When some children remain disinterested in writing and are continually moaning, "But I don't know what to write!" this can be a source of frustration to the conscientious teacher who wants to inspire *every* child to write. This chapter has offered teachers three different kinds of suggestions for dealing with the omnipresent reluctant writer: the first suggestion is for teachers to broaden their definition of what can be regarded as "creative" so that they might encourage the unique imaginative qualities that exist in every child. A more inclusive perspective of creativity will free children to experiment and take risks with language without fearing negative or restrictive evaluations.

The second set of suggestions deals with ways to create a classroom atmosphere most conducive to creative expression, where the gamut of ideas that children just naturally come up with can flourish and be recognized.

The final set of suggestions are specific writing activities that have been used successfully by practicing teachers to pique the imaginations of their reluctant writers. In an ideal affective language arts classroom these and other writing motivators are skillfully combined with an atmosphere that frees children to believe that they really can write because they have something exciting to say. That sad lament, "But I don't know what to write!" is gradually replaced with, "I can't write fast enough!" and it is indeed music to the affective teacher's ears.

References

Applegate, Mauree. *Freeing Children to Write.* New York: Harper & Row, 1963.

Burton, William H., and Helen Hefferman. *The Step Beyond Creativity.* Washington, DC: National Education Association of the United States, 1964.

Gurney, Nancy and Eric. *The King, the Mice and the Cheese.* New York: Random House, 1965.

Jarrell, Randall. *The Gingerbread Rabbit.* New York: Macmillan, 1964.

Chapter Six

Build-Me-Ups: Enhancing the
Self-Concept through the Language Arts

Jennifer is off to her first day at school. Will she be successful at learning how to read and write? Will she "pass" first grade? How can we predict?

More than likely, Jennifer has already been given an entire battery of tests to determine her state of readiness to begin reading and writing. She has been given intelligence tests, the verbal sections of which seem to be tied to later achievement in reading. She has also been given standardized reading readiness tests to see if her ability to make auditory and visual discriminations of letters and words is fine-tuned enough so that she will be as ready as others her age to learn to decode words. Additionally, Jennifer's teachers may have filled out check lists that help to show a profile of the child's mental alertness, her verbal prowess, and her ability to concentrate--all factors that help to signal that a child is ready to learn to read.

One crucial readiness area, however, is not routinely tested. It is an area that we know to be highly correlated with success in reading and writing; in fact, certain researchers go so far as to assert that it is THE most important predictor of success in reading: it is the "self-concept" of children like Jennifer and her classmates. We have indeed been aware since the early 1920s that a strong interactive effect exists between the self-concept and reading and writing success, yet we have failed to place a self-concept building program in most elementary curricula in any kind of thoughtful way, nor have we used it as a screening device for beginning reading instruction.

I remember countless curriculum planning meetings with classroom teachers and administrators to decide upon the educational goals for the coming academic year. Invariably, the enhancement of the self-concept of the children in the school would be mentioned as a global priority, and all the educators would solemnly avow that they were committed to the idea of improving the self-image of their charges. Yet these commitments always seemed to remain as lofty objectives, but were rarely translated into any real systematic classroom practice. What gives?

The reason for this apparent lack of carry-through may well be that there is no precise way to accurately measure the self-concept of children in numbers that will clearly go up, as achievement tests do, when we have made appropriate curriculum interventions. Particularly in our current climate of accountability for all that we do, pre-tests and post-tests are utilized to make most of the judgments about what is and what is not successful, with fractions of percentage points often dictating what will stay and what will be shelved in an academic program.

Although the self-concept cannot hope to be measured in such precise quantitative terms, the affective teacher, as a professional, should be the judge of whether the self-concept of each of her pupils is increasing or decreasing. She knows, because she is keenly tuned in to her pupils' feelings, but she may lack necessary statistics. She CAN show "numbers" in terms of the books that have been read, the number of pages written, the number of thoughts and ideas willingly shared, or the number of social overtures made by a once withdrawn child, but unfortunately, these are not the "magic figures" that carry clout in terms of accountability, even though they are desperately important.

An affective teacher need not lose heart, however. It is quite possible to add activities into the language arts program that have as their objectives the enhancement of the self-concept of children while giving them the kind of practice in reading, writing, listening, and speaking that will just naturally increase achievement scores in these areas. But like the other components in an affective language arts program, they will also help to create in children more positive attitudes toward themselves as readers, authors, and thinkers, as well as unique human beings.

Enhancing the Self-Concept through Bibliotherapy

An ideal way to develop the self-concept of children in an Affective Language Arts program is by showing them how to use literature to help them cope with their problems and identify with fictional characters who may have concerns similar to theirs. This process, called bibliotherapy, allows teachers to show children how certain books just naturally portray some of the conflicts that children may be facing in their lives. There are stories that can sensitize children to the plights of others who may be experiencing death, or divorce in their families, a physical or mental handicap, or perhaps just the "ordinary" pain that can come from the tribulations of being a child growing up in a most confusing world.

Bibliotherapy works when a bond begins to develop between the reader (or listener) and the main character in a story. A child typically goes through three stages toward greater self-understanding as a result of this bond: 1) identification, where the child feels close to the character because he begins to see that he is not the only one to have experienced this problem; 2) catharsis, when the child shares the characters' feelings as he works out the conflict in the story, and 3) insight, as the child's attitudes toward the problem are modified and the child feels a bit more confident about dealing with his problem (Corman, 1975).

To use bibliotherapy in an Affective Language Arts program, the teacher may on some occasions decide that the whole class needs to become more sensitive to a certain issue, such as racism. She would then select a book that deals with this theme, read it aloud to the class, and then discuss it with the class. In other cases, an individual child may be in much anguish when her mother remarries. In this instance, the teacher may suggest that that child read a book which deals sensitively with the problems that a stepchild may face. Later the teacher could ask the child how she felt about the main character and how she dealt with her problem. To assist a teacher in quickly identifying books that have the necessary themes at the appropriate age levels, *The Bookfinder* (Dreyer, 1977) is an invaluable resource. It contains over 1,100 children's books categorized into such topics as aggression, disabilities, death, divorce, moving and loneliness, and can help the teacher match a child who has a particular problem with a book that just might help him through it a little bit easier.

The remainder of this chapter contains a panoply of other language arts activities designed to foster more positive self-concepts in children.

Activities to Create a
Positive Classroom Climate

Welcoming Postcards. When the affective teacher first receives his class roster, a postcard can be sent to each of the new students explaining how very happy the teacher is to have this student in his class and describing a few highlights that the children can look forward to in the coming year.

Individual Chalkboards. When children are doing spelling, it is helpful for them to be able to write on individual chalkboards that can be made inexpensively out of cut pressed wood, masonite board, or similar substances and then painted over with chalkboard paint. Then, after spelling words have been dictated, the board can be held up for the teacher to correct. She can give each child a response without any of the other children seeing, so no child has to feel embarrassed in front of his peers.

Mail Service. A mailbox is a "must" in an affective classroom so that students can communicate in written form to each other and to the teacher. The teacher can utilize the service to reiterate that something in class was done particularly well or that the student has been especially kind to a troubled classmate, or any number of other messages that can make individual students feel better about themselves. The teacher can keep a roster of students' names to check off to make sure he is not overlooking any child.

Personalized Spelling. Using each child's name in spelling lists and spelling dictation is a wonderful way to combine enhancement of the self-concept with a basic spelling lesson. Students will learn how to spell each other's names and also discover new things about each other when the teacher dictates a sentence like, "Ramon likes to collect stamps of different countries."

Torture the Teacher. A great way to encourage students to gain positive academic self-images is to teach them some things that others (particularly adults!) do not know. This is especially true when working with children labeled "slow" or placed in special classes. In teaching spelling to such children, the teacher can include a few very difficult words, such as "proselytize" or "scrupulous," that even the so-called "smart" students don't know. Also, when starting a new unit in a content-area subject, the teacher can invite students to look through the text and find words that they think are unusually difficult to try to "stump" the teacher. If the teacher cannot correctly define the word or concept (and it is most helpful for affective teachers to admit that they do *not* know everything!), then the children "win."

Spread Rumors. Children feel very good about themselves when something they have done--a kind word or deed--has been recognized and affirmed. Teachers should make a point of describing such activities to the class without directly mentioning the student's name, but in a thinly-veiled manner. When a teacher says, "I noticed someone being especially courteous to Josh during recess," the entire class feels good.

Person of the Week. A bulletin board labeled "Very Important Person of the Week--(VIP)" can allow each child in your class to be highlighted and feel very special when he or she is featured. Baby pictures, toys that have been kept, plus a simple autobiography done by the parents with the child's help can be a self-concept enhancing focus of a classroom. The child can be encouraged during his week to tell the class about the baby pictures and read his autobiography or to tell a funny story about what he was told he did as a baby.

**Activities to Create
Confident Speakers and Writers**

I Am. To highlight what makes individual children unique, children can draw a picture of themselves including any physical (or other) characteristic that makes them different from others. Then ask them to finish the sentence, "I am . . ." at least five times at the bottom of the drawing. Encourage them to elaborate on all the things that they feel contribute to making them unique. Provide some time when children can share their pictures and tell others a bit about themselves. Arrange the pictures around the room for several weeks to give all children a chance to look them over before they are taken down and put away for safekeeping to be used later in the year. This activity should be repeated toward the end of the year. If the class has spent much time in the interval in an Affective Language Arts program, obvious differences will be noted in the students' responses.

Be Your Thingo. A wonderful exercise that helps students explore the unique qualities of themselves and others in this class is "Be Your Thingo." Each child is given a dittoed grid portioned off like a bingo card. Then a master card with instructions is put on the blackboard or overhead so that students know what to write in each space. Next, students are asked to write in the appropriate words and phrases to describe their characteristics. Then the students write each of these characteristics on a small square of paper so that it can be put in the "pot." Beans are used as markers and the game then proceeds like bingo. Example:

- THINGO -

Colors	Name	Place	Family Members	Likes
your hair (brown)	yours (Ben)	born (Indiana)	me (brother)	1st choice (camping)
your eyes (brown)	mother (Heather)	would like to go (Australia)	mother	2nd choice (reading)
your house (red)	a friend (Ray)	wouldn't like to go (South Africa)	father	3rd choice (football)
favorite (light blue)	favorite (Matt)	have visited (Canada)	brother or sister (Rian)	4th choice (baseball)
least favorite (light grey)	book character (Sherlock)	have read about (Israel)	pet (fish)	doesn't like (jumprope)

I'm For Sale! After a unit on newspapers or advertising techniques, a good way to incorporate enhancement of the self-concept is by asking students to write original advertisements trying to "sell" themselves. First, the students must think about their best qualities as well as several things that they are able to do well. Then these positive items are integrated into the ad along with some salient "likes" and "dislikes." For example, "For Sale: A tennis-playing eleven-year-old girl with freckles, pig-tails (sometimes) and a sunny disposition. Very friendly and likes to talk to everyone. Likes her room very neat, but doesn't like spinach. Is able to sew and knit wonderful things, but is also in Little League. Reasonable."

Picture Perfect. To encourage each child in the class to begin to focus on the positive, rather than the negative qualities of each other, take photographs of each child and hang them up around the room. Discuss with the class that every person has good qualities and the class will be exploring these for each member of the class. Any time they wish to, they may write something "true" and "good" about a person in the class under his or her picture. The teacher, too, should feel free to add comments and encourage the children to read and discuss the comments written on the sheets of other classmates. At the end of the week, have a discussion about how people's attitudes change toward each other when they are concentrating on and looking for only the good.

Person Match. To help children develop relationships based upon respect and understanding, and to bring out the "shy" child, have students complete these sentence starters on a 3"x5" card, such as:

My favorite song is ("Don't Worry, Be Happy").

The place I go to be alone is (Science hill).

The person I most admire is (Bishop Tutu).

If I could have one wish, I'd wish for (an end to all wars).

The best book I ever read was ("Jumanji").

Instruct students *not* to put their names on their papers, and distribute them, making sure no child gets his or her own. After all students have read the answers, children try to find the person who wrote the paper by asking questions based upon the information given in the paper, e.g., "Is Mother Teresa the person you admire most?" Even if the answer is "no," the person must share who the person he admires most is. Students sit down and chat with their person when they have found him.

Lifelines. In order to fully appreciate why they are the way they are, children must learn to reflect on the important events of their lives. A good precursor to an autobiography is to ask students to list the five most important things that have happened in their lives and to write down how old they were when these events occurred. Then help them to make a scroll using parchment paper attached to two popsicle sticks. Help them to place their events in the order in which they took place (most children begin with their birth). Let them make a brief presentation to the class about their choices. They then have an outline to fill in for their autobiographies.

**Activities to Create Children
Confident in Oral Language**

Who Are You? To help children to identify what is unique and special about themselves, a series of forced-choice questions can be asked that allow them to creatively reflect upon their personal qualities. Children are asked, "Are you more like . . .
    . . . a rose or a dandelion? Why?
    . . . the sun or the moon? Why?
    . . . cotton or wool? Why?
    . . . a cat or a dog? Why?
    . . . red or blue? Why?
    . . . "head in the clouds" or "feet on the ground"?
        Why?
    . . . breakfast or lunch? Why?
    . . . the mountains or the ocean? Why?
    . . . fall or spring? Why?
    . . . a baby or an elderly person? Why?
After children have written down their responses, ask for volunteers to tell orally why they chose the answers they did. Emphasize that there are many different ways to be, which is why the world is such an interesting place!

Happy Circle. A routine that goes a long way toward encouraging children to look at the positive things in themselves and others and helps them to feel comfortable sharing in front of a group is the happy circle. For a few minutes every day, children sit in a circle and everyone gets to add one thought to a common theme, such as saying one positive thing about a selected student, e.g., "I like the way Wendy smiles," or "Wendy is always there with a joke; she makes me happy when I feel bad." Or the circle might begin with everyone relating one positive thing that has happened that day, or "one thing that made me happy today." Done on a daily basis, this technique goes a long way toward building healthy self-images and improved interpersonal relationships, as well as confident speakers.

Slogan Statements. What people say through their T-shirts and on their bumper stickers can tell us something about their beliefs. Over a two or three day period children can keep a list of the slogans that they notice on people's T-shirts and bumper stickers. Collect the lists. Have children play a combination of twenty questions and charades by first having other classmates figure out the slogans by using only questions that can be answered "yes" or "no." Then, if it is unlikely the slogan has been heard before, charades can be used to get the specific words. As slogans are guessed, write them on the blackboard. Afterwards, have a discussion about why people might advertise their beliefs in this manner and what can be learned about them from the slogans they display.

The Secret Me. For several days, have children collect things from home and at school to go on a collage--things they like to do, places they have been, people they admire, possessions, opinions, etc. Display anonymous collages around the room. Beneath each one put a box. Children can then try to guess who each collage belongs to and why, and put that child's name in the box. Then let each child share his or her collage and the meaning of the items in it. Discuss what surprises cropped up. Then talk about the damage that can be done when opinions based on preconceptions of a person are made before actually getting to know that person.

Good and Bad. This activity shows children how it feels to receive negative *or* preferential treatment based upon superficial characteristics. After allowing two or three students to leave the room, choose a characteristic such as the opposites "short" and "tall." Then go around the room telling tall students they are "bad" and short ones they are "good." The children who left the room then return and try to guess the criterion by which the students were labeled. After several rounds, explore such concepts as value judgments, stereotyping and prejudicial treatment. Solicit input from those who were labeled to see how they felt when others were responding to them negatively. What were their feelings toward those placing arbitrary value judgments upon them? Then contrast the feelings of the "good" and "bad" students. A lot of insights can occur.

Natural Resources. Often children feel powerless when they can indeed do many things, but haven't considered all the things they *can* do. Their self-worth can be enhanced by asking them to make a list of all the things they can do, such as sew, paint, rake leaves, read, dance, tell jokes, do dishes, etc. Then they can be instructed to consider what tools they have at their disposal to accomplish some of the things they can do. These items might be things like a rake, needle and thread, cooking utensils, etc. Then have them draw an outline of themselves and on the picture they can write, "I can do these things; I can use these tools." Have them cut out their outlines and paste them on a piece of construction paper and decorate it to look like themselves. Hang these from the ceiling over each child's desk. For several days emphasize the idea that "we have a roomful of marvelous human resources and potential" and let them discuss their abilities.

Acrostic Poems. Children feel good about themselves when their special qualities are recognized by others. The acrostic poem lets them concentrate on each other's positive qualities. After dividing children into pairs, let each write a simple, unrhymed poem about the other child using the letters in the other child's name to start each phrase. All phrases must reflect some "good" and "true" qualities in the other child. Example:

Never a frown,
Always smiling,
Not a care in the world,
Can you be her friend?
You will want to be!

Let the writer of the poem read it while the recipient of such positive comments beams!

Who Are You? Interviewing skills can be enhanced while children learn to better appreciate one another through this activity: After pairing off students (the more unlikely the pair, the better!), tell them they are going to make a book about the person with whom they are paired. Each week allow the pairs to meet for twenty minutes to discuss past events ("When did you learn to walk and talk?") or recent events in the lives of their partners ("What did you do over summer vacation?"). Then let the children write about what was discussed in the current session, illustrating the piece if desired. At the end of the school year, each child will have a biography presented to him or her that can be shared with the class and read again and again.

Summary

Although educators have known for years that the self-concept is strongly related to successful achievement in all facets of language skills, most schools have not placed the enhancement of the self-concept into their curriculum in any systematic way. This may be because teachers and administrators are keenly aware of the need for achievement scores that reflect growth in academic areas, and the improvement of the self-concept is not easily put into numbers, even though the majority of practitioners include it among their primary goals for their students. Fortunately, there are ways to enhance the self-concept of children through activities that also give much-needed practice in the language arts of reading, writing, speaking, and listening.

Bibliotherapy is a technique that can be used in an Affective Language Arts program to aid children in their ability to come to terms with their problems and to feel more capable of their ability to handle them. The affective teacher can help match a child to a main character with a similar concern through the use of *The Bookfinder* which contains over 1,100 titles categorized by subject area and age level.

To enhance the self-concept of her children, the affective teacher need not sacrifice sound teaching that will help her students to achieve in the language arts. Fortunately, there are many classroom activities that skillfully combine the language arts of reading, writing, speaking, and listening with the enhancement of the self-concept by having children discover new things about each other and teaching them to look for the positive qualities in each other as well as themselves. Many such activities have been described in this chapter.

References

Beane, J. and R. Lipka. *Self-Concept, Self-Esteem and the Curriculum.* Boston: Allyn and Bacon, 1984.

Corman, C. "Bibliotherapy--Insight for the Learning Handicapped." *Language Arts* 52 (1975): 935-37.

Dreyer, Sharon Spredemann. *The Bookfinder.* Circle Pines, MN: American Guidance Service, 1985.

Edwards, P.A. and Simpson, L. "Bibliotherapy: A Strategy for Communication Between Parents and their Children." *Journal of Reading* 30, no. 2 (1986): 819-21.

Gibson, Janice T. *Psychology for the Classroom.* Englewood Cliffs, NJ: Prentice-Hall, 1976.

Hummel, Jeffrey and Nancy Lee Cecil. "Self-Concept and Academic Achievement." *Journal of Humanistic Education and Development.*

Purkey, W. *Self-Concept and School Achievement.* Englewood Cliffs, NJ: Prentice-Hall, 1970.

Samuels, Shirley. *Enhancing Self-Concept in Early Childhood.* 1977.

Chapter Seven

The Newspaper: Conduit to our Reading Culture

While visiting small fishing villages along the Eastern seaboard of Canada, I have been continually fascinated by the ease with which children living in these tiny villages become active members of their fishing culture. From the time they can first walk and talk they joyfully experience all the facets of fishing, from making the fishing nets to the intricacies of baiting and casting a line. To such children these activities are as natural as breathing. Because their parents and everyone they know participate in some aspect of fishing, the children, too, grow up learning to fish and enjoy it.

Thus it should be in our culture with reading. The activity is certainly as necessary for survival in our society, yet reading is not an activity that is visibly modeled by all adults in our culture. So unfortunately, the message that reading is a vital activity does not naturally come across to our children as strongly and loudly as we might hope.

One type of reading, however, seems to be more visibly modeled than others by adults in our culture; indeed, it might be considered to be as much a part of the American lifestyle as the morning cup of coffee: the local newspaper, though not often lauded for its literary merit, belongs in an Affective Language Arts program because it is one of THE major reading activities by which we demonstrate that we really are a reading culture. For children to become familiar with this pervasive adult institution is to have them begin to take part in a tradition that they are apt to see many adults modeling on a routine basis.

Another reason for including the newspaper in an Affective Language Arts program is that children get to see another valid reason for reading--to gain information about what is currently happening in the world. Unfortunately, the major thrust in many language arts programs is often so heavily geared toward story or narrative structure--picture story books in the primary grades evolving to short novels in the intermediate grades--

71

that we tend to overlook the fact that for some children (and adults) reading for information will always be the preferred genre. We have for too long subtly implied to children that only those who love reading "books" and "novels" could possibly be considered true lovers of reading! This is as sad as it is untrue.

For these reasons, I have chosen to include a chapter which looks at how the local newspaper can be used in an Affective Language Arts program. This chapter will include activities to familiarize children with the newspaper, and activities that stimulate them to write and think critically, as well as a section on creating a classroom newspaper. Additionally, "just for fun" newspaper activities are included for the purpose of building positive associations with this important conduit to our reading culture.

Introducing Children to the Newspaper

Perhaps the best way to introduce children to the newspaper is to initially discuss some of the vocabulary that is common to this particular medium: editorial, obituary, headline, dateline, advice column, classified, advertisement, horoscope, weather, entertainment, index, and features, are a few of the words and phrases with which they need to become familiar. Besides using these words as the weekly spelling lesson, a scavenger hunt can be employed to make sure that children can find examples of each of these items by looking carefully through the newspaper.

A subsequent scavenger hunt might require children to scout through the newspaper to find these items that can be found daily in every newspaper:

A picture of an animal	A comic strip
A famous sports figure	A fact
A word describing you	A graph or chart
A crime committed	Name of your state
A crossword puzzle	Another word game
An ad for a car	An opinion
A movie you want to see	A TV show you like
A crisis situation	

To show children the scope of services provided by the newspaper, have them participate in a third scavenger hunt that instructs them to look for specific advertisements that might appeal to the following groups:

Men	Mothers
Women	All adults
People looking for recreation	People wanting to save money
People needing a vacation	People looking for a new home
Children	People with pets
People who smoke	People with a hobby
People in search of a job	People who are hungry

To graphically illustrate to children the way headlines are used to grab people's attention with a minimum of words, the teacher can write the headline, "Teacher Caught Stealing" on the blackboard. Solicit many ideas as to what this headline might mean. Then explain that this headline is the lead-in for an article about a local faculty-student softball game in which the music teacher was tagged while attempting to "steal" second base! Let children draw their own conclusions as to why such a deliberately misleading headline might have been created for the article. Then encourage children to try to find other headlines that attract attention in a similar way.

Finally, to help children to begin to understand the succinct nature of newspaper journalism, have them practice choosing articles and then determining just how quickly the facts of "who," "what," "when," "where," "why," and "how" are revealed. After doing some practice articles orally with the whole class, let children pair off, select an article, and then answer these questions which can be typed onto a ditto master:

What is the headline of your article?
Who is the subject(s) of your article?
What is the main idea, or topic, of your article?
When did the event take place?
Where did the event take place?
According to your article, *why* did the event take place?
How is the event happening?

Using the Newspaper to Motivate Writing

After children have become familiar with the newspaper and feel comfortable working with it, the following activities can be used to stimulate writing.

* *Antonyms.* Have children look through advertisements in the paper to find a product that they

dislike. Have them make a list of positive descriptions that have been used and then find words that mean just the opposite of these words. Instruct them to then rewrite the advertisement telling people what the product is *really* like, in their opinion.

* *Questions.* Help children to select a feature article which interests them, such as a piece about a recent lottery winner. Ask them to write a list of ten questions they would like to ask the person if they had the opportunity to interview him or her. Then have them make some predictions about what possible responses might be based upon their hunches about the individual.

* *Imaginary Conversations.* Students will enjoy finding pictures of two people in the news with whom they are especially fascinated. Instruct them to place the two pictures on top of a piece of paper to look as though the two people are having a conversation. Using dialogue format, have children then make up the fictional conversation that might have taken place between the two individuals--in a humorous or serious vein.

* *Lost and Found.* From the classified ads in the newspaper have children select an item that has been either lost or found and then let them write a short piece-- silly or serious--about how that item came to be lost or found, who lost it, where it was lost, and the feelings of the person who lost (or found) it.

* *Recipes.* Encourage children to find a recipe in the newspaper that sounds like a food they might enjoy eating. Point out how the ingredients are usually listed in a recipe, but that often the directions for combining the items are not clearly sequenced for the reader. Ask the children to rewrite the instructions in a paragraph format, using words that clearly signify sequence, such as "first," "next," "then," "finally," etc. Then let them actually prepare their chosen food and write a critique of the results in the same language that the restaurant critic in the newspaper might use.

* *Mock Mugging.* Help a group of students to prepare to stage a "mock mugging" or accident for the rest of the class. Instruct other members of the class to write a newspaper article about the incident as they saw it. Encourage class members to formulate questions for interviews with the "victims" and other persons involved in the mock incident. Discuss variations in the written accounts of the incident and brainstorm some possible reasons for the variations as well as the implications of those variations for the readers of the news.

* *Controversy.* Guide a class discussion about some controversial topic of current interest in the news, such as the efficacy of nuclear power. In two separate columns on the blackboard or overhead, write down children's comments, pro and con, about the issue. Then encourage each child to write an editorial (his or her personal opinion) on the topic.

* *Personal Letters.* Have students find a feature article about someone who has experienced a major good or bad event recently--for example, the loss of a beloved animal, winning the lottery, or some personal triumph over adversity. Review the different reasons one might have for writing a letter to someone--to express sympathy, to extend congratulations, etc. Let children draft a letter to the person they have selected from the newspaper. After revising and editing letters with the help of peer editors and/or a teacher conference, let the children send their letters to their chosen person, in care of the local newspaper.

* *Restaurant Critic.* After discussing the specific style of writing of restaurant critics, allow children to review (tactfully) a lunch served in the school cafeteria, or a bag lunch from home. If the class has its own newspaper, encourage children to let the review become a standard feature of the paper.

* *Smart Consumer.* Have children find a half page or full page advertisement in the newspaper. Tell them to read all the information in the ad and then write down all the factual information that is included about the product, deliberately ignoring any glamorous or "hype" words. Based upon this activity, have them then write a paragraph stating whether or not they would buy the product and why or why not. Encourage them to also include any additional information they might need before they could make a decision.

Activities to Expand Critical Thinking

Newspapers can provide some excellent fodder for critical thinking, and provide a more realistic context and refreshing change from workbooks purporting to teach these skills. With teacher guidance, children can grow in their ability to analyze information through the following activities:

* *Analyzing an Article.* Have the children find an article in the paper that relates to a topic that they have been studying. Then ask them to complete these steps for

analyzing the article: 1) Read the article carefully; 2) Circle the important facts and factual statements; 3) Write a summary of the article; 4) Identify the topic that they have already studied and explain how the article relates to it; 5) List any *new* information that has been gained about the topic.

    * *Facts and Opinions.* From the editorial page, let children choose an editorial. Divide the blackboard or overhead into two sections, labeled "Facts" and "Opinions." On the fact side, solicit from the children all the statements that can be proven. On the opinion side write down all statements that are just one person's opinion. Help children to look for techniques that might lead them to question what the author is saying: Does the author show bias? Are the author's ideas based on faulty assumptions? Does the author use any propaganda techniques (e.g. emotionally laden words or name-calling)?

    * *Article Summaries.* After students have selected an article of their choice, have them read it carefully and respond to the following questions:

    1) What are two conclusions you could draw from your article?

    2) What are some questions you would like to ask the writer of this article?

    3) What are some ways the information in this article could affect *you?*

    4) What groups of people might be pleased by the information in this article?

    5) What groups of people might be upset by the information in this article?

    * *Time Capsule.* Tell students to imagine that they are in charge of preparing a time capsule for children in the year 3000. They would want to reveal to the people of that era as much as they could about life today. Instruct them to cut out the ten items (using pictures or words) from the newspaper that would best describe what their life is like. Allow children to orally defend their selections.

    * *SQ3R.* Newspapers provide excellent practice material for study skills. Have each child choose an article. Then ask each child to go through the following five steps:

    1) Skim your article quickly.

    2) List four questions you have about your article.

    3) Read your article to answer your questions.

    4) Rewrite the article, answering your own questions.

    5) Recite from memory all you have learned from the article.

6) List any questions you still have about the topic.

   * *Political Propaganda.* Instruct children to find examples of candidates' campaign statements. Divide the blackboard or overhead into two columns: specific and general. Solicit responses from children about each statement as to whether it gives very general promises or solutions to problems, or very specific, explicit ideas as to what the candidate will really do.

   * *Community Concerns.* Let children select articles from the local newspaper about city problems such as water shortages, traffic congestion, vandalism, etc., and have them make suggestions as to how each problem might be solved. After brainstorming as a class, encourage children to write letters to appropriate city officials outlining their recommendations for solutions.

Just For Fun

The following motivational activities tend to promote growth in the various subskills of the language arts and are valuable with all grade levels to help build positive associations with the newspaper:

   * *Cartoon Dialogue.* From the comics section, have each child cut out a favorite cartoon. Let each paste his cartoon on construction paper and then use white-out to erase the dialogue in the cartoon bubble. Instruct each child to look at the cartoon and, from the action portrayed by the pictures, write new dialogue in his own words.

   * *How-To.* Ask children to find a "how-to" article from the home section of the newspaper. Show them how to write each step on a separate strip of paper. Mix the steps and allow children to exchange their how-to articles and attempt to put them back into the correct sequence.

   * *Sports Verbs.* Discuss with children several examples of terms used on the sports page to denote that one team has triumphed over the other: "Cubs *blitz* the Red Sox"; "Lakers *jolt* Kings." Keep a running classroom list of all the different verbs that are used to indicate success and failure in the sports headlines.

   * *Match the Headlines.* Cut out articles from the newspaper and paste them on construction paper or tagboard. Separate the headlines from the articles and place several combinations in a bag. Ask children to shake the bag, select an article, skim it, and then see if they can find the appropriate headline for that article.

   * *My S-E-L-F.* Have children cut out the capital letters that make up their first names from the headlines

in the newspaper. Then ask them to look through the rest of the paper for twenty-five words that they feel describe who they are. Help them to paste the words, collage-fashion, on sheets of colored construction paper.

   * *Mars Adventure.* Tell children they are about to go on a pretend adventure to the planet Mars for an extended period of time. Instruct them to look through the newspaper, find, and cut out five items (using only pictures or words) that they feel would best help them survive their ordeal. Advise them that their allotted space would be no larger than their desks. Have them paste their five items on construction paper and then orally defend their choices.

   * *Newsmakers.* Make a bulletin board of photos of people who are currently in the news. Put a blank sheet of paper underneath each person and allow children to cut out and paste words from the newspaper which describe each person.

   * *Mystery Person.* From the newspaper have each child cut out appropriate words and phrases to fill in the following blanks:

   My age is _____.

   My favorite food is _____.

   My favorite sport is _____.

   I sometimes wear _____.

   I can be described as _____.

   My favorite TV show is _____.

   This makes me angry: _____.

   This makes me happy: _____.

Collect the "mystery" sheets and read them out loud. Let children try to guess who each mystery person is.

   * *Rapid Recall.* Ask each child to choose an interesting picture from the newspaper. Allow each child to study her picture carefully for two minutes. Then tell all the children to turn their pictures over and try to write down as many things as they can remember about their picture. Then let pairs of children evaluate each other's recall.

   * *Role Plays.* From an advice column such as Dear Abby, have several children role play a situation of their choosing. Let other children in the class volunteer to get

up and simulate possible solutions to the problem. Discuss the benefits of each suggested solution.

Creating a Classroom Newspaper

After children have become familiar with the newspaper and its particular brand of journalism, they will often be eager to institute their own classroom newspaper. This venture is an optimal way to provide plenty of integrated reading, writing and re-writing practice. Additionally, it serves as an important forum for the publication of children's work, and reinforces content area curricular classroom activities and field trips by allowing children to write about them for their own paper.

I can best attest to the value of a classroom newspaper from my own experience: I don't remember the publication of my first journal article as a professor nearly as vividly as I do the time I had an article published in our sixth-grade newspaper. The positive feedback I was given from teachers and peers is *still* fresh in my memory. Many children have told me similar tales of their feelings about having published their work in classroom newspapers.

Having children select a name for the classroom newspaper is crucial because it clearly establishes the students' ownership and authorship of the project. Allow children to first do some research into some names of local newspapers and then encourage the whole class to vote on a name that is personal yet in the language of newspapers--such as "The Sixth Grade Centurion" or "The Renton School Reporter."

Next it is time to decide how the class newspaper will be produced. Help the children discuss the following issues:

1) Will the newspaper be photocopied or mimeographed?

2) Will you sell the papers for a fee, or will the class ask for help from the PTA?

3) Will the paper be sold to the whole school, or just the class that is producing the paper?

4) Do you want to include art work?

5) Will the newspaper be typed or printed?

6) Who will duplicate the paper?

Organizing the Class

Let the class determine an editor for each page. That editor will be responsible for all the stories and art work on that page. The teacher can serve as "publisher" and thus supervise all work, but the class should agree on and set deadlines and the publication date.

As a class, discuss the stories that must be in the paper and the stories that would be desirable. The class newspaper should contain news stories, feature stories, sports and editorials. To keep the newspaper current, have children check the school calendar and plan which events to cover and promote in the paper. The following are other possibilities to consider as part of the paper:

Book review	Classified
Advice column	advertisements
Weather report	Crossword puzzle
School lunch review	School-wide contests
Fun page (jokes	Original stories
and riddles)	and poems

Each editor should make an assignment sheet for his page and post it where everyone can see it. The editor may assign stories to certain students in the class, or children may sign up for the stories they wish to write. In either case, the teacher and editors should see that every child, including the editors, makes at least one written contribution.

Features, Sports and Editorial

Feature stories can allow children to interview people involved in significant school events and create human interest, instead of the usual news story written in the past tense. Feature writers should be encouraged to write stories that are more creative and less "condensed" than news stories.

Sports writers should know that their best choice for the classroom newspaper would be the sports feature story, allowing them to do in-depth interviews with a team member or a story about the sport itself.

Caution students about editorials: guide them to realize, through their familiarity with "real" editorials, that this piece of writing can commend as well as criticize something. Tell children that an editorial should state a problem, analyze it, and then offer a constructive solution. Stress that any editorials printed must be fair, and provide space for letters to the editors by readers who disagree with the editor's point of view.

Editing and Layout

When the stories are finished, they should first be read by the editor, then revised and resubmitted if the editor suggests any changes. If there are none, the child should schedule a conference with the teacher to go over the story for any mechanical problems. When the story has been rewritten to the satisfaction of the student, the editor, and the teacher, it should be put in an envelope for the page on which it is supposed to appear. The editor should then check off each completed story on the assignment sheet.

Once all the stories for a page are finished, the editor should take a sheet of paper the size of the completed newspaper page and lay out the page, noting where each story and piece of artwork is to be placed.

The most important story on each page should be placed in the upper left-hand corner, except for the front page, where it should be placed in the upper right-hand corner.

Each story should have a headline, which will typically grab the reader's attention with a minimum of words. Headlines can be typed or hand lettered on the master.

The art work needs to be measured exactly for size and space left for it on the master so that it can be transferred just before the paper is mimeographed or photocopied.

Then the stories, headlines, and art work should be sent to the typist, word processor or hand printer. When the papers come back, they should be proofread and corrected by the editors and teacher before being run off.

When the pages have been run off, they can be collated and stapled by the class. Distribution might take place at lunchtime, before or after school, or to individual classrooms. A treasurer should be appointed to keep track of all money received.

Summary

Newspapers can be dynamic teaching tools for an Affective Language Arts program. The wide scope of material in the average local newspaper makes it an ideal stimulus for critical thinking and a wide array of writing activities that cross the entire curriculum. Additionally, many of the subskills of the language arts can be practiced and reinforced in motivational ways using some of the newspaper exercises suggested in this chapter. Too, familiarity with the newspaper's format and style of journalism often spurs children to want to develop their *own* classroom newspaper, providing an excellent forum for the students' own writing. Thus, an even more pressing reason to complete the arduous task of writing, revising, and editing naturally comes to light in the classroom.

Perhaps more importantly, though, children start to recognize the value of newspapers in a free and literate society. They begin to take part in one of the few reading activities in American culture that is actively modeled and enjoyed by a large number of adults on a routine basis. When they have been introduced to the "newspaper habit," children feel they have somehow entered the grown-up world of our reading culture. Though some children may never grow up and experience the joys of the wide spectrum of other literary genres available to them, at least this one important door will have been opened wide.

Chapter Eight

The Wonder of Words

Since words are the obvious building blocks of sentences and thus ALL writing, a classroom in which the teacher and children enjoy playing with words is usually one in which children also enjoy writing. In such a classroom, all the children are delighted when Chrissy suddenly chirps, "A clink is like a pink drink of water!" because word play is just naturally pleasing to their ears, and they know the teacher thinks so too. In such a classroom, also, when John asks how to spell the word "succeed" because he wants it for his journal entry, the teacher does not demand that he "look it up." The wise teacher realizes that this would be one of the surest ways to dampen John's burgeoning enthusiasm for the dictionary as the "house of words," and she is also quite certain that the next time he would hesitate before asking for her assistance when spelling a word he didn't know. So, instead, she patiently shows him how to spell his word so that he can get back, without serious interruption, to the important business of writing down his thoughts.

Because children begin their lives with an intense curiosity about words, the affective teacher of language arts has a very special mission in regard to the teaching of vocabulary. She can: 1) perpetuate the children's interest (if she is lucky, and too many "look it up's" haven't already destroyed it); or she can 2) try to rekindle the interest if she finds that her students have become dictionary-shy and word-weary; or, 3) she can actively build into her language arts program some exciting activities that can help make vocabulary development an outgrowth of children's natural linguistic play, rather than the more common tedium of looking up isolated words and then writing them in sentences that occurs in drearier classrooms.

This chapter contains suggestions to make the third option a reality. A potpourri of teacher-tested activities will be described that can be used to cultivate, nourish, and enrich children's listening, speaking, reading, and writing vocabularies. Activities are also included for the purpose of building positive associations with the dictionary as a useful "friend" that tells readers and writers things they want to know about words. Finally, a few words of caution are offered about some unfortunate prevalent practices that can easily extinguish the love of learning flame. Instead, by implementing some of the ideas set forth in this chapter, teachers can actively fan the flame by encouraging children's natural fascination with words. Such teachers will more than likely be rewarded with students who will risk penning their ideas in fresh and interesting ways.

Stimulating Interest in Words

Teachers can help children appreciate the connection between words in our language through an enjoyable look at some verbal relationships via these vocabulary-enriching activities.

* *Novel Appellations.* Children are intrigued by adages such as the following examples for which synonyms have been used for each original word or phrase, although the meaning has been kept intact. Introduce children to the Thesaurus as an invaluable aid in translating them:

Members of an avian species of identical plumage congregate. (Birds of a feather flock together.)

All articles that coruscate with resplendence are not necessarily auriferous. (All that glitters is not gold.)

The stylus is more potent than the claymore. (The pen is mightier than the sword.)

Male cadavers are incapable of yielding testimony. (Dead men tell no tales.)

It is fruitless to attempt to indoctrinate a superannuated canine with innovative maneuvers. (You can't teach an old dog new tricks.)

After "decoding" these sentences into their more common form, children will be eager to similarly encode other common phrases, titles of books, or popular songs with the help of the Thesaurus, for other members of the class to decode. A further challenge is to ask them to design phrases that mean the opposite of the originals that they have collected. For example, "All that glitters is not gold," might become, "None that tarnishes is silver."

   * *Classifying Grid.* To allow children to gain enjoyable practice categorizing words, a classifying grid can be used. The name of a child in the class is selected and then other class members determine five to ten categories that they would like to encounter. Then in groups of four or five, children try to fill in the grid, trying to think of an item to fill every cell, as in the following grid:

	J	A	N	E
animal	jaguar	armadillo	newt	elephant
tree	juniper	ash	nut	elm
flower	jonquil	azalea	narcissus	easter lily
food	jam	asparagus	nutbread	egg
color	jade	avocado	nilegreen	eggshell
country	Japan	Antarctica	Nigeria	Ethiopia

   To score the grid, groups get one point for every cell that is correctly filled in and three points for items that no other group mentioned.

   * *Semantic Mapping.* An excellent way to help children understand how words relate to one another is through the semantic map. This technique can span all content areas and is especially useful for crystallizing concepts with which students have been introduced. Before or after studying gas, for example, children can be asked to contribute everything they can think of about the subject while the teacher records what is said in columns on the blackboard, according to the categories in which they might fit. With the teacher's guidance, the children later go back and label the categories, gaining a much greater insight into how the more abstract, superordinate

concepts, and the concrete, subordinate concepts might fit together, like so:

GAS
Related to:
molecular movement
chemical changes
states of matter
evaporation & condensation

abstract
superordinate
concepts

Uses	Kinds	Properties	
heating	natural	expands	more concrete
illuminating	helium	colorless	subordinate
putting people	neon	fills space	concepts
to sleep	chlorine	no volume	

Understanding the major meaning-bearing affixes in our language can be extremely helpful when trying to determine the meaning of unfamiliar words, but can also become a creative and motivational classroom project by implementing this teacher-tested idea:

* *Wacky Word Book.* After some direct instruction about the organization of a dictionary and the meaning of some of our most commonly used roots, prefixes, and suffixes, children will be interested in creating their own classroom dictionary of "wacky words." The teacher can give each child a list of these roots and affixes and then group children into threes to cooperatively create a list of ten "new" words by combining prefixes, suffixes, and roots in novel ways. Next the groups should be instructed to think up some humorous (or realistic) meanings for their newly coined words. Examples:

au'to.therm"ist, n. one who sets himself on fire.

cir'cum-hy.dri"tis, n. the state of walking around puddles instead of through them.

mul'ti.vi"tish, adj. having several lives.

ret'ro.cel"er.ide, n. the act of running quickly backwards.

Then each group should present its new words to the other members of the class who can try to guess the definitions of the words from their own knowledge of the various word parts. Finally, the class can create their own "wacky word book" for publication by entering all their new entries into a dictionary.

An understanding of how words can be used to actually "paint pictures," much as an artist mixes colors to get just the right hues, can be developed by helping children to become aware of the fine shades of meanings of words in our language. The next two activities can help to heighten this awareness:

* *Cloze Stories.* To use the instructional cloze to build an appreciation of fine shades of meaning, the teacher can take a short (approximately 250 words) article from a children's magazine, a young people's encyclopedia, or even a lengthy advertisement from the newspaper, and delete every other adjective. She should then display the original passage, with deletions, on an overhead projector, after children have filled in their own adjectives. Let the children then contribute their own word choices for the deletions. Discuss with children how certain words make a clearer visual picture for the reader than others. For example, in the sentence, "The _____ lady lumbered down the street," the use of the word "lumbered" should suggest to children that the lady talked about is quite large, and a choice of the word "obese," "hefty," or "stout" for the blank would make the image more clear than the choice of a more generic word such as "big." Stress that while many words are acceptable, there are some words that serve to enlighten the reader more completely than others.

* *Assembling and Disassembling Sentences.* An excellent way to teach subject and predicate agreement (as compared with the more traditional language text exercise of putting one line under the subject and two under the predicate) is to show children how to assemble and disassemble their own sentences. The activity can be introduced by having children close their eyes and visualize a sentence, such as, "The wind whipped." Then ask them to compare their visual impressions of the same sentence "dressed up" in the following manner: "On a frigid afternoon in January, the strong, biting wind whipped through the swaying, swirling branches of the towering oak tree growing on the far side of the farmer's snow-covered field." After allowing children to disassemble many sentences into their simple components in this way, let them try their hands at assembling such sentence germs as "The man cried," or "the canary warbled." For the latter sentence, the children may come up with vastly differing visions: "The arthritic old canary, having led a rich and full life in the Buddhist monastery, warbled his last tuneful notes, slipped off his perch and died"; "The peach-colored canary warbled a sweet song of love for his tiny mate, then died of a broken heart when she heard that he

had been given to his owner's sister." When sharing assembled sentences, discuss the differences in visions from one sentence to the next. This routine practice of assembling and disassembling sentences will not only promote an appreciation for the richness of our language and the utter power of words, but will also lead to an intuitive understanding of grammar. Moreover, used daily, children grow in their desire and ability to write more finely-shaded sentences.

Finally, word games such as Scrabble and crossword puzzles can become lifelong habits that foster a love of words. In a similar vein, the following word games are guaranteed to provide positive experiences with words for even the most reluctant students:

* *Hinky Pinky.* A "hinky pinky" consists of two rhyming words that must be discovered by figuring out the meaning of a cryptic, two-word clue. Example: "A fatter arachnid" would be a "wider spider." Children very much enjoy doing this activity, especially in groups of three or four or as an overnight assignment for which the dictionary may be consulted, or parents involved if they wish. (Many parents have told me that this was the most "academic" fun they had ever had with their children!) Not only does this activity offer an enjoyable experience with words, but also a realistic need for the dictionary, as well as a better understanding of synonyms and their use. The following ten hinky pinkies--my favorites--can be used for an introductory contest; later children can be encouraged to devise their own for other classmates to decipher.

1) foul-smelling jam: **smelly jelly.**
2) an evil pastor: **sinister minister.**
3) a citrus bell: **lime chime.**
4) decayed material: **rotten cotton.**
5) an ebony slit: **black crack.**
6) a facile acne: **simple pimple.**
7) a clever elf: **bright sprite.**
8) a gaunt horse: **bony pony.**
9) an unclear pestilence: **vague plague.**
10) an abrupt pocketbook: **terse purse.**

* *Twisted Stories.* Twisted stories (also called "Mad Libs," which are available commercially) are "blind" stories that the children can help the teacher to write by providing some of the words. To do this activity the teacher does not show the story to the children so that they, without the benefit of the context of the story, shout out

specific parts of speech as they are solicited by the teacher, while he writes them down in the appropriate spaces. Then the finished story is read aloud to the entire class. After the teacher has initiated a few of these Twisted Stories, a greater benefit comes from having the children write their own stories, making blank spaces to be filled in by their classmates. A possible story to use to introduce this activity is included here, along with the final "product." The blank spaces were filled in by members of a fourth-grade class:

The Vacation

Last summer I traveled to _(city or country) Japan_ with _(person) Clint Eastwood_ and _(person) Abe Lincoln_ to see as many _(adjective) gross_ _(plural noun) erasers_ as we could find. It was a/an _(adjective) flimsy_ trip. We packed enough _(articles of clothing) socks_ to stay _(number) 103_ days. One day we visited the famous _(adjective) Sneaky_ _(noun) Bubblegum_ State Park. It was there I saw my first _(adjective) silly_ _(color) purple_ _(noun) pencil sharpener_. I took a picture of the _(animals) snakes_. They're so _(adjective) joyful_! I bought a souvenir tee-shirt that said, _(adjective) "Moldy_ _(plural noun) books_ love _(color) pink_ _(liquid) milk_." Later we went to a ball game. The _(animals) cats_ played the _(number) 62'ers_. It was very _(emotion) sad_. The game was very _(adjective) stubborn_. But we had to leave _(adverb) gently_ because I said, _(exclamation) "Holy Cow!"_ to a _(noun) garbage can_. On the last night of our trip we went to a _(type of music) rock 'n' roll_ concert. The well-known band, _(adjective) Interesting (noun) Finger_ was on stage. I saw one musician _(verb) vacuum_ his _(musical instrument) clarinet_ using his _(body part) lung_. I was so _(emotion) jealous_ that I bought a _(noun) banana_ and mailed it home. My vacation

taught me one lesson: Never give a (noun) stethoscope to a
(adjective) rad   (noun) mouse !

Fostering Positive Associations
with the Dictionary

The dictionary is quite a complex reference tool
without which many readers and writers would undoubtedly be lost. Many adults (I count myself among them) who
read and write frequently will readily admit that they still
look up several words a week through their routine contact
with print. Because the dictionary can be so helpful in
helping children learn to communicate more effectively,
we must make certain that they feel comfortable using it.
The use of the dictionary requires a hierarchy of abilities:
children must first be taught to 1) locate the words, which
are arranged in alphabetical order; 2) understand how to
use the pronunciation guides if they are to use the word
orally, and 3) find the appropriate meaning of the word.
Moreover, it is simply not sufficient to teach children to
rely on superficial verbalizations for words that are
prompted when they are asked to memorize isolated word
lists. A child, for example, who has remembered by rote
that "frantic" means "wild" may then try to tell how he
was picking "frantic flowers," and a child who has
learned that "athletic" means "strong" might tell you
about pouring "athletic vinegar" on her salad!
Rather than providing meaningless word lists and
demanding that children always look up unfamiliar words,
dictionary games can help children acquire a feeling of
confidence and ease with the dictionary, while making it
much more likely that the use of this important tool
becomes a habit.
I have found the following motivational games very
successful for building positive attitudes toward the dictionary. The practice afforded by such games automatically reinforces children's ability to perform the rudimentary
skills just mentioned.
* What Would You Do With It? From the dictionary,
select a word that is probably unfamiliar to your students.
Write the word on the blackboard and solicit hunches
about the word's use. For example, the word "freshet" is
written on the blackboard and pronounced. The children
are told that the word is a noun, or the name of a person,
place, or thing. Then children are asked what they would
do with a "freshet." Answers may range from "hang it in

my closet, because it is probably a sweet smelling bag of herbs" to "step on it, because it's probably an insect of some sort." After all who want to have guessed, allow all of the children to look up the word. Children will be surprised and amused to find that a "freshet" is a flooded stream and will want to compare their hunches with the actual definition.

  * *Camouflage.* This game combines motivational dictionary practice with non-threatening extemporaneous speaking and oral creativity. To introduce the game, the teacher must first explain what the word "camouflage" means and then tell children that to play this game, they must camouflage, or hide, a word. Then give children slips of paper, each of which contains a word that is just above children's oral (speaking) vocabularies; that is, words that they would not use in their everyday conversations. Ask them not to show their words to anyone else, but encourage them to consult a dictionary to get a broad feeling of the word's meaning. Next, either demonstrate yourself, or select a confident and easily verbal risk-taker to go first. Have another member of the class volunteer to ask the child a very general question, such as, "What is your favorite thing to do?" or, perhaps, "Would you rather live in this country or China?" After considering the question for a few seconds, the first child must then loosely answer the question, trying to sneak in the word that was on the slip of paper. An obvious strategy is to utilize all the "big" words that the child can think of in answer to the question in order to throw the other children off. When the child is finished answering the question, other members of the class try to guess which word was being camouflaged. The first child "wins" if the number of children who guess the camouflaged word is fewer than the sum total of incorrect guesses.

  * *Clue.* The game "Password" is very popular with children and has great merit in giving children practice in thinking about the meaning of words. Unfortunately, only five can play the traditional version of this game at one time. A variation of this game, suitable for the whole class, is "Clue." One child is selected to sit facing the front of the classroom with a word that she has not seen taped to her back. Other children are put into two teams and, armed with student dictionaries, take turns offering one-word synonyms that they hope will cause the child to guess the word. As words are offered, they are written on the blackboard so that the child who is guessing can try to synthesize all the definitions that the other children have

contributed. The team that says the clue that causes the child to say the word wins the round.

* *Torture the Teacher.* Often the reason children are intimidated by the dictionary is because it is so full of words they don't know, but somehow feel they *should* know. They feel somewhat comforted when they realize that no one knows ALL the words in the dictionary . . . not even their teacher! Using an unabridged dictionary, let children on a daily basis, take turns hunting for a word for which they think you might not know the meaning. For their part, they must provide the word, its pronunciation, and its part of speech. You, then, must give a reasonably accurate sense of what the word means. If you do know the word's meaning, you win for the day. If you don't know the meaning of the word, they win, and they feel smug and most pleased with themselves. Warning: this activity is NOT for the insecure!

* *Farkle.* When children become familiar enough with the peculiar stilted language of dictionary definitions, Farkle can be a fun way to practice dictionary skills while fostering creativity at the same time. To do this, select a word that is probably unknown to the class. On the blackboard, write the word, its part of speech, and its pronunciation using diacritical marking. Example: pur-lieu (per'loo), n. Then ask the children, using their imaginations, to create a definition for this word on a slip of paper using their best imitation of dictionary language. Meanwhile, the teacher writes out the actual dictionary definition on a slip of paper. Slips of paper are then collected, shuffled, and numbered. Then all the definitions are read to the class once so that class members can hear all the definitions and try to determine which is the real one. Then the definitions are read a second time and children "vote" for the one definition they think is the actual one. When the voting is completed, all children look up the word to find its true definition. The made-up definition that received the most votes wins.

Final Axioms for Guiding Growth in Vocabulary

The underlying supposition in an Affective Language Arts program is that learning to communicate should be rewarding and enjoyable; the vocabulary-building activities just described will certainly help make it so. But because I have recently seen so many routine classroom practices that could seriously dampen this enthusiasm, I would like to offer a few words of caution here:

1) DO NOT consistently tell children to look up words they don't know or can't spell. For spelling purposes, it is better to just show the child how to spell the word, or let him try to sound it out, to be edited at a later time. For meaning purposes, at times just tell the child what the word means. Also, encourage children to keep personal VIP word books in which they write down any unfamiliar words which they have encountered in school or while reading at home. Later, when they have accumulated 10-15 such words, they can look them up all at once. Encourage them to share some of the VIP words that they especially like with the rest of the class.

2) DO NOT give children words to memorize that have been taken from commercial word lists. Words memorized in isolation have little meaning or interest to children and will soon be forgotten. The words that children readily want to learn and have the best chance of remembering come from topics they are currently studying or, even better yet, words for which they have expressed an interest in knowing themselves.

3) DO NOT give children simple synonyms for words. Instead offer them the whole sense of what the word means, moving from the general to the specific, and telling them what the word is like and what the word is unlike compared with that which they already know. For example, to explain the word "sword" you might say that it is something to cut with, like a knife, but much sharper and bigger; but unlike a knife, it is usually used as a weapon.

4) DO NOT use the dictionary as a "tutor" for students learning English as a second language. I have been in too many classrooms where a child who speaks little or no English is put by himself in the back of the classroom to "learn English" by copying dictionary pages. Not only does he learn to despise the dictionary, but by being segregated from the rest of the class he is denied the language interaction that is the best possible environment in which to acquire a second language.

5) DO NOT use the dictionary as a punishment. As much as I would like to believe that this final caveat goes without saying, I am still observing practices in otherwise fine school districts where children are instructed to copy whole pages from dictionaries as punishment for minor rule infractions! Besides the fact that the punishment has nothing to do with the "crime," the practice will very quickly counteract any positive feelings that have been connected with the dictionary.

Summary

The affective teacher of language arts can joyfully capitalize on the fact that it is in the nature of the child to love words and word play. If she can then simply take advantage of the myriad of occasions during the day when children are directing their own language through play, she can quite naturally integrate vocabulary development into the entire curriculum.

The teacher can also plan special experiences for children that can be presented in such an interesting and inviting way that children will begin to appreciate the various shades of meaning possible in our language, the interesting ways that words relate to one another, and how the dictionary can become a liberating tool that will allow independent investigation of words. A host of activities leading to these ends have been presented in this chapter. In a classroom where words are exciting for both the teacher and the students, great things often happen. Just the right word is eagerly sought to convey an intense feeling or a physical description; sentences, too, are now designed to create a precise message or personal vision. Children begin to understand that if they think something, they can say it or write it. It is indeed a revelation to children when they first see that they will soon have the very tools at their command to communicate clearly what is in their hearts and minds. The key to a more dynamic interaction with the rest of the world is within their grasp.

Chapter Nine

Visualization Activities: Why the Book Was Better Than the Movie

There is probably a good reason for the often heard cliche, "It was a great movie, but the book was even better!" Most people who really do enjoy reading use the incredible resource of their own imaginations while reading a good book. They actively bring their own myriad of life's experiences to the text, allowing their minds to vividly color the characters and events exactly the way they wish them to be. The text comes alive for them in the most personal and intense kind of way. No wonder the film--always a far cry from what the fertile imagination has conjured--is a disappointment to them!

In today's high-tech world, the old cliché is not heard as often among young people and I worry that we are short-changing them by taking away the imaginative challenges in their recreational activities. Instead of children making up a fanciful dialogue with their teddy bears, for example, the toys can now instigate and control sophisticated "conversations," while video games have become so frighteningly graphic that virtually nothing needs to be imagined. Even popular songs now provide lavishly-produced videos, dismissing the need for youngsters to call up any of their own images to make the lyrics come alive.

Because children are being given fewer and fewer opportunities to use their imaginations naturally, it becomes crucial to include visualization activities in an Affective Language Arts program. For one thing, when children are in the midst of the writing process they must be able to consult their own personal "mind pictures" to decide what should come next in their work. Visualization exercises can strengthen this ability, making it almost second-nature to children. As a result, they become more confident and capable writers.

Additionally, encouraging children to actively visualize words and concepts may not only help them to enjoy reading more thoroughly, but it can also improve their understanding of what they read. As an example, a program focusing on the skill of using visual imagery was implemented in the Escondido Union School District. Gains in comprehension were shown that were over three times that of previous years (Escondido Union School District, 1979).

The following chapter will give the affective teacher specific steps, guidelines, and visualization activities that can be used as motivational pre-writing prompts and will also help children to glean more pleasure from reading by becoming better able to use their imaginations to appreciate sensory and descriptive imagery. Additionally, the chapter will describe some ways teachers can familiarize their students with the metacognitive strategy of turning to their own personal mind pictures for guidance when writing.

Guidelines for Using Visualization

To obtain the optimal affective benefits from the routine use of visualizing, the sensitive teacher may want to keep in mind the following general guidelines (Fredericks, 1986):

1) Children first need to be reassured that there are no "correct" or "incorrect" mind pictures; whatever their imaginations dictate are valid responses.

2) Children must learn to respect each other's mind pictures, understanding that the images that pop into one's mind are often influenced by one's own past experiences.

3) Children need enough "wait time" to bring forth their images. If they are rushed, some children will draw blanks and begin to believe that their imaginations are somehow inadequate.

4) Allow sufficient time to discuss images in a supportive, cooperative and informal atmosphere that conveys the feeling to children that everyone's images are worth exploring.

5) Help children to develop the skill of elaboration by actively seeking details about their contributions. For example, if a child offers, "I see a blue house," the teacher might reply, "Oh--that's interesting. Can you tell us more about the blue house?"

Activities to Foster Visualization

For some fluent children, visualization comes quite naturally, and they write prolifically without interruption. Others may need practice creating images in their minds as a precursor to writing.

Mundell (1985) has presented a four-step process for helping children to more actively use their imaginations:

1) *Give children practice visualizing concrete objects.* Allow children the opportunity to look very carefully at everyday objects, such as the pencil sharpener, a favorite toy, or their tennis shoes. Have them close their eyes and try to recreate every detail of the object in their minds, and then with their eyes open, compare their mental image with the actual object. Finally, let them verbally or pictorially try to recreate the object, attempting to include even those details they had overlooked the first time.

For an added oral language dimension to the previous exercise, have one child select an object and put it in a bag so that it is out of sight to the other members of the class. Let the child describe all the visual attributes of the object that would help the other children identify it while the others try to draw the object from the child's description. Then compare the object with the children's drawings and discuss the reasons for the sometimes humorous discrepancies between the drawings and the actual object.

A "human" variation of this activity is to select a child to leave the classroom for a few moments. Have the rest of the children in the class describe the absent child by trying to visualize everything the absent child was wearing, and his or her height, weight, and eyes and hair color. When the child reenters the classroom compare the class members' visual memory with the child's actual appearance.

2) *Give children practice recalling scenes or experiences from outside the classroom.* To help children become more accurate observers, ask them to close their eyes and picture their family car (or pet, or living room, etc.). As they are thinking about it, orally "walk" them around the outside of the car, telling them to try to imagine the wheels, the hub caps, the doors (two or four?), the color of the paint, the grille, the license plates, etc. Next, have the children draw a picture of the car with as much detail as they can remember. Then ask them to take their drawings home and compare them with the actual vehicles.

Every child has watched a helium-filled balloon go up into the sky until it is out of sight. Key into this experience common to children by showing them the film *The Red Balloon.* Then follow the viewing with the reading aloud of Shel Silverstein's poem "Eight Balloons" while children close their eyes (this poem describes the journey of eight balloons whose sad fates range from landing on a frying pan to entering a crocodile's mouth). Ask the children to now imagine that they are holding their own helium-filled balloons which suddenly escape into the air. Give them a few moments to image the flight of their balloons and then encourage them to give an oral or pictorial account of the balloon's journey.

Finally, to demonstrate to children how their visual and olfactory memories combine to create even stronger memories, bring in several items with strong aromas without revealing to the children what they are. Have the children close their eyes and sniff the items whose smell usually evokes explicit memories of past experiences, such as leather, pine cones, a plastic doll, bubble gum, or lavender sachet. Ask children to then share the mental images that come to their minds of people or places that they may associate with these scents.

3) *Give children practice listening to high imagery stories and relating them to their own experiences.* Read stories aloud to children that contain a great deal of visual imagery, such as the books *Tuck Everlasting* or *Julie of the Wolves*. Stop every so often and allow children to share their mental images of how the characters, settings, or events have come to life in their minds.

Also, do "mental adventure" exercises on a routine basis. While having children close their eyes, orally give them a guided imagery of a situation such as a safari in deepest Africa or a tamer adventure, like a walk in the forest:

"Picture yourself in a forest. You are strolling among the trees on a well-worn path. What is the weather like? (Pause to let children imagine.) As you walk along, you see a person. You exchange glances with the person, and then that person runs quickly in the other direction. Why? (Pause.) You continue walking and soon come to a body of water. What is it? How deep, how wide, how cold? (Pause.) You cross it--how? (Pause.) You find the path again on the other side and begin walking again. Soon you almost trip on a cup lying in the middle of the path. You stoop to pick it up and examine it carefully. What does it look like? (Pause.) You put it down. Why? (Pause.) You keep walking until the path leads to a fence. You climb over the fence and see a house. What does the house look like? (Pause.) You enter the house and find yourself in the kitchen. What is the kitchen like? (Pause.) You sit down at the kitchen table and see that there is something interesting on the table. What is it? (Pause.) While you are looking at it, the person whom you saw in the forest walks into the kitchen. Describe him or her."

Ask the children to then retrace their individual journeys orally for the class or, at later stages, in written form.

Allow pairs of children to act out their journeys for the rest of the class if they wish.

Another high-imagery listening experience that you can provide for your class is to have them listen to *The Adventures of Robinson Crusoe, The Cay,* or *Swiss Family Robinson.* Have them close their eyes and visualize their own versions of a shipwreck. Then, over the period of time during which the story is read, ask them to write a series of journal entries of their adventures on their own make-believe islands, encouraging them to "borrow" as much as they would like from the text. Let each child select his own favorite entry to dramatize into an original one-act play for the rest of the class.

**Trusting Mind Pictures to
Tell What Happens Next**

To provide children with the "ignition key" that will always be at their disposal when they are writing independently, spontaneous story technique (SST) (Kolpakoff, 1986) can serve as the bridge between a child's pictorial imagination, oral language, and writing. This method is ideal for use at all grade levels, but requires much practice and the initial enthusiastic participation of the teacher as storyteller.

To begin using this technique, children should be gathered around the teacher in a relaxed fashion, preferably on the floor. Then the teacher instructs her students to close their eyes and make their minds as empty as possible. The rest of a typical SST exercise goes something like this:

"Now your mind is empty. But as soon as you 'see' something, raise your hand."

(The teacher then solicits responses as to what individual children have visualized and encourages elaboration.)

"Again, I want you to make your mind as empty as possible, but this time I'm going to ask you to do something very strange! When I tell you NOT to see something, try as hard as you can, NOT to see it! Now--DO NOT see a pink monster!"

(Stop and discuss with children how many of them actually did see a pink monster and have children share what their various monsters looked like. Continue in this manner with several other examples of things you tell children NOT to see.)

"Now I want you to make your mind empty once more and hold it on empty for as long as you can. When a picture does come into your mind, raise your hand."

(Wait until all hands are raised and then solicit the children's images. Praise effective elaboration that allows other children to "see," too.)

"I am now going to ask you to put your last picture back in your mind again. Hold that picture there as long as you can. When that picture goes away or changes to a new picture, please raise your hand."

(When all children have new pictures, let them share them.)

After a number of SST sessions, when children have become much more confident about using their imaginations and are willingly sharing their images, they are ready to begin to use these visual skills to problem-solve endings to stories. They can now be assured that they can *always* know what comes next in a story; all they have to do is to allow their minds to create the next picture. At this stage, the teacher will want to have a session include a "cliff-hanger" story told first by the teacher, but in later sessions, made up by student volunteers. A cliff-hanger story might go like this:

"Close your eyes and let your mind be empty. Now I want you to picture yourself entering a room in an old attic. It is raining and you can hear the soft patter of raindrops on the roof. Hear them? (Pause.) You wander around the stuffy attic and notice an old rocking horse and a stuffed rabbit with an ear missing. You walk toward a broken window and see a large spider web. The spider suddenly swoops down to look at you (pause for squeals from the squeamish), and then scurries quickly away. Your eye catches a large mirror on the far wall of the attic. It has fancy gold decorations on all sides and is covered with several layers of dust. You move over to it and start to brush off some of the dust when you discover, to your surprise, that you can walk through the mirror. You push your body through the mirror and you see . . ."

At this critical point, ask children to open their eyes and share their visions of what was on the other side of the mirror.

Other visualization stories that could be expanded and used in a similar way are these:

* "You are exploring a deep, dark cave. You suddenly hear a strong, frightening voice. You try to find your way back to the entrance, but it seems that all the rooms in the cave look very much alike. You panic as you realize the voice is coming closer and closer. Suddenly, you see who it is . . ."

* "You are flying in an airplane over some cornfields in the Midwest. Suddenly the engine starts to sputter and the plane begins to lose altitude. You decide to bail out and so you quickly put on your parachute. You are as scared as you have ever been, but you jump out of the plane, and . . ."

* "You are skindiving off the coast of Australia. You are having fun playing hide and seek with the groupers and friendly parrot fish. Suddenly you spy an old abandoned ship and you dive down to explore it. You open the door to the captain's quarters and are amazed to find . . ."

When children are feeling confident that they now can "know" what will happen next in a story through their mind pictures, they are ready to begin using story boards to help them finish the rest of their stories. The "story board" for very young children is simply a piece of paper divided into six panels on which children pictorially sequence the next six events in the story. For older children, the panels are the next six pages of text.

Individual tape recorders are sometimes useful to help children make the transition from "mind pictures" to the oral telling of incidents, to the written version. With the tape recorder, the children can revise and expand their text until they are completely satisfied with their story before writing anything. Then they can use their recording to help them transcribe the text onto paper, continually checking with their mind pictures for any new information.

While the children are busy writing, the teacher's role is to interact with his students in a non-directive way to help them to work through their writing problems and temporary blocks. Kolpakoff suggests three specific interactive techniques that can enable the teacher to become a more effective writing facilitator:

1) *Marking time.* When children tell the teacher that they don't know what comes next, the teacher may deliberately NOT respond to this lament and, instead, distract the child from the writing task by instigating a very brief

chat about something totally unrelated to the child's current writing. This chance for the child to "get away" from the intensity of creating for a few seconds often allows that child to then get back to her writing with fresh ideas and immediate inspiration--a ploy used often by professional writers.

2) *Next picture.* When a child is "stuck," another technique is to read the child's work and then offer a snippet of an idea which could lead to a new set of possibilities. For example, a child writing about the mirror in the attic may be blocked when he sees a picnic area on the other side of the mirror, but can't get an idea what happens there. The teacher might suggest, "I see a little boy running away from his parents into the woods and . . ." At that point the teacher smiles and walks away, promising to check back later to see how the author is doing.

3) *Writer's talk.* Because the teacher is ordinarily so engrossed in her role of support person, often the only real intellectual interchange between teacher and young author is of the offer to help or request for assistance variety. Another important role for the teacher when children are writing from their imaginations is simply to talk to each child, author to author, making respectful comments about each one's imaginative thoughts and ideas. Teachers are then able to be perceived as helpful collaborators rather than "powerful beings with all the answers."

Visualization across the Curriculum

The skill of visualizing should have a prominent place in many areas of a whole language elementary curriculum, where the language arts are thoroughly integrated, especially when abstract concepts and ideas need to be made more concrete and meaningful for the younger child. Social studies, for example, requires children to do much writing of an analytical/expository nature, but when guided imagery is used to mentally "walk" children through the content areas, children can become more personally involved through the sensory/descriptive information that visualization provides for them.

Sprowl (1986) uses the image of present, familiar situations to help children relate to difficult and abstract concepts. For example, to show children how technology has affected their lives, he asks them to close their eyes and imagine that it is early morning and they are in the bathroom trying to get ready for school. He then has them mentally take away any machines that they would normally use, such as electric toothbrushes, hair dryers or electric rollers. Of course, there is no light in the bathroom. Next he has them picture themselves walking to their bedroom, erasing the images of their radio or stereo, or even any clothing that was made by machine. On the way to the kitchen they pass through the living room and the children are told it is now bereft of the telephone, television, VCR, and again, lights. The children must then try to imagine their kitchen without the stove, refrigerator, washer, dryer, or dishwasher. Finally, children are instructed to do away with even the walls and the carpets, as these items, too, are made by machines.

Because this mental voyage is so graphic and personal for children, they truly begin to understand, in a very memorable way, the concept of a world without the modern technology that they quite naturally take for granted. Such guided imagery can also be used to effectively introduce other important global concepts such as poverty, racism, nuclear war, or life in another country, to name just a few.

Summary

Visualization activities invest children with the ability to look inside themselves to "see" stories more clearly and to trust that their own minds will know what should happen next for their own creations. The skill is a fundamental technique that should be at the core of any affective language arts program, for it quite clearly demonstrates to children that they must be active, rather than passive, participants in their own development as writers. Visualization gives them, also, one more important tool that will allow them to communicate effectively. It is a tool that almost all children naturally possess, but somehow, somewhere, it is often discarded in deference to other external demands that are placed upon them.

This chapter offers guidelines for using visualization activities in the classroom and includes a variety of fun exercises to help children relearn this important skill. By so doing, children's writing, thinking, and enjoyment of reading will be positively impacted. More importantly, children will no longer have to be dependent upon the teacher to help them make decisions about "what should come next" in their writing. Through the tremendous power of their fertile imaginations, children will most likely be delighted to find that a whole army of wonderful ideas is very much alive somewhere in their minds, patiently waiting to be invited onto the page.

References

Escondido Union School District. *Mind's Eyes--Creating Mental Pictures from Pirated Words.* Escondido, CA: Escondido Union School District Board of Education, 1979.

Fredericks, Anthony. "Mental Imagery Activities to Improve Comprehension." *The Reading Teacher* 40 (October, 1986): 78-81.

Kolpakoff, Ivan. "Spontaneous Story Technique," unpublished manuscript, 1986.

Mundell, Dee Dee. *Mental Imagery: Do You See What I Say?* Oklahoma City, OK: Oklahoma State Department of Education, 1985.

Pressley, G. M. "Mental Imagery Helps Eight Year Olds Remember What They Read." *Journal of Educational Psychology* 68 (1976): 355-59.

Sprowl, Dale. "Guided Imagery in the Social Studies," in *Practical Ideas for Teaching Writing as a Process.* Sacramento, CA: California State Department of Education, 1986.

Chapter Ten

Role-Playing: Trying Life on for Size

In one classroom, a small boy is very hungry and watches while others eat voraciously, then smiles gratefully when a little girl shyly offers him half of her sandwich. In another classroom, a child proudly explains to her peers how she helped hundreds of slaves escape to freedom using the underground railroad. A glimpse into a third classroom finds a little girl leaving home for an exciting land far, far away, wondering if she'll ever again see her parents.

Transported by the evocative magic of role playing, these children put themselves in the places of other people. In so doing, they begin to learn how it feels to be someone else. Role plays like these, when used as tools in an Affective Language Arts program, can open a child's eyes to see and her heart to listen and understand.

The term "role playing" is used to refer to a type of play-acting in the classroom. By definition, it is a dramatic oral language activity in which children explore, in the most intimate way, the relationships of human living for the purpose of acquiring needed understandings and intrapersonal communication skills. But unlike children's free play, which is unstructured, role playing can occur under a teacher's guidance. Yet, unlike the more formally structured "drama" in which set lines are read or memorized, role playing unfolds rather spontaneously, without a predetermined script. It uses the dramatic elements of characterization and dialogue. Empathy is unusually intense in a role play because the actor is attempting to take on the internal characteristics of the person she is fashioning.

In the elementary classroom, role plays can grow out of current daily situations, problems, past episodes, or concepts that have implications for learning in the content areas. Sometimes the actual situation itself is the point of departure; other times, the teacher arranges the environment. Still another approach is to bring to life a beloved children's story in which there are relationships to be understood and rich opportunities for characterization.

105

But whether the point of departure is a real life experience, an important concept, a story, or a hypothetical event, the process through which learning can evolve the most dynamically is through role playing. This is the premise of this chapter: let children be actors and in acting they will learn. Let them engage in creative make-believe and they will discover what no teacher can teach them. Let them reflectively reenact arguments and they will develop insight and problem-solving skills. Let them simulate concepts and that which is unclear will be understood and that which is remote will become near and alive.

Role Playing to Reverse Bad Situations

Consider the following scenario that occurs daily, in various formats, on playgrounds across the country at recess:

Jimmy: I'm getting tired of playing kickball every day. Today why don't we play soccer instead?

Ryan: Nah, let's not play soccer. I don't know how to play soccer. Besides, soccer's a sissy game. Let's either play kick ball or baseball.

Jason: No. I like Jimmy's idea. Let's play soccer for a change. I'll be the captain and Jimmy can be the other captain. Let's choose up sides!

Ryan: No WAY! I have the ball, and you can't have it if you're going to play soccer!

Jimmy: I'm telling the teacher on you, you creep!

Ryan: Go ahead! She'll take my side!

Jason: All right, just give me the ball RIGHT NOW, or I'm gonna beat you up!

Ryan: Oh yeah? You and whose army?!

In the next few moments, of course, the argument escalates into fisticuffs between Ryan and Jason. Normally, the situation ends with angry feelings all around, as all three boys are reprimanded and/or sent to the principal's office by the teacher on recess duty. Everyone involved is thoroughly disgruntled and little, if anything, has been learned through the ordeal. The weary teacher and the three boys then go back to the classroom, still upset about what happened, but trying to put their minds to more academic concerns.

Role playing is the vehicle through which this unfortunate scenario might have been transformed into a dynamic oral language/social science lesson, not only for the boys involved, but for the rest of the class as well. Role playing can make positive use of an event that has just occurred, or even one that is fictitious, and make it immediately come alive for children to act out, and then think about and discuss. The activity can help children to consider the variety of alternative solutions available for handling problems and it can provide a deeper understanding about what causes crises to occur and what the effects are likely to be.

If a teacher wanted the children to gain insight from the aforementioned scenario, for example, he would need to guide his students through these steps:

1) Have a neutral observer from the class give his or her version of what happened;

2) Select children to play the roles of each person involved;

3) Ask the actors to take a few moments to prepare two skits: the first an actual reenactment of the situation as it actually happened, and a second skit that changes the outcome to a more positive, alternative ending to the conflict;

4) While the actors are preparing their skits, instruct the other children to, "Watch what the actors do and say. Try to put yourselves in their shoes and feel what they must be feeling. As you are watching, be thinking of some other ways in which the conflict could have been resolved."

5) Have the actors present their skits in the center of the classroom, surrounded by the other class members;

6) In sequence, reflect upon the differences in the two skits. Encourage other class members to contribute their alternative solutions to the problem;

7) Finally, discuss the "cause" and "effect" patterns in the two skits in terms of words or actions and resultant feelings.

For this particular playground scenario, Jason and Ryan, the two children who were involved in the original altercation, might be asked to play themselves in the reenactment or, to develop more insight into each other's point of view, they could also be asked to switch roles. The two boys' alternative solution to the conflict might turn out to be Jason conceding that they will play kick ball again, as they always do. Other class members who have watched both skits as dispassionate observers may have some different suggestions for them: Since Ryan has admitted that he doesn't know how to play soccer, why don't Jason and Jimmy teach him how to play? Or, why don't they set up a rotating schedule of playing kick ball one day, baseball the following day and soccer the next? Or, what would happen if they were to agree to toss a coin each day to decide which game was to be played?

Finally, through a guided reflective discussion, all the children in the class can begin to see exactly what turn of events caused the build-up of bad feelings that resulted in two friends having a fist fight. More importantly, they have themselves problem-solved some ways to lessen the chances of the unfortunate situation from recurring.

Role Playing Fictitious Events

While it is always a good idea to "catch the moment" in order to turn a bad situation into a good one, as in the previously mentioned scenario, it is also of great benefit to role play hypothetical situations to ward off certain problems *before* they occur. By being "tuned in" to certain age-related behavioral characteristics, the affective teacher can help children consider in advance certain situations that can often cause conflict. Consider these common scenes from elementary classroom life:

1) Cheryl, Jennifer, and Lisa are talking about Brittany's pajama party which is coming up on the weekend. Shirley strolls over to them and asks what is happening. At first they don't answer, but she presses them, so they tell her about the party, to which they know she would never be invited. Shirley blurts out, "Will you ask Brittany if I could come too?" The other girls just laugh at Shirley. She gets angry and calls them names.

2) Lunch money is missing from Zack's desk. Three boys, John, Mark, and Jesse say they know who took it, but they are afraid to tell. Zack confronts Mark and tells him if he doesn't tell who took his money, he will beat him up. Mark names an innocent child, Tam, who gives Zack his own lunch money and cries the rest of the day.

3) David's father has been sent to prison. A group of boys, Kevin, Josh, and Tim, taunt him about it, saying that his father is a murderer and a thief and David must be bad, too. David retaliates by making up lies about Kevin's mother, vowing to hurt Tim's little brother, and tripping Josh as he gets out of his seat. At recess, the three boys beat David up.

4) Returning to the room from lunch, Denise cannot find her pencil. She cries out in a loud voice, "WHO STOLE MY PENCIL?" When no one answers her question, she turns to Billy, who sits behind her, and takes one of the pencils from on top of his desk. "Hey. . . that's MY pencil!" Billy yells, and the two stage a heated tug-of-war over the pencil.

Having children act out the above situations and then reflect upon possible solutions provides an excellent forum for the verbalizations of their opinions, attitudes and emerging values. Additionally, consistent role playing of these and similar situations that they may soon encounter leads to four positive outcomes in the classroom:

1) The common problems of human interaction are personalized and made concrete so that children can clearly look at them and learn to proactively communicate their feelings about them;

2) When the entire class is involved in reflecting on possible alternative solutions, each student begins to take personal responsibility for *all* problems that arise in the class;

3) Sometimes problems are actually resolved before they ever occur through the group interaction and joint verbal commitments to solutions;

4) Finally, children come to understand that satisfactory solutions and positive changes in behavior are generally brought about through thoughtful discussion, rather than through impulsive reacting or aggression.

Role Playing Characters
in Children's Literature

When reading a book with many complex characters to a group of elementary children, role playing can help make the characters in the book come alive and help children to discover the relationship between what they are reading and their own lives.

This role playing of literature can be used with many favorite children's stories, such as *Peter Pan*. First of all, students work in pairs so that every child is involved. Partners are assigned, rather than allowing students to choose their own, to make sure that shy children are paired with more outgoing ones. Each pair of children is assigned one role as a character or to the author, or adaptor. The characters to be assigned for *Peter Pan*, for example, might be these:

Author	Wendy	Mrs. Darling
Captain Hook	Peter Pan	John
Mr. Darling	(1) pirate	Tinker Bell
Michael	Nana	the crocodile

After reading the story, all the children are then asked to study the text in light of their own character's personality and motivation during every part of the text. To clarify confusing points, pairs should be encouraged to consult the teacher as character to reader or reader to reader.

For the second part of the project, each pair draws up a list of questions--at least one question for each of the other characters in the book and one for the author. The questions might be those a reader would ask about the story, or even those a character might ask another character. Also, children should be urged to include some questions that go beyond the scope of the book, such as, "Peter, do you ever see Wendy anymore now that she's grown up?" or "Pirate, what do you think your punishment would have been for making people walk the plank if you had been caught?"

After this preparation has been completed, the children are ready for the role playing. Each pair wears character name tags so that class members will have no problem identifying the character they wish to question. Members of each pair take turns answering questions, although they are free to collaborate.

The teacher opens the session by asking the pair on her right the first question, "Mrs. Darling, how did you feel when you first learned that your children were gone from the nursery?" Then the children go around the circle, asking a question of a different character each time, unless someone wants to ask a follow-up question related to the previous one, such as, "If you were so sad about losing your children, Mrs. Darling, why didn't you call the police or the FBI?"

At first, expect the questions and answers to be somewhat stilted. Children may initially ask obvious, factual questions eliciting responses that rely solely on textual information, like, "Captain Hook, who cut off your hand?" As they get more into the spirit of role playing, however, they begin to ask more probing questions that get them interacting in more personal ways. For instance, Peter Pan might be asked, "Can you explain why it is that you don't want to grow up?" to which Peter might reply, "As a child, I can always do just exactly as I wish and fly around having fun. If I don't grow up I will never have to go out and get a job."

Another child counteracts with, "But won't it make you sad when all of your friends grow up and then you have no one to play with? I felt kind of like that when my sister got married and moved away!"

Similar role plays can be used with any number of children's books that contain a large cast of interesting characters that in some way reflect real life. Children not only gain a deeper appreciation of the characters and new insight into themselves, but they can actually bring the whole story to life, investigating one another's feelings and motives. At times they find themselves becoming frustrated, puzzled, and even angry, but always enlightened by the characters, who have become infinitely more memorable.

Role Playing Mock Debates and Interviews

Some years ago, Steve Allen used to host a program called "Meeting of the Minds" on which he would interview actors and actresses who would be playing the part of certain serious personalities of the past, such as Marie Curie or Sigmund Freud. A fascinating discussion would take place as Steve asked his pretend guests all those probing kinds of questions that we would like to ask those persons if they were alive in today's world.

Children, too, will thoroughly enjoy similar role plays in the classroom. Such an activity becomes a self-motivating reason to do historical research because such labor will, in this instance, lead to an exciting and challenging chance to become, for a while, a very famous person.

To prepare for the presentation, pairs of children must decide on a character from history, preferably one who is somewhat familiar to the other members of the class. The pair must then research the person thoroughly--using a wide spectrum of media including videos, if available--so that they can become acquainted with the facts of the person's life, significant events, his or her per-sonality or style of dress, opinions or political orientations, mannerisms, accent, and perhaps even memorize some of the quotations for which the person is best known. Among the historical figures who will work well for this activity would be:

Albert Einstein	Will Rogers	Mahatma Gandhi
Eleanor Roosevelt	Jesse Owens	Albert Schweitzer

Martin L. King, Jr.   Walt Disney   Abraham Lincoln
Harriette Tubman   Clara Barton   Amelia Earhart
John F. Kennedy   Paul Revere   King George III

Next, from the research the pair will draw up a list of provocative questions that would ask the historical figure to project how he or she would respond to current world issues or events. For example, Abraham Lincoln might be asked, "What are your thoughts on apartheid?" and his response would be largely based upon what the two researchers have discovered about Lincoln's contributions to the abolition of slavery, as well as their general understanding of the man's values.

For the presentation, the pair would decide who would play the part of the historical figure while the other would be the interviewer and ask the prearranged questions. After the interview session, the rest of the class, who have been taking notes, would be encouraged to ask their own questions of the person while the historical person tries to "think in character," and respond as the person might actually have responded.

The follow-up discussion is a time for the teacher and the students in the "audience" to try to clear up any obvious inconsistencies in the historical figure's responses by providing documented reasons for their objections. For example, if a student playing the role of Dr. Martin Luther King, Jr., has stated that he would support the war in Nicaragua, it would be important to remind the student about the implications of King's credo of passive resistance. Most importantly, during the reflective discussion there must be ample time to share new appreciations and insight into the historical figure in his or her now human, multi-dimensional form, and to explore any new questions or concerns that were raised.

Understanding Concepts through Simulation

Sometimes in the course of teaching children it becomes clear that all the verbalization in the world is failing to get across a certain important idea. The teacher knows that the abstract concept she is trying to convey is just not making any sense to her concrete, hands-on learners. In this situation it is sometimes advisable to pre-plan experiences where the children can actually simulate-- or vicariously play act--the concept. This acting out of an idea brings about a sense of discovery of just what the teacher is talking about as well as, in some cases, a visceral response that is not soon forgotten. Setting the stage for such a discovery often takes a good deal of time and effort, so it is therefore not feasible for every concept that is addressed. However, some concepts, such as the three described below, because of their complex nature, cannot truly be internalized by children without the total self-involvement that simulation affords.

Haves and Have Nots

Hopefully, most of the children that we teach will never have had the experience of going to bed hungry, but therefore they cannot always empathize fully with the two-thirds of the world's people who are starving. Children take for granted that their basic needs will be met and therefore grow up quite insulated from the desperate concerns of those who are more unfortunate. To give children a very basic glimpse of how inequitable it is to have the world's wealth so unevenly distributed, arrange with the school cafeteria to provide lunch for only one-third of your class for one day. For another third, bring small amounts of rice. The remaining third will have no lunch. To begin the simulation, allow children to draw straws numbered one, two, or three to determine what their lunch fare will be. Explain to them that they are taking part in a very important experiment and you will discuss the reasons later, but that they should write down all questions, feelings, and complaints that they have. There will, of course, be much moaning and groaning from those who have been given only a bowl of rice; more so from those children who have received no lunch. Make it clear to the "no lunch" group that they must not buy food from any other source, but that they may ask children with regular lunches to share, although those children are not obligated to do so. At a later time (when hunger and anger have abated), encourage the three groups of children to vent their feelings and share their written records. As the third group complains that being given nothing to eat was unfair, they are ready to hear that millions of people are starving daily. Have those children in the simulation who shared and those who received this charity share their feelings. Finally, allow children to brainstorm some things that they now feel could be done to ease world hunger.

Bartering

Economic concepts such as "supply and demand" and why money is used as an exchange medium are best conveyed through a simulation of bartering, much like people did in the days before money, as we know it, was used. For this activity, provide a variety of small toys and objects so that there are enough for each child in the class to be given five identical items. Distribute the same set of five items to several children--such as five paper clips to six children--but give sets of the more desirable items, like balloons or pencils, to only one child each. On the blackboard list all the items that have been distributed and the number of each that there are. Then tell children that they will have five minutes to trade their objects with as many other class members as they need to in order to end up with exactly what they want. When they have finished trading, ask them to sit down and recount the exchanges they had to go through to get what they have. Next ask children to orally share their bartering experiences. Some children who had items that were in abundant supply or of lesser intrinsic value (such as the paper clips) will have had a difficult time and will probably not have ended up with what they wanted. Other children, who started out with scarcer or more desirable items, will have happier tales to tell. Finally, discuss: What happened when there were too many items? What happened when someone had the most desirable items? In what way would money have made the trading easier? How do you think the worth, or value, of objects is determined?

Prejudice

Much has been written about some very intense simulations of prejudice that were carried to such an extreme that children were psychologically damaged when the teacher and perpetrators apparently began to lose touch with what was simulation and what was reality. Rest assured that a more reasoned simulation can have the desired effect without causing lasting harm.

For this simulation children need to be artificially categorized as "good" or "bad" according to some God-given trait over which they have no control, such as gender, or color of hair or eyes. If eye color is chosen, for example, children would be told that those children with brown eyes would be first to go to recess and the drinking fountain. Throughout the day they would receive many other small privileges. When children question this favoritism, tell them that brown-eyed children are receiving differential treatment because some ignorant people might believe that they are simply "better" than those with blue or green eyes. Because of the anger and frustration that this situation quite naturally produces, the activity should not continue for more than a morning or afternoon, at most. After that time, the blackboard should be divided into two columns. First have the brown-eyed children share their feelings and reactions, and then the non-brown-eyed. Tell children that while this was only a rather unhappy game, some people really do judge people on the basis of such superficial traits in real life. Discuss how people really *should* be evaluated and how this simulation might help these people who judge others on traits that they can do nothing about. Finally, ask children to elaborate on how this activity might change the way they behave toward other people in the future.

Other important concepts to be assimilated can also be understood on a deeper level by following this rudimentary framework for guiding simulation activities:

1) Strip the concept to its most basic form and decide upon what methods and materials would be most effective in getting the point across. Allow a sufficient block of time for the activity, and be sure to communicate to parents and administrators ahead of time exactly what you are trying to do.

2) With minimal explanations, have children act out the concept. Ask them to write down questions and feelings about what is going on.

3) Let children describe what happened in their own words. Explain the concept they were simulating and ask them, "What did you learn about _____?" "Who do you think might benefit from also doing this activity?" "Did you think of any *new* problems to be solved as a result of doing this activity?"

Summary

We know that young children are concrete, hands-on learners whose preoccupation is mainly with themselves. This should not be cause for dismay, for it is exactly in this search for self-understanding that children start to make sense of the world around them. And because this is so, there is no more effective approach to the task of teaching interpersonal communication skills than by first observing the way children orient themselves to their environment as they seek self-understanding through role playing.

Seeking to understand who they are and what their relationship to other people, situations, and concepts are, children will role play life as they see it. Using their imagination, they create make-believe worlds that, like a prism, illuminate and clarify in miniature the meanings and values they are discovering in living with other human beings. Role-playing, they push themselves out into the world of others and in so doing, take stock of their own values and ideas. Deeper insights develop as children stretch the boundaries of their own life space.

In short, through role playing children begin to try on life for size, but they do so in the relative safety of an affective classroom environment where it always fits each child perfectly.

Chapter Eleven

The Integrated Teaching Unit: Tying It All Together

Many years ago when I was doing my undergraduate work in teacher education, the "buzz word" was UNIT. The unit was touted to be THE hottest, most innovative way to teach and if you didn't know how to teach using this approach, you were led to believe that you would quickly be considered a teaching "dinosaur."

Teaching by means of the unit, which was developed in the John Dewey Schools of the late twenties and early thirties, is still alive and well today and by most accounts, considered an effective strategy for fulfilling the instructional goals of the modern elementary curriculum. It also seems suited to the objectives of an Affective Language Arts program because it so effectively encourages individual creativity and language development. Yet the field of social studies has long claimed the teaching unit as its own exclusive property. How, then, is it possible for unit teaching to serve as a vehicle through which to more expansively teach the language arts as well as the content areas, such as social studies?

Regardless of the separate categories by which they are normally organized, the content areas and language arts are integrally related. Language in its four basic forms--reading, writing, listening, and speaking--is the means by which children obtain and convey information about *any* subject in the curriculum. On the other hand, the content areas provide the substance which serves to stimulate children's need to communicate. Moreover, thought processes central to learning, such as remembering, organizing, and evaluating information, cut across the entire curriculum. Organizing themes in children's literature and history, for example, call upon children to collect information, consider its worth, and then arrange that information into some kind of logical form. Additionally, recent research has made it increasingly evident that children learn communication skills not by the artificial practice found in most language textbooks, but by engaging in real "languaging" activities that allow them to

117

listen, speak, read, and write in natural and meaningful contexts (Halliday, 1982).

The content areas are abundantly rich with ideas and concepts that can come to life through the use of a variety of language arts activities. Accordingly, there is growing insight into the premise that substantive and varied language activities used for content area instruction actually serve to clarify and strengthen children's understanding of the subject matter (Tovey and Weible, 1981, 1979; Dolgin, 1981). And as children hear, talk, read and write about topics in that content area through the integrating vehicle of a unit, they become thoroughly involved in making sense of the material, relating it to what they already know, and formulating some brand new ideas of their own. It is highly likely that careful integration of the two spheres will result in mutual reinforcement and increased facility in *both* areas, as well as creating children who are sensitive to each other and eager learners.

Goals of an Integrated Unit

"Unit teaching" simply means that the chosen subject matter is organized into one complete whole, rather than taught as a series of isolated subjects. The body of knowledge to be conveyed to children is related, integrated, and correlated with memorable experiences so that the intellectual, social, emotional, and physical needs of children can be met on an individual basis (Smith, 1979). Through unit use, the teacher can develop group concepts without sacrificing the individual development of each child. The bottom line is that unit teaching can be viewed as a cross-curricular method of teaching that has the best chance of developing both the understanding of concepts and the creative intrapersonal communication skills that are needed in an Affective Language Arts program.

An effective integrated teaching unit should have these distinguishing characteristics:
1) It has a central, dominating theme;
2) It is based on the needs of a particular group of children;
3) It is planned cooperatively with that group of children;
4) It cuts across subject lines;
5) It provides a wide range of experiences so that children can grasp the concepts according to their own level of maturity;

6) It develops critical thinking skills;
7) It guides children toward creative thinking and self-realization;
8) It provides open-ended experiences which allow children to problem-solve;
9) It fosters good human relationships among children;
10) It requires a large block of time.

Planning an Integrated Unit

Often a unit of study is launched when a question is raised by the children in a particular classroom. The question might address some practical problem of society that could be adjusted for study at the elementary school level. Such a problem might be local, such as "What can we do to increase the ecological awareness of the people of Greenville so that Bond Lake might again be clean enough for swimming?" Or the question could be more global in nature, such as, "How did the problems that Blacks encountered before the Civil Rights Movement of the '50s compare with the Apartheid Policy in South Africa today?" These kinds of questions require in-depth exploration and discussion in order to develop the understandings necessary to really answer the questions; children must obtain a great deal of information, but it goes much deeper than that. Children will also need to become aware of the feelings and attitudes of people, discover how values, appreciations and character are developed in people and learn how to empathize with them so that the question can be seen and felt from a variety of viewpoints. The process of answering the question, then, becomes more important than the "solution" itself. For it is in the process of exploration that a unit provides that children come face to face with situations that force them to develop sensitivity to others while learning how to make their own decisions. In short, by using a unit approach to answer children's self-initiated questions, they learn about themselves and how to live with other human beings.

When beginning a unit, the major task of the teacher is to stimulate all the children in the class to be invested intellectually, socially, emotionally, and physically in the topic to be studied. Superficially, the interest would seem to be already there, as the original question has emanated from the group as a whole. But a deeper motivation stems from the act of establishing a sense of group mission that will ensure cooperative effort on the part of the teacher

and students over a protracted period of time. Involving
ALL the children is of vital concern and is best addressed
by thoughtfully planning a large variety of ways for children to set about exploring the question so that each child
can learn in the manner that he or she learns best.

To plan a unit which has the greatest chance of
deeply involving all children in the exploration of the
question, the teacher must be well planned. First of all, she
needs to be thoroughly versed in the subject matter, or the
unit will certainly lack direction, focus and cohesion if
she "learns as she goes." Secondly, she needs to outline the
unit and gather relevant materials by following a
guideline such as the one provided by these nine questions:

1.   Why did you select this particular unit?
     ○ Did it spring from questions the children have
     asked?
     ○ Are *you* interested in it?
     ○ Is the topic timely?
     ○ Are materials available for use by or with the
     children?
2.   What are the global cognitive and affective
     objectives you have in mind as important in
     developing through the unit?
     ○ What are your long-range objectives?
     ○ What are the children's objectives?
     ○ What are the outcomes you anticipate?
3.   What are some motivational ways you can intro-
     duce the unit that will enlist the commitment of
     ALL learners?
4.   What are the principles, understandings, or
     general information you want the children to
     come away with?
5.   What activities and/or experiences can you plan
     that will span the entire curriculum and arouse
     the interest of each learner?
     ○ What community resources (e.g., guest speakers)
     are available?
     ○ What trade books can be gathered on the
     topic?
     ○ What research can be correlated with the
     topic?
     ○ What field trips could be planned?
     ○ What creative experiences could enhance the
     topic? (Drawings, paintings, murals, recipes,
     poems, plays, songs, folk tales, dances, etc.)
     ○ What other language experiences could be
     planned? (Debates, buzz groups, mock game

shows, panel discussions, choral readings, discussion groups, etc.)

6. What culminating activity can you plan that will provide closure to the whole unit? (Dramatic production, assembly program, parents' night, feast, party, excursion, etc.)
7. What materials can you use as resources? (Community members, learning centers, bulletin boards, filmstrips, videos, movies, textbooks, etc.)
8. What materials can be provided for the children? (Trade books on different levels, commercial games, songs, teacher-made games, computer simulations, etc.)
9. How will you evaluate the effectiveness of the unit?
   - Criterion tests (pre- and post)?
   - Attitude scales?
   - Daily observation?
   - Individual conferences?
   - Anecdotal records?
   - Essays requiring analysis?
   - Creative work springing from the topic?

Constructing a Curriculum Web

When all of the above questions have been considered, the teacher will be ready to organize the materials and activities for the duration of the unit. A graphic way to do this is through the use of a device known as the curriculum web (Moore et al., 1986). This framework helps the teacher to think of many possible ideas for the unit and then provides a visual structure which aids in the daily planning of the unit. To construct such a web, the teacher simply writes the question that the children have asked in the center of a large sheet of poster paper or tag board. Then he lets obvious subtopics branch off from the question by brainstorming available materials and activities that could be included to span all areas of the curriculum for each subtopic. For example, the following would be a sketch of a curriculum web for the question, "How are modern times rooted in the Middle Ages?"

**Social Life
Activities**
Diorama of medieval life
Reenact a joust
Construct a medieval
   castle
Display of medieval garb
Crafts popular during
   the era
Medieval feast

Books
Knights of Old
Folk Tales of the
   Middle Ages
Anne: Child of the
   Middle Ages
Life in a castle

**Culture
Activities**
Tell stories of knights
   going to battle
Research medieval
   religions
Perform a medieval skit
Lecture by members of
   historical society
Sing ballads from the
   Middle Ages
Perform folk dances of
   the era
Make individual
   Coats-of-Arms

Books
Culture of the
   Middle Ages
Growing Up in the
   Dark Ages
Medieval Ballads

**HOW ARE MODERN TIMES
ROOTED IN THE MIDDLE AGES?**

**Political Issues
Activities**
Maps of ancient
   boundaries
Design a feudal pyramid
Computer simulation:
   Feudalism

Books
The Feudal System
The Dark Ages: A
   Political Perspective
The Feudal Pyramid

Language Activities
Research history
   of languages
Trace language to roots
Explore worlds of
   Middle Ages

Books
Tracing Our Language
Language in the
   Middle Ages
A Brief History
   of Languages

Teaching an Integrated Unit

If a teacher were to decide to explore the unit based upon the curriculum web just presented, his objectives might be to acquaint children with the people, institutions, customs, and events of that thousand year period, and to help children to recognize, through this encounter, that some aspects of modern society have their roots in ideas and events of the Middle Ages. A variety of multimedia activities and cross-curricular experiences could be included to capture children's attention, to stimulate their thinking, and of course, to promote development in reading, writing, speaking, and listening skills.

From the start, children would be actively involved in discussing the proposed course of study. A teacher-written overview of concepts, vocabulary, and instructional goals might provide a springboard for reflection and a sharing of more new questions. Children would be encouraged to think about what facets of the unit might especially appeal to them, to share any prior knowledge about the topic, and to speculate on the importance of the unit to their own lives.

The dominant vehicle for unifying the content area of social studies with the language arts might, in this case, consist of a newspaper project in which children must report with as much historical accuracy as possible, life as it was in the Middle Ages. Although children would be well aware that newspapers were nonexistent in the Middle Ages, they could still use that well-known medium to convey their knowledge about the era to others. This extended project would involve children in a variety of language-centered activities, from seeking and gathering information to evaluating the importance of that information. Although the medieval newspaper would be the focal point of the unit, a number of other activities could be closely linked to it. These activities might include lectures on medieval life by costume-garbed members of a local historical society and demonstrations of arts and crafts that were popular during the era. Throughout the unit, classroom interactions would be varied, allowing children to work individually as well as in small and large groups.

Children's work would be evaluated continuously. Sometimes the evaluation might take the form of direct oral feedback to a child on work-in-progress via an informal conference. At other times, the evaluation could be offered as written comments or a grade on completed, formally submitted tasks.

Students' listening skills would be tapped by videos, filmstrips and books read to them about medieval life. Children would discuss social happenings of the nobility, the clergy and peasants, and simulate these events through computer programs. They would also talk about the economic and political issues of the time. These discussions, supplemented by films, computer programs, stories, and skits, would take on added importance because children would be aware that the knowledge gleaned would soon be transmitted to others through their newspaper articles and illustrations.

Throughout the unit, the most valuable sources for developing communication proficiency would undoubtedly be the children themselves as they interact with each other and the teacher. Effective listening and speaking are most critical when children are engaging in the hands-on projects that could be offered: the construction of a small-scale medieval castle, the creation of a personal coat of arms, and the assembling of several displays of medieval tools, clothing, personages, and scenes.

As children progressively gather more information and increase their understanding of the unit's concepts, they would be asked to share this new knowledge through formally and informally structured presentations; for example, groups of children might take turns role-playing different medieval scenarios. During these language activities children would be dramatically increasing their communication skills while literally immersing themselves in medieval life and tradition.

Children's awareness and appreciation of cultural and linguistic differences could be heightened with this unit by tracing the Spanish and English languages back to their Romance and Germanic roots. Children would also be exploring the different functions of *all* languages by using language for a number of different purposes: as they describe and reenact a sports event, such as jousting; as they invent and tell stories laced with imaginary episodes of knights going into battle; or as they recount and explain the symbolic information in their coats-of-arms.

By using the language arts in this wide variety of ways, children would be exercising their burgeoning understanding of concepts while stretching their intrapersonal communication abilities as well.

One added bonus to the unit approach is that, because of its interdisciplinary nature, the teacher need not worry that one isolated subject is "suffering" when the class is concentrating so intensely on the concepts of another isolated subject. Therefore, any unit need not be terminated until: 1) all the resources for the unit have been depleted, or 2) children's questions have been answered to their satisfaction and the teacher's objectives have been met, or 3) the interest of the class has waned, which may well never happen!

Literature-Based Units

An equally valid way to approach an integrated unit of study is through literature. Using this approach, instead of content area material being taught through the language arts, children's literature is the focus and is enhanced by spilling its message over into all crannies of the curriculum. Every goal of an Affective Language Arts program can be accomplished using children's literature in this way: listening improves as children listen purposefully, with rapt attention, to stories they grow to love; speaking improves as they eagerly discuss their reactions to the story. Many pieces of children's literature are excellent models for children's writing, and they can inspire students to try their hands at creating their own stories. And, of course, because they are not fraught with the idea of tedious skill development and stilted, controlled vocabulary, children's books are those that can most easily motivate children to read--for their own enjoyment.

Not only does children's literature provide a holistic framework for the development of listening, speaking, writing, and reading, but it can also be the cornerstone of a unit that provides stimulating lessons in all the other areas of the curriculum. This can be seen in the example of a unit centered around the book for primary-aged youngsters, *The Gingerbread Boy* (see page 126).

Summary

The teaching unit has been around for many years, but has traditionally been thought of as the exclusive domain of the social sciences. In light of what we now know to be true of the need to integrate the language arts into meaningful contexts, the unit would seem the natural vehicle through which this integration could best flourish. With careful planning on the part of the teacher, the very important questions that children ask can become dominating themes for language-centered units that cross every boundary of the curriculum, providing stimulating experiences that totally immerse children in the process of answering their own questions. And through this special process, children learn to empathize with another's point of view and crystallize their *own* viewpoints at the same time. They learn to work cooperatively in small groups, large groups, and by themselves under the teacher's watchful guidance. The variety of activities offered allows all children, regardless of their ability, to understand at some level the major concepts of the unit, according to their own styles of learning.

Math
Make gingerbread cookies following a recipe and measuring ingredients.
Discuss ordinal numbers that could be used in the story: first he ran from the bird, second from the rabbit, etc.

Art
Paint a sequential mural of events in the story.
Make papier-mache masks of characters in the story for use in retelling.
Make a diorama of a favorite scene from the story.

THE GINGERBREAD BOY

Language Arts
Have children tape their version of the story.
Compare the story with The Bun (Brown).
Create a skit of the story.

Science/Health
Research what all animals in the story really eat.
Discuss how gingerbread cookies can fit into a balanced diet.

Music
Make up a song about the Gingerbread Boy.
Listen to "Peter and the Wolf" while doing other activities.
Discuss what instruments could be used for animals in "The Gingerbread Boy."

Social Studies
Make a topographical map of the Gingerbread Boy's journey.
Discuss the natural enemies of all the animals in the story.
Discuss the cookie's behavior to his parents.

This integration of the curriculum can also spring from the exciting world of children's books. Any one of a number of excellent selections from children's literature could be expanded to include tangential lessons spanning the entire curriculum, while enhancing and deepening children's understanding of and appreciation for those books.

The integrated unit--whether germinating from a child's question or from children's literature--has one overriding characteristic that would earn it a place of honor in an Affective Language Arts program: this unique approach makes the learner a vitally active participant in the learning process. For too many years educators have labored under the arrogant assumption that students must learn solely from their teachers. It takes only one well-planned unit to graphically illustrate to all who care to observe that yes, children do learn from the teacher, but they can also learn many, many important things by themselves and from each other.

References

Brown, Marcia. *The Bun.* New York: Harcourt Brace Jovanovich, 1972.

Dolgin, A. B. "Teach Social Studies through Writing." *Social Studies* 72 (January-February 1981): 8-10.

Halliday, M. A. K. "Three Aspects of Children's Language Development: Learning Language, Learning through Language, and Learning about Language." In Y. Goodman, M. Hausler and D. Strickland (eds.). *Oral and Written Language Development Research: Impact on the Schools.* National Council of Teachers of English, 1982.

Holdsworth, William Curtis. *The Gingerbread Boy.* New York: Farrar, Straus, & Giroux, 1968.

Moore, David W., Sharon A. Moore, Patricia M. Cunningham, and James W. Cunningham. *Developing Readers and Writers in the Content Areas.* New York: Longman, 1986.

Smith, Frank. *Writing and the Writer.* New York: Holt, Rinehart and Winston, 1982.

Smith, James A. *Creative Teaching of the Social Studies in the Elementary School.* Boston: Allyn and Bacon, Inc., 1979.

Tovey, D. R., and T. D. Weible. "Social Studies, Thought, and Language." *Social Studies* 70 (July-August, 1979): 167-69.

Tovey, D. R., and T. D. Weible. "Extending Social Studies Understanding through Language Activities." *Social Education* 45 (May 1981): 367-69.

Chapter Twelve

Learning Stations:
Child-Centered Language Learning

Mr. Trainor has just been assigned his very first class--a fourth grade--and he surveys his eager charges with mounting dismay. He finds that within his class are Jesus, age seven; Michael, age eight; Dorothy, age nine; Debra, age ten; and Martha, age eleven. There is one other seven-year-old like Jesus, a half dozen eight-year-olds, like Michael, and almost a dozen nine-year-olds like Dorothy, as well as a couple more eleven-year-olds, like Martha. The ages of Mr. Trainor's students just mentioned are not their chronological ages, but their mental ages, or the ages at which they are currently functioning intellectually. This intellectual spread is not at all unusual in a fourth grade classroom, and the differences of the children do not stop there. Mr. Trainor also finds that his students vary widely in the styles in which they learn best, and the pace at which they can assimilate concepts. He also notices an enormous discrepancy in the kinds of activities and reading materials that appeal to the children of this class, as well as their command, in some cases, of English as a second language.

But poor Mr. Trainor's curriculum is all planned for his fourth-graders; his textbooks were purchased with the "average" nine-year-old in mind, and he is duly expected to get all the children ready for fifth grade by the end of the year. This is the dilemma of teachers everywhere; Mr. Trainor's class is no exception. And as long as we ignore the realities and act as though the differences do not exist, we will ALWAYS continue to struggle with the dilemma, and neither carte blanche promotion nor a return to systematically retaining "underachievers" will make it go away.

The development and use of learning stations is one effective method of achieving some measure of individualization of instruction. It is not intended as a panacea to all classroom problems and it will certainly not satisfy *all* the needs of *all* the learners in a classroom. But it can be an effective approach for moving children away from rigidly uniform whole-group learning experiences targeted to the "average" child in a classroom, and toward student-selected, individual and small group learning experiences.

The learning station is *not* meant to replace the teacher and his humanizing influence in the classroom, nor can a station be expected to be the prime source of instruction in the classroom. It can, however, be used in an Affective Language Arts program to provide the necessary reinforcement for expansion on, and enrichment of, those concepts and skills which have previously been introduced by the teacher. Moreover, a well-planned learning center is often so attractive and inviting that even the most reluctant learner is easily lured to it. Children, before the teacher's very eyes, become intensely involved in exploring a wide variety of interesting topics in the way that youngsters feel the most comfortable--by actively experiencing them, at their own pace, through their senses.

Pre-planning for a Learning Station

In developing educationally sound, stimulating learning stations which have the best chance of meeting the needs of the children in a particular class, the secret is pre-planning. Each center should be carefully planned with specific objectives in mind for the need of the range of learners in the class. Each center must not only meet the needs of the average and slow learners, but challenge the intellectually talented as well.

The following criteria are helpful to consider when first attempting to construct learning stations (Smith, 1979):

1) A learning station should have specific objectives. A survey of student needs through pre-testing may be the teacher's best guide to the type of center to be developed. First, the teacher must determine the center's major objective. Second, the teacher must decide upon a variety of activities which will help children to realize that goal. Finally, the teacher needs to plan a method of evaluating whether or not the children have met the objective. For example, the purpose of one learning station might be to familiarize children with folk tales from other countries. The teacher's specific objective might be stated like this: "As a result of the activities in this learning station, the children will be able to write a new folk tale based upon the fictitious customs of a country which the child has created."

2) A learning station must be well equipped. In order to present a broad scope of multisensory activities which will best accommodate the range of learning styles in a classroom, a wide variety of materials must be gathered. For instance, a folk tale center would need a globe, maps of the various countries represented, trade books of folk tales from other lands, filmstrips, a tape recorder for the oral telling of stories, puppets and a puppet theater in which to perform folk tales, shoe boxes for dioramas, writing paper and utensils, encyclopedias, a dictionary, a file of duplicating masters, and a costume box with costumes to inspire skits, and packets for individual contracts.

3) A learning station should be colorful and attractive. Whether the intent of the learning station is skills development, enrichment, or sheer fun (or, ideally, a combination of all three), inviting packaging will enhance the appeal and greatly increase children's motivation to spend time there. The overall impression children should have as they approach the station is one of very high visual attractiveness, cohesion and harmony. Even if "beauty is only skin deep," the look of the station should grab children's attention and make them eager to explore its contents.

4) A learning station must be functional. A functional station is well aligned with the purposes of the Affective Language Arts program. This means that the station must be well-planned in keeping with the station objectives, inviting enough to attract children, and equipped with enough language activities and equipment so that all children may independently learn from working in it without direct teacher supervision. There must also be provisions for small groups of children to work together cooperatively.

5) The activities in a learning station must facilitate self-learning. Once the overall instructions and objectives for the learning station have been explained by the teacher to the entire class, children should be able to be in charge of their own learning by means of contracts between the teacher and student, records kept by the teacher and student, and evaluations in which children play an active role. Additionally, many activities may be designed so that they are programmed or involve self-checking, so that children can begin to monitor their own progress.

Arranging a Learning Station

The best room arrangement technique, particularly when a teacher is planning to use more than one learning station at a time, is to make small clusters, or "learning pockets" around the periphery of the room, but there is really no right or wrong way to arrange a learning station. The teacher must simply use his imagination and resources to make the center physically fit the needs of his students within the constraints of his own classroom.

The flat-topped, individual desks or large four- to eight-student tables with separate chairs are the most convenient to use for learning stations, but slanting desks can be used for individual study centers or individual activities. Also, slanting desks can be effectively used as writing surfaces when the stations are located on shelves or walls. Games could be played on an old shag rug on the floor. Other pieces of furniture that can assist in organizing the station would be bookcases, dividers, book racks, and painting easels. Overstuffed chairs, a couch, or bean bag chairs will also add to the physical appeal of a station and might be used for a reading or library corner. Bulletin boards should be an integral part of a station, and bright contact paper and paint could be used to liven up drab pieces of furniture. Children are usually happy to assist in these refurbishing chores and such tasks add to their sense of ownership of the learning station.

Scheduling for Learning Stations

The amount of time to be scheduled at learning stations depends upon what kinds of activities are contained in the station and how the activities have been integrated across the curriculum. Obviously, there is no right or wrong scheduling plan as long as the teacher feels comfortable with the time spent in the station, the children are actively engaged in learning through station activities, and the needs of the entire range of students are being met.

Schedules provide children with an outline for using their time beneficially. Moreover, the children develop a sense of security as well as a sense of responsibility by keeping track of what they will be doing daily at the station. There are two basic systems for scheduling students into stations, by rotation and by contract.

Rotational

When multiple stations are being used in a classroom, rotational scheduling is a good introductory format because it allows the children to sample a bit of everything that is offered in the classroom. Using this scheduling format, stations are set up around the room and children can be managed by use of an "assignment wheel" such as this one:

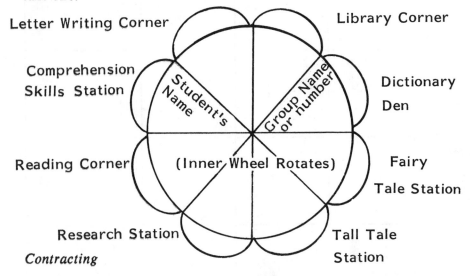

Letter Writing Corner   Library Corner

Comprehension
Skills Station   Student's Name   Group Name or number   Dictionary
Den

Reading Corner   (Inner Wheel Rotates)   Fairy
Tale Station

Research Station   Tall Tale
Station

Contracting

A "contract" is a written agreement between student and teacher, and can be drawn up for each child after a new learning station has initially been introduced to a group of children. Each child decides exactly what he would like to accomplish in a station in order to meet the specific goals that the teacher has established for the station. Student-teacher conferences are arranged in which the child shares orally what he has agreed to do in his written contract. By this method, children learn to monitor their own work habits and use of time. Often children put too much in their contract and are then unable to complete the work by the date to which they have agreed. The teacher then needs to help the child to realistically determine a reasonable amount of work to be included on a contract.

A simple contract might be put onto a ditto master and made available within the learning station. Page 134 shows an example of a learning station contract.

CONTRACT FOR: _____

Date Started: _____

Activity	Comments	Activity	Comments

Date completed: _____

Teacher signature: _____

Student signature: _____

Comments: _____

_____

_____

_____

Record Keeping for Learning Stations

In order to properly evaluate each child's progress in a learning station, the teacher must keep adequate accounts of what each child is doing. This is a continuous process involving both the teacher and the child. Records show the kind and the amount of work a child accomplishes. An evaluation, on the other hand, reflects the quality of that work. The type of records that need to be kept will vary depending upon the areas covered by the learning station.

One common type of record keeping for a station is the student file of completed work. For this file, the teacher and child set priorities for work to be completed and then establish a schedule for daily, weekly, and monthly activities. To each file is attached a teacher comment sheet. Comments are written in the file every week so that children can modify their work habits. These comments also help to prepare the teacher for the student-teacher conferences.

A chart showing what each child has read is another record keeping device that is of supreme importance in a learning station. Because the information on this chart is a tangible reflection of accomplishment, it serves to satisfy the child's need for recognition of progress and achievement. It also encourages recreational reading in areas that may have been new to the child. The reading chart should be displayed in or near the learning station so that the children themselves become responsible for updating the record as more and more books are completed.

Records can also be kept for a station that is accentuating specific skill development. For this type of record keeping, the teacher needs to list the specific skill objectives on the student record sheet. Each station should have a sheet that lists all tasks, each one of which would be designed to reinforce a certain skill. Older children would be able to check off the tasks as they are completed. Younger children can color a square or have the teacher check off the task. An example of a record-evaluation sheet for a set of tasks in a learning station is on page 136.

Sample Evaluation of Student Work at Station

Marking System:
+ understands concept; assign to more challenging task
/ meeting objective; continue through task
- needs assistance, reteaching

TITLE OF ACTIVITY: Dictionary Teasers

Objective: Using the dictionary, the student will be able to sort sets of twelve words into the categories of animals, plants, or inanimate objects.

Date	Name:	1	2	3	4*	5	6	7	8	9*	10
Comments:											

*Tasks that require teacher correction.

Suggestion: Use graph paper to make record sheets.

Holistic Evaluation in a Learning Station

Evaluation of a child's work at a learning station is much more than a letter grade at the completion of some self-selected station activities; it is an ongoing, continuous affair. Evaluations included on all record sheets in the form of comments and self-correcting materials, give children immediate feedback for self-appraisal. During student-teacher conferences children offer and receive suggestions for improvement. "Spot checking," too, is an important evaluation tool as children are actively involved in independent learning. As the teacher makes observations, he writes anecdotal comments on the child's work folder immediately. Additionally, children may share projects orally with the whole class and relate their new discoveries and experiences, giving the teacher an even greater insight into what his students have assimilated.

But evaluation in an Affective Language Arts program means much more than just looking at children's cognitive accomplishments. The affective teacher is interested in the growth of the whole child: the rate, the process, the child's reactions and attitudes, his products, and any new behaviors that have developed in the child as a result of working in that station.

There are several kinds of positive attitudes and behaviors that ideally should evolve from a learning station experience:

- Children will have worked in groups, cooperatively and productively.
- Children will have grown in independent work habits.
- Children will have demonstrated increased ability to plan their time.
- Children will have discovered some creative new ways to work together and by themselves.
- Children will have explored some new areas of interest.
- Children will have participated in the evaluation of their own work.

Based upon these expectations, the evaluation form on the next page might help the teacher to look more thoroughly at how the "whole child" has benefited as a result of working at the learning station.

Summary

Learning stations work in an Affective Language Arts program because it is a truism that no two children are exactly alike, and the station allows the teacher to develop a variety of inviting activities and materials which actually cater to individual differences. The affective teacher in today's schools is sensitive to the vast differences in ability, learning styles, and interests of her pupils; indeed, it is not uncommon for five or six grade

Evaluation of Child's Learning Station Experience

Student: _____

Date : _____

	Rating Scale	Comments
	1 2 3 4 5	
	Low High	

A.   How well does this child:

1. Follow oral & written
   directions? .... 1 2 3 4 5   _____

2. Complete station tasks?
   .... 1 2 3 4 5   _____

3. Interact with other children in a
   helping or sharing
   situation? .... 1 2 3 4 5   _____

4. Take responsibility for group
   learning? .... 1 2 3 4 5   _____

5. Use his/her time? .... 1 2 3 4 5   _____

6. Explore new areas of
   interest? .... 1 2 3 4 5   _____

7. Ask questions that go beyond the scope
   of the activity? .... 1 2 3 4 5   _____

8. Communicate thoughts and ideas to
   classmates? .... 1 2 3 4 5   _____

9. Devise ways to use materials or
   make suggestions for the
   stations? .... 1 2 3 4 5   _____

10. Complete plans made in student-
    teacher conferences?
    .... 1 2 3 4 5   _____

Comments: _____

_____

levels of ability and achievement to be represented in a single classroom! This reality tends to make assignments targeted to the class as a whole a waste of time for many children. There is no longer any justifiable reason for every child in a class to always learn the same thing, in the same way, in the same amount of time, from the same material, with the same amount of interest. The learning station seems to be one viable solution to this dilemma.

Learning stations build stimulating group experiences into the learning process. The child is offered these group situations, but is also offered opportunities to work independently. By working together cooperatively, children learn how to respectfully exchange ideas and share the responsibility for learning.

If, in the development of an exciting and inviting learning station, the teacher is attentive to individual interests, learning styles, ability differences, and the range of achievement in the class, the learning station will probably be a success. When in addition, each child is involved in setting goals, the selection of the learning activities and materials, the pace at which she will work, and the evaluation of that work, then success is virtually assured. These successful experiences will, in turn, enhance the self-concept of the child. Too, the chances are then excellent that the teacher will be forever "hooked" on the learning station approach to learning as an affective way to help meet the needs of *all* children.

References

Blitz, Barbara. *The Open Classroom: Making It Work*. Boston: Allyn and Bacon, 1973.

Gagne, Robert. *The Conditions of Learning*. 3rd ed. New York: Holt, Rinehart & Winston, 1977.

Johnston, Hiram, et al. *The Learning Center Ideabook*. Boston: Allyn and Bacon, 1978.

Musgrave, Ray G. *Individualized Instruction: Teaching Strategies Focusing on the Learner*. Boston: Allyn and Bacon, 1975.

Petreshene, Susan S. *Complete Guide to Learning Centers*. Palo Alto, CA: Pendragon House, 1978.

Rapport, Virginia, ed. *Learning Centers: Children on Their Own*. Washington, DC: Association for Childhood Education International, 1970.

Smith, James A. *Creative Teaching of Social Studies in the Elementary School*. Boston: Allyn and Bacon, 1979.

Appendix

Appendix

Appendix One
Predictable Books

Predictable books: language patterns, repetitive words, phrases, questions, story patterns, cumulative tales, numerical sequences, days of week, months, hierarchies, songs, and rhymes.

Aardema, Verna, reteller. *Why Mosquitoes Buzz in People's Ears.* Illustrated by Leo and Diane Dillon. Dial, 1975.
Aardema, Verna, reteller. *Bringing the Rain to Kapiti Plain: A Nandi Tale.* Illustrated by Beatriz Vidal. Dial, 1981.
Adams, Pam. *This Old Man.* Grossett, 1974.
Alain. *One, Two, Three, Going to the Sea.* Scholastic, 1964.
Aliki. *Go Tell Aunt Rhody.* Macmillan, 1974.
Aliki. *Hush Little Baby.* Prentice-Hall, 1968.
Aliki. *My Five Senses.* Crowell, 1962.
Allen, Pamela. *Bertie and the Bear.* Coward, 1984.
Asch, Frank. *Monkey Face.* Parents, 1977.
Balian, Lorna. *The Animal.* Abingdon, 1972.
Balian, Lorna. *Where in the World is Henry?* Bradbury, 1972.
Bang, Molly. *Ten, Nine, Eight.* Greenwillow, 1983.
Barchas, Sarah E. *I Was Walking Down the Road.* Scholastic, 1975.
Barrett, Judi. *Animals Should Definitely NOT Wear Clothing.* Atheneum, 1970.
Barton, Byron. *Buzz, Buzz, Buzz.* Macmillan, 1973.
Baten, Helen and Barbara Von Malnar. *I'm Going to Build a Supermarket One of These Days.* Holt, 1970.
Battaglia, Aurelius. *Old Mother Hubbard.* Golden, 1972.
Baum, Arline and Joseph Baum. *One Bright Monday Morning.* Random House, 1962.
Becker, John. *Seven Little Rabbits.* Illustrated by Barbara Cooney. Walker, 1973.
Beckman, Kaj. *Lisa Cannot Sleep.* Watts, 1969.
Bellah, Melanie. *A First Book of Sounds.* Golden, 1963.
Berenstain, Stanley and Janice Berenstain. *The B Book.* Random House, 1971.
Bishop, Gavin. *Chicken Licken.* Oxford University Press, 1985.
Bonne, Rose, and Alan Mills. *I Know an Old Lady.* Rand McNally, 1961.
Brand, Oscar. *When I First Came to this Land.* Putnam, 1974.
Brandenberg, Franz. *I Once Knew a Man.* Macmillan, 1970.
Brennan, Patricia D. *Hitchety Hatchety Up I Go!* Illustrated by Richard Royevsky. Macmillan, 1985.

Brooke, Leslie. *Johnny Crow's Garden*. Warne, 1968.
Brown, Marc. *Witches Four*. Parents, 1980.
Brown, Marcia. *The Three Billy Goats Gruff*. Harcourt, 1957.
Brown, Margaret Wise. *Four Fur Feet*. William R. Scott, 1961.
Brown, Margaret Wise. *The Friendly Book*. Golden, 1954.
Brown, Margaret Wise. *Goodnight Moon*. Harper, 1947.
Brown, Margaret Wise. *Home for a Bunny*. Golden, 1956.
Brown, Margaret Wise. *The Important Book*. Harper, 1949.
Brown, Margaret Wise. *Where Have You Been?* Scholastic, 1952.
Brown, Ruth. *A Dark, Dark Tale*. Dial, 1981.
Burningham, John. *Mr. Grumpy's Outing*. Holt, 1971.
Burningham, John. *The Shopping Basket*. Crowell, 1980.
Cameron, Polly. *I Can't Said the Ant*. Coward, 1961.
Carle, Eric. *Do You Want to Be My Friend?* Harper, 1971.
Carle, Eric. *The Grouchy Ladybug*. Crowell, 1977.
Carle, Eric. *The Mixed-Up Chameleon*. Crowell, 1975.
Carle, Eric. *The Very Busy Spider*. Philomel, 1984.
Carle, Eric. *The Very Hungry Caterpillar*. Collins World, 1969.
Carlstrom, Nancy White. *Jesse Bear, What Will You Wear?* Illustrated by Bruce Degen. Macmillan, 1986.
Charlip, Remy. *Fortunately*. Parents, 1964.
Charlip, Remy. *What Good Luck! What Bad Luck!* Scholastic, 1969.
Considine, Kate, and Ruby Schuler. *One, Two, Three, Four*. Holt, 1965.
Cook, Bernadine. *The Little Fish That Got Away*. Addison-Wesley, 1976.
Cummings, Pat. *Jimmy Lee Did It*. Lothrop, 1985.
de Paola, Tomie. *Tomie de Paola's Mother Goose*. Putnam, 1985.
de Paola, Tomie. *When Everyone Was Fast Asleep*. Holiday House, 1976.
de Regniers, Beatrice Schenk. *Catch a Little Fox*. Seabury, 1970.
de Regniers, Beatrice Schenk. *The Day Everybody Cried*. Viking, 1967.
de Regniers, Beatrice Schenk. *How Joe Bear and Sam the Moose Got Together*. Parents, 1965.
de Regniers, Beatrice Schenk. *The Little Book*. Walck, 1961.
de Regniers, Beatrice Schenk. *May I Bring a Friend?* Atheneum, 1972.
de Regniers, Beatrice Schenk. *Willy O'Dwyer Jumped in the Fire*. Atheneum, 1968.
Domanska, Janina. *If All the Seas Were One Sea*. Macmillan, 1971.

Domanska, Janina. *The Turnip*. Macmillan, 1969.
Duff, Maggie. *Johnny and His Drum*. Walck, 1972.
Duff, Maggie. *Rump, Pum, Pum*. Macmillan, 1978.
Eastman, P. D. *Are You My Mother?* Random House, 1960.
Einsel, Walter. *Did You Ever See?* Scholastic, 1962.
Emberley, Barbara. *Drummer Hoff*. Illustrated by Ed Emberley. Prentice-Hall, 1967.
Emberley, Barbara, and Ed Emberley. *One Wide River to Cross*. Illustrated by Ed Emberley. Scholastic, 1966.
Emberley, Ed. *Klippity Klop*. Little, Brown, 1974.
Ets, Marie Hall. *Elephant in a Well*. Viking, 1972.
Ets, Marie Hall. *Play With Me*. Viking, 1955.
Farber, Norma. *As I Was Crossing Boston Common*. Illustrated by Arnold Lobel. Dutton, 1975.
Flack, Marjorie. *Ask Mr. Bear*. Macmillan, 1932.
Flora, James. *Sherwood Walks Home*. Harcourt, 1966.
Fyleman, Rose. "The Goblin." *Picture Rhymes from Foreign Lands*. Lippincott, 1935.
Gag, Wanda. *Millions of Cats*. Faber and Faber, 1929.
Galdone, Paul. *The Gingerbread Boy*. Seabury, 1975.
Galdone, Paul. *Henny Penny*. Scholastic, 1968.
Galdone, Paul. *The Three Bears*. Scholastic, 1973.
Galdone, Paul. *The Three Billy Goats Gruff*. Seabury, 1973.
Galdone, Paul. *The Little Red Hen*. Scholastic, 1973.
Galdone, Paul. *The Three Little Pigs*. Clarion, 1970.
Gerstein, Mordicai. *Roll Over!* Crown, 1984.
Ginsburg, Mirra. *The Chick and the Duckling*. Macmillan, 1972.
Ginsburg, Mirra. *Good Morning, Chick*. Illustrated by Byron Barton. Greenwillow, 1980.
Greenberg, Polly. *Oh Lord, I Wish I Was a Buzzard*. Macmillan, 1968.
Greene, Carol. *The World's Biggest Birthday Cake*. Illustrated by Tom Dunnington. Childrens Press, 1985.
Guilfoile, Elizabeth. *Nobody Listens to Andrew*. Scholastic, 1957.
Guthrie, Donna. *The Witch Who Lived Down the Hall*. Illustrated by Amy Schwartz. Harcourt Brace Jovanovich, 1985.
Hale, Irina. *Brown Bear in a Brown Chair*. Atheneum, 1983.
Hawkins, Colin, and Jacqui Hawkins. *Old Mother Hubbard*. Putnam, 1985.
Hayes, Sara. *This Is the Bear*. Illustrated by Helen Craig. Lippincott, 1986.
Hill, Eric. *Nursery Rhyme Peek-a-Boo*. Price/ Stern/ Sloan, 1982.
Hoffman, Hilde. *The Green Grass Grows All Around*. Macmillan, 1968.

Howell, Lynn, and Richard Howell. *Winifred's New Bed.* Knopf, 1985.

Hutchins, Pat. *Don't Forget the Bacon.* Puffin, 1985.

Hutchins, Pat. *Good-Night, Owl!* Macmillan/ Penguin, 1982.

Hutchins, Pat. *Happy Birthday, Sam.* Puffin/ Penguin, 1981.

Hutchins, Pat. *Rosie's Walk.* Collier, 1968.

Hutchins, Pat. *Titch.* Collier, 1971.

Hutchins, Pat. *You'll Soon Grow into Them, Titch.* Greenwillow, 1983.

Hutchins, Pat. *1 Hunter.* Greenwillow, 1982.

Isadora, Rachel. *I Touch. I See. I Hear.* (3 titles) Greenwillow, 1985.

Joslin, Sesyle. *What Do You Say, Dear?* Scholastic Press, 1958.

Joyce, Irma. *Never Talk to Strangers.* Golden, 1967.

Keats, Ezra Jack. *Over in the Meadow.* Scholastic, 1971.

Kellogg, Steven. *Much Bigger than Martin.* Dial, 1976.

Kent, Jack. *The Fat Cat.* Parents, 1971.

Klein, Lenore. *Brave Daniel.* Scholastic, 1958.

Kraus, Robert. *Whose Mouse Are You?* Illustrated by Jose Aruego and Ariane Dewey. Greenwillow, 1986.

Kraus, Ruth. *Bears.* Scholastic, 1948.

Kraus, Ruth. *The Carrot Seed.* Illustrated by Crockett Johnson. Harper, 1945.

Kraus, Ruth. *A Hole Is to Dig.* Harper, 1952.

Kroll, Steven. *That Makes Me Mad.* Starstream, 1980.

Langstaff, John. *Frog Went a-Courtin'.* Harcourt, 1955.

Langstaff, John. *Oh, A-Hunting We Will Go.* Illustrated by Nancy Winslow Parker. Atheneum, 1970.

Laurence, Ester. *We're Off to Catch a Dragon.* Abingdon, 1969.

Lexau, Joan. *Crocodile and Hen.* Harper, 1969.

Lloyd, David. *Bread and Cheese.* Illustrated by Deborah Ward. Random House, 1984.

Lloyd, David. *Jack and Nelly.* Illustrated by Clive Scruton. Random House, 1984.

Lobel, Anita. *King Rooster, Queen Hen.* Greenwillow, 1975.

Lobel, Arnold. *The Rose in My Garden.* Illustrated by Anita Lobel. Greenwillow, 1984.

McGovern, Ann. *Too Much Noise.* Scholastic, 1967.

Mack, Stan. *10 Bears in My Bed.* Pantheon, 1974.

McMillan, Bruce. *Kitten Can . . .* Lothrop, 1984.

Mars, W. T. *The Old Woman and Her Pig.* Western, 1964.

Martin, Bill, Jr. *Brown Bear, Brown Bear, What Do You See?* Illustrated by Eric Carle. Holt, 1983.

Martin, Bill, Jr. *Fire! Fire! Said Mrs. McGuire.* Holt, 1970.

Martin, Bill, Jr. *A Ghost Story.* Holt, 1970.

Martin, Bill, Jr. *The Haunted House.* Holt, 1970.

Martin, Bill, Jr. *Old Mother Middle Muddle*. Holt, 1970.
Martin, Bill, Jr. *Up and Down the Escalator*. Holt, 1970.
Marzollo, Jean. *Uproar on Hollercat Hill*. Illustrated by Steven Kellogg. Dial, 1981.
Mayer, Mercer. *If I Had . . .* Dial, 1968.
Mayer, Mercer. *Just For You*. Golden, 1975.
Memling, Carl. *Ten Little Animals*. Golden, 1961.
Mendoza, George. *A Wart Snake in a Fig Tree*. Dial, 1968.
Miller, Edna. *Mousekin Takes a Trip*. Prentice-Hall, 1976.
Milne, A. A. "Puppy and I," *When We Were Very Young*. Dutton, 1924.
Moffett, Martha. *A Flower Pot Is Not a Hat*. Dutton, 1972.
Most, Bernard. *If The Dinosaurs Come Back*. Harcourt, 1978.
Munari, Bruno. *The Elephant's Wish*. Philomel, 1980.
Munari, Bruno. *Jimmy Lost His Cap, Where Can It Be?* Philomel, 1980.
Muntean, Michaela. *Bicycle Bear*. Illustrated by Doug Cushman. Parents, 1983.
Palmer, Janet. *Ten Days of School*. Bank Street College of Education, Macmillan, 1969.
Parkinson, Kathy, reteller. *The Enormous Turnip*. Whitman, 1985.
Patrick, Gloria. *A Bug in a Jug*. Scholastic, 1970.
Pearson, Tracey Campbell. *Old MacDonald Had a Farm*. Dial, 1984.
Peek, Merle, adapter. *Mary Wore Her Red Dress and Henry Wore His Green Sneakers*. Clarion, 1985.
Peppe, Rodney. *The House that Jack Built*. Delacorte, 1970.
Peterson, Jeanne Whitehouse. *While the Moon Shines Bright: A Bedtime Chant*. Illustrated by Margot Apple. Harper, 1981.
Piper, Walter. *The Little Engine That Could*. 1976.
Polushkin, Maria. *Mother, Mother, I Want Another*. Crown, 1978.
Pomerantz, Charlotte. *The Piggy in the Puddle*. Illustrated by James Marshall. Macmillan, 1974.
Preston, Edna Mitchell. *The Sad Story of the Little Bluebird and the Hungry Cat*. Illustrated by Barbara Cooney. Four Winds, 1975.
Preston, Edna Mitchell. *Where Did My Mother Go?* Four Winds, 1978.
Quackenbush, Robert. *No Mouse for Me!* Watts, 1981.
Quackenbush, Robert. *She'll Be Comin' Round the Mountain*. Lippincott, 1973.
Quackenbush, Robert. *Skip to My Lou*. Lippincott, 1975.
Rice, Eve. *Benny Bakes a Cake*. Greenwillow, 1981.
Rice, Eve. *Sam Who Never Forgets*. Greenwillow, 1977.
Rockwell, Anne. *Honk, Honk!* Dutton, 1980.

Rokoff, Sandra. *Here Is a Cat.* Singapore: Hallmark Children's Editions, n.d.

Scheer, Julian, and Marvin Bileck. *Rain Makes Applesauce.* Holiday House, 1964.

Scheer, Julian, and Marvin Bileck. *Upside Down Day.* Holiday House, 1968.

Shulevitz, Uri. *One Monday Morning.* Scribner's. 1967.

Skaar, Grace. *What Do the Animals Say?* Scholastic, 1972.

Slobodkin, Esphyr. *Caps for Sale.* Addison-Wesley, 1947.

Sonneborn, Ruth A. *Someone Is Eating the Sun.* Random House, 1974.

Spier, Peter. *The Fox Went Out on a Chilly Night: An Old Song.* Puffin, 1984.

Stanley, Diane Zuromskis. *Fiddle-I-Fee.* Little, Brown, 1979.

Stover, JoAnn. *If Everybody Did.* David McKay, 1960.

Sutton, Eve. *My Cat Likes to Hide in Boxes.* Scholastic, 1973.

Tafuri, Nancy. *Have You Seen My Duckling?* Greenwillow, 1984.

Tolstoy, Alexei. *The Great Big Enormous Turnip.* Watts, 1968.

Watanabe, Shigeo. *What a Good Lunch!* Illustrated by Yasuo Ohtomo. Philomel, 1980.

Watanabe, Shigeo. *Where's My Daddy.* Philomel, 1982.

Welber, Robert. *Goodbye, Hello.* Pantheon, 1974.

Wells, Rosemary. *Noisy Nora.* Dial, 1973.

Westcott, Nadine. *I Know an Old Lady Who Swallowed a Fly.* 1980.

Wildsmith, Brian. *The Twelve Days of Christmas.* Watts, 1972.

Wolcott, Patty. *Double-Decker, Double-Decker, Double-Decker Bus.* Illustrated by Bob Barner. Addison-Wesley, 1980.

Wolkstein, Diane. *The Visit.* Knopf, 1977.

Wondriska, William. *All the Animals Were Angry.* Holt, 1970.

Wood, Audrey. *King Bidgood's in the Bathtub.* Illustrated by Don Wood. Harcourt, 1985.

Wood, Audrey. *The Napping House.* Illustrated by Don Wood. Harcourt, 1984.

Zemach, Harve. *The Judge: An Untrue Tale.* Illustrated by Margot Zemach. Farrar, Straus, 1969.

Zemach, Margot. *The Teeny Tiny Woman.* Scholastic, 1965.

Zolotow, Charlotte. *Do You Know What I'll Do?* Harper, 1958.

Appendix Two

Two Field-Tested Units

UNIT I

Title: How Do Pioneers of Today Compare with Those of the Past?

Brief Description: A three-week unit of study geared for a third-grade class comparing pioneers of the 1800s with pioneers of today.

I. **Major Concept:** There are many similarities between pioneers of the past and pioneers of today.

II. **Learning Goals:**

    A. To compare and contrast the pioneers of the 1800s with those of today.

    B. To help students evaluate the pioneers' use of resources and analyze what solutions to problems may have been possible.

    C. To allow students to identify with several famous pioneers and explore the characteristics that made them famous.

III. **Teaching Objectives:**

    A. To impart some factual information about these areas of pioneer life:
        1. Travel
        2. Homes
        3. Food
        4. Clothing
        5. Education
        6. Religion
        7. Social Activities

    B. To study several famous pioneers to gain perspective on what might have made them famous.

IV.   **List of Materials**

     A. Pictures depicting frontier life
     B. Construction paper, glue, scissors, etc.
     C. Computers and software
     D. Typical pioneer clothes
     E. Small jars with lids, whipping cream, crackers, knives
     F. Records of pioneer songs

V.   **List of References**

     A. Books
         1. *American Folk Poetry* (Emrich)
         2. *Pioneer Tenderfoot* (Estep)
         3. *Never Miss a Sunset* (Gilge)
         4. *Cowboys and Cattle Company* (American Heritage Publ.)
         5. *The California Gold Rush* (American Heritage Publ.)
         6. *The Pioneer Twins* (Perkins)
         7. *Little House on the Prairie Series* (Wilder)
         8. *Dan Frontier Series* (Hurley)

     B. Media
         1. Songs of the Trail (RCA Victor)
         2. 45 Songs Children Love to Sing (RCA Camden)
         3. Oregon Trail (MECC)
         4. The Opening of the West (filmstrip)
         5. Americans Move West (picture cards)

VI. **Enabling Activities**
     A. Use math skills of addition and subtraction to compute distances between cities on the Oregon Trail.
     B. Hypothesize about supplies needed for a trip West.
     C. Analyze effects of natural events on the move West.
     D. Learn several songs depicting pioneer life.
     E. Participate in several folk dances.
     F. Compare modern clothing with pioneer clothes.
     G. Write a story in the person of a modern pioneer or one living in the 1800s.
     H. Make butter and discuss the time and effort involved in making food this way.

    I.   Listen to stories about early and modern pioneers.
    J.   Simulate the journey West via the Oregon Trail.
    K. Construct a scale model of a pioneer cabin.
    L.   Help to paint a mural of The Westward Journey or America's exploration of outer space.
    M. Participate in a skit of either early or modern pioneer life.
    N. Compose a ballad for modern pioneers.

VII. **Culminating Activities**
    A. Hold a parent's night, featuring folk dances of the pioneers of the 1800s and the skits of early and modern pioneers.
    B. Make a class book of early and modern pioneers.
    C. Hold an "open house" of completed projects for other classes.

VIII. **Evaluation Procedures**
    A. Pre- and post-test on factual information of the pioneers of the 1800s.
    B. Essay discussing how early and modern pioneers are the same and different.
    C. Observation of student behavior, attitude, and understandings while doing projects.
    D. Student-teacher conferences on projects.
    E. Creativity expressed in projects.

UNIT II

Title: What Have We Learned About Outer Space?

Brief Description: A three-week unit of study for fourth-graders concerning past and current work done in space exploration; what an astronaut does; and how rockets are designed.

I.   **Major Concept**: Valuable work has already been done in space exploration, but there are still new areas to be explored.

II.   **Learning Goals**:
A.   To compare and contrast views of outer space before and after man landed on the moon.
B.   To value the work already done in space, and hypothesize about what the future holds for space exploration.
C.   To identify with the feelings of astronauts as they explored outer space.

III.   **Teaching Goals**:
A.   To impart some factual information about the following areas:
1.   The earth and the planets
2.   Early space exploration
3.   The Apollo program
4.   Firing a rocket
5.   Skylab
6.   The space shuttle

B.   To help children understand what the job of an astronaut entails and have them become familiar with several astronauts' lives.

IV.   **List of Materials**
A.   Computer and software
B.   Rocket display
C.   NASA patches
D.   Paper plates
E.   "Star Wars" music; tape recorder
F.   Moon myths
G.   "Mission to Mars" game
H.   Apollo diagram
I.   Tape of dialogue between NASA and Skylab

V. **List of References**
A. Books
1. *Space and Beyond* (Montgomery)
2. *Space Cat* (Marshal and Ruthven)
3. *Barney in Space* (Goff)
4. *First Men in Space* (Clark)
5. *A Space Age Cookbook for Kids* (Porentea)
6. *If You Were an Astronaut* (Moore)
7. *SPACE: An Easy-to-Read Fact Book* (Crowley)
8. *Space Shuttle* (Jay)
9. *Easy to Make Spaceships that Really Fly* (Blockma)
10. *Astronomy for Everybody* (Newcomb)

B. Media
Filmstrips
1. Moon, Sun, Stars
2. Beyond the Solar System
3. The Solar System

Movie
1. A Trip to the Moon
2. Flash Gordon's Old Movies

VI. **Enabling Activities**
A. Complete a cumulative notebook (space log).
B. Build and decorate a spacecraft for a "Great Space Race."
C. Collect data at the Great Space Race and make hypotheses.
D. Label diagrams of spacecrafts.
E. Complete math warp project.
F. Play "Mission to Mars."
G. Simulate space voyage on computer.
H. Participate in gravity experiment.
I. Graph the planets.
J. Listen to tape of dialogue between NASA and Skylab.
K. Do research on astronaut of choice.
L. Complete time line of space history.

VII. **Culminating Activities**
A. Present space logs at open house.
B. Compile a classbook of astronauts researched.
C. Set off rocket in field for other classes.
D. Space Age luncheon with food eaten by astronauts.

VIII. **Evaluation Procedures**
    A. Pre- and post-tests on factual information about our solar system and the space program.
    B. Essay synthesizing understandings about what we have learned through space exploration.
    C. Observation of student behavior, attitudes.
    D. Student-teacher conferences about projects.
    E. Creativity expressed in projects.

Appendix Three

Sample Learning Stations

COMPREHENSION SKILLS CENTER

Purpose of Center: To provide reinforcement experiences with comprehension skills.

RIDDLE MATCH

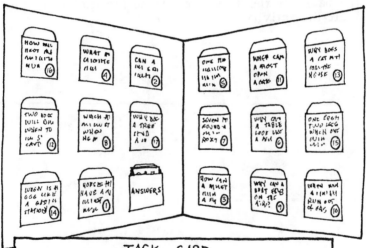

TASK CARD

1. READ THE RIDDLES ON THE POCKETS.

2. FIND THE ANSWERS IN THE ANSWER CARD POCKET.

3. PUT THE ANSWER CARDS IN THE RIGHT POCKETS.

4. CHECK YOUR WORK BY SEEING THAT THE NUMBER ON THE POCKET, AND THE NUMBER ON THE ANSWER CARD MATCH.

Materials: Two 14" x 20" pieces of cardboard
    Two 14" x 20" pieces of colored tagboard to cover cardboard
    One roll of mystik tape to make hinges for the cardboard and to bind the edges
    Eighteen library book pockets
    Adhesive dots
    Eighteen 3" x 5" index cards

Procedure: One student reads the riddles on the library book pockets. Another student finds the answer to the riddle on one of the cards in the "Answer Pocket." The card is placed in the correct pocket.

Evaluation: Adhesive dots with numbers corresponding to the numbered dots on the library book pockets are placed on the backs of the answer cards, so the student is able to evaluate the activity.

COMICS SEQUENCE

Materials: Cartoon pictures which have been cut apart. These may be obtained from newspapers or comic books.
   Twenty-four 5" x 7 1/2" envelopes
   3" x 5" index cards for mounting comics

Procedure: The student arranges the cartoon frames in their correct sequence.

Evaluation: An answer key should be provided so that the activity is self-correcting. Symbols work well as a coding system (see illustration).

PARAGRAPH SEQUENCE

Materials: Twenty-four 9" x 12" pieces of tagboard or cardboard

Twenty-four stories, cut into paragraphs. These may be obtained from discarded texts, children's magazines, or written by the teacher and students.

Twenty-four plastic sleeves or clear contact paper to protect the materials.

Wax marking pencils

Carpet squares for erasing

Procedure: The child reads the paragraphs and numbers them in correct sequence.

Evaluation: A correcting key may be provided or a key placed on the back of each card in order to make the activity self-correcting.

MAKE THE HEADLINES

Materials: Twenty-four 6" x 8" cards
Newspaper articles
Wax marking pencils
Carpet squares for erasing

Procedure: The student reads the article on the card and then writes a headline for the article. The actual headline is attached to the reverse side of the card.

Evaluation: Student evaluated.

"AD CONCENTRATION"

Materials: Thirty or forty 3" x 5" cards
Labels from products, magazine advertisements, etc.
Glue

Procedure: The cards are placed face down on a table or the floor. The first player turns over any two cards; if they are a match he keeps them and continues to play until he misses. The player with the most cards at the end of the game is the winner.

Evaluation: Student evaluation or teacher observation.

PLAYER CONTRAST

KEN STABLER | J___ ___MLY |

___me_____ Card #___

What are the names of the 2 players?

A _____

B _____

2. What position does each man play?

A _____

B _____

3. Which team does each man play for?

A _____

B _____

4. Which player is older?

_____

5. Which player is taller?

_____

Materials: 24 baseball, football, or basketball cards. These can be purchased from variety stores, markets, or vending machines.

Twelve 5" x 8" plain index cards. These are folded and stapled 1 1/2" from the bottom to make a pocket in which to place the player cards.

Adhesive dots for coding.

Procedure: The student takes a pocket from the set. He reads the questions, locates the answer on the backs of the cards, records the information on the answer sheet.

Evaluation: An answer key is provided so the activity is self-correcting.

WHAT'S THE STORY

Materials: Four ring binders or manila folders
Pictures from magazines and newspapers
Tagboard or construction paper for mounting pictures
3" x 5" index cards
Corner mounts
Four 5" x 8" envelopes for holding story cards.

Procedure: The student reads the paragraph on the index card, finds the picture that the paragraph tells about, and fits the card in the corner mounts under the picture.

Evaluation: The pictures and cards may be coded so that the activity is self-correcting.

QUESTION MATCH

Materials: Five phrase cards telling WHO
Five phrase cards telling WHAT
Five phrase cards telling WHERE
Five phrase cards telling WHEN
Five phrase cards telling WHY
Five phrase cards telling HOW

Sixty 2 1/4" x 3 1/2" cards, distribution as follows:
Five question cards asking WHO
Five question cards asking WHAT
Five question cards asking WHERE
Five question cards asking WHEN
Five question cards asking WHY
Five question cards asking HOW

Procedure: Two to four children may participate in the game. The cards are shuffled and five are placed face up in the center of the table. The first player examines the five cards to determine whether or not there is a match--a match being a phrase card that answers a question card. If there are matches, the child identifies them and picks them up, laying down other cards to fill their places. He then turns up a card from the top of the deck and determines if he can make a match. He may continue to turn up cards until he cannot make a match, in which case he places the card face up with the others. There must be five cards turned up as each player begins his turn. The player having the most cards at the end of the game is the winner.

Evaluation: Teacher observation or participation.

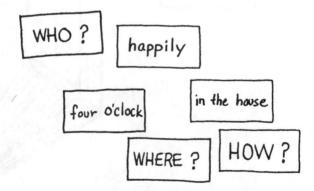

TALL TALE CENTER

Purpose of Center: To provide children with the opportunity to read and enjoy tall tale stories.

VIEWING STATION

Materials: One piece of cardboard, 18" x 22"
      Two pieces of cardboard, 11" x 22"
      One piece of tagboard for back cover, 18" x 22"
      Four pieces of tagboard, 11" x 18" for sides
      One piece of white tagboard, 18" x 22" for viewing
screen
      Mystik tape 1 1/2" wide for hinges
      Contact paper (do not put on screen)
      Filmstrip projector
      Filmstrip
      Pencils
      Paper
      Task Cards (optional)

Procedure: Children will view filmstrip. Questions may be written on task cards or they may be asked orally.

Evaluation: Answer sheet or teacher observation

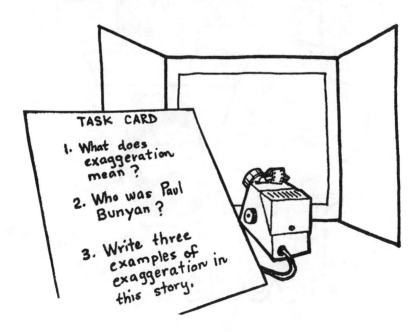

TASK CARD

1. What does exaggeration mean?

2. Who was Paul Bunyan?

3. Write three examples of exaggeration in this story.

CREATIVE WRITING STATION

Materials: Three manila folders for story wheels
Three shape books
Pencils
Writing paper
Construction paper
Scissors
(See Fairy Tale Center)

Procedure: Child will choose one creative writing activity. If the child chooses to do a shape book, he must trace the pattern on his writing paper. After the story has been completed the child can make a shape folder for his story.

Evaluation: Teacher corrected

STORY STARTER WHEELS

Make three 5" circles. Make three windows 2" by 3/4" (see drawing for placement of windows).

Use one-inch brads to mount circles to manila folder.

On top wheel put nouns or noun phrases. On middle wheel put verb phrases and on last wheel put prepositional phrases and/or objects.

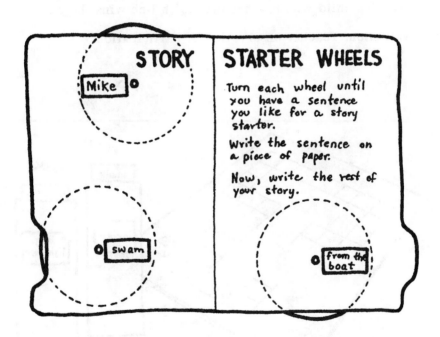

GAME STATION

Materials: One game board
Vocabulary cards
Markers
Dice
Three pocket windows
Word strips

Procedure: Children will roll the die to see who starts the game. The child looks at the first word in his window and must pronounce it correctly and give a definition. The definition will be written on the back window. If he is correct, he will roll the die and move the corresponding number of spaces. If the child is incorrect, he loses his turn. The child who reaches the finish line wins the game.

Evaluation: Teacher observation or participation

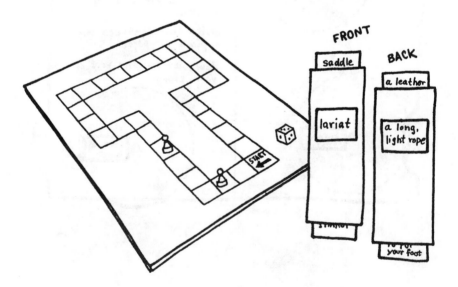

ART STATION

Materials: Pencils
Crayons
Construction paper 12" x 18"
Task Cards

Procedure: Child will take one art task card from the box. On the task card will be written a descriptive scene from one of the tall tale stories. The child will illustrate the scene he has chosen.

Evaluation: Teacher observation

READING CENTER

FREE READING STATION

Materials: Books
     Table
     Rug (if possible)
     Couch or chair (if possible)
     Pillows (if possible)

Procedure: Child will pick a book from the shelf to read

Evaluation: Need not be evaluated

FAIRY TALE CENTER

Purpose of Center: To provide children with the opportunity to read, listen, and dramatize the literary form of fairy tales in conjunction with English skills.

LISTENING STATION

Materials: 30 minute tape
    Tape recorder
    Books with tape
    Set of earphones
    Double -- 12" circles -- one for each story
    Brass paper fasteners
    4 1/4" x 5 1/2" ditto answer sheets
    8 1/2" x 11" castle-shaped task card
    Pencils

Procedure: The children read the task card and follow the directions step-by-step. (See sample task card and script that follow.)

       TASK CARD
     * Listen to tape.
     * Choose a wheel about a fairy tale.
     * Answer the questions on an answer sheet.
     * Now, choose a story to read or listen to
        the tape of a story.

Tape Script

    Many, many years ago most people did not have books. Instead of reading books people told stories. Sometimes the stories were changed as one man told another. That is why today there are different beginnings and different endings to the same tales. You will even find different names for the various characters.

    At this center you will find some library books and some of my books with many fairy tales. Fairy tales are special stories that we read over and over again. They are fun to tell each other too. Maybe some boys and girls will write new fairy tales for our class.

    Since fairy tales were told to people before we had books, you do not have to read all the fairy tales. We have some fairy tales on tape for the tape recorder. A friend may read a story to you, or you may read a story to yourself.

    To help you decide what story you would like to read there are wheels of questions. Try to answer the questions on a wheel. If you cannot answer two questions correctly, then read the story.

    Fairy tales are fun, so have a good time!

Evaluation: Fairy tale answer sheets.

VOCABULARY STATION

Materials:
    Carrell:
        One piece of cardboard 19" x 26"
        Two pieces of cardboard 13" x 19"
        Two pieces of colored tag 19" x 26"
        Four pieces of colored tag 13" x 19"
        One folded piece of tag 12" x 12" for pocket
        One roll 1 1/2" mystik tape
        Clear contact paper.
    Task Cards:
        5" x 8" cards
        Pencils
        Writing paper

Procedure: The child will select a task card and follow the directions. (See sample of task cards which follow.)
    TASK CARD #1   Don't forget your NAME!!

    You will need: Paper
                   Pencil
    Put the vocabulary words in alphabetical order.
    Pick 6 words. Write each word in a sentence.
    Put paper in folder.

    TASK CARD #2   Don't forget your NAME!!

    An *antonym* is a word having the *opposite* meaning of another word.
    Example: *hot   cold*
    You will need: Paper
                   Pencil
    Pick 6 vocabulary words. Write an antonym for the words you choose.
    Put paper in folder.

    TASK CARD #3   Don't forget your NAME!!

    You will need: Paper
                   Pencil
    Use the vocabulary words.
    A *noun* is a person, place, or thing.
    List all the nouns from the "fairy tale" vocabulary list.
    Draw a picture of 3 of the words you listed.
    Have a friend check your work. Then put in folder.

Evaluation: Teacher corrected

SYLLABLE CHIP ACTIVITY

Materials: Five 10" x 10" cards, divided into 2" squares
One box
100 poker chips
100 adhesive dots to label poker chips

Procedure: Child takes a word card. He says each word quietly. He counts the number of syllables he hears. He places a numbered poker chip on the word to show how many syllables it has.

Evaluation: Answer key is provided for self correction.

FAIRY TALES				
village	princess	throne	golden	fairy
tale	handsome	elf	castle	tower
enchant	prince	creature	king	fortune
kingdom	witch	magic	peddler	knight
beast	dragon	queen	treasure	robber

ANSWER KEY				
2	2	1	2	2
1	2	1	2	2
2	1	2	1	2
2	1	2	2	1
1	2	1	2	2

SYLLABLE CHIPS

CREATIVE WRITING

Materials: Two pieces of cardboard 13" x 19"
Four pieces of colored tag 13" x 19"
One folded piece of colored tag 8" x 12" for pocket
One folded piece of colored tag 12" x 12" for pocket
Clear contact paper
Six 5" x 8" cards
Mystik tape
Student writing paper

Procedure: The student will choose one of the story starters. The first paragraph of a fairy tale is on the card. The student will copy the paragraph and finish the story.

Evaluation: Teacher corrected

SAVE THE PRINCESS

Materials: One piece of cardboard 13" x 19"
One piece of colored tag 13" x 19"
Clear contact paper
Four markers
One die
Deck of vocabulary cards

Procedure: Children take turns rolling the die, reading a word and moving the number of spaces on the die. If a child is unable to read a word he loses a turn.
The first child to the castle is the winner.

Evaluation: Teacher observation or participation.

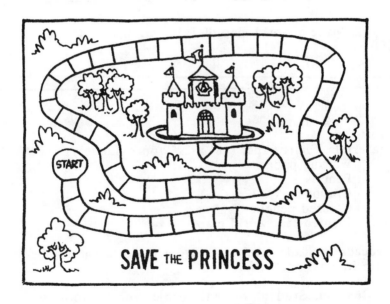

RESEARCH CENTER

PROJECTS

1. Compare two fairy tales.

   List: Characters Vocabulary Events

   _____

   How are they alike

   _____

   How are they different

   _____

2. Make a world map of fairy tales.

Materials: Chart paper (18" x 22" approximately)
Writing paper
Pencils
Crayons
Colored pencils
Printed flat world map

Procedure: Student selects a project. Research may be done both in class and at home.

Evaluation: Student presents project orally to class or to teacher.

Index